W9-AHK-484

SELECTED POEMS

*Other Macmillan editions of
John Masefield's works:*

THE BIRD OF DAWNING

JIM DAVIS

SALT-WATER POEMS AND BALLADS

THE TAKING OF THE GRY

VICTORIOUS TROY OR, THE HURRYING ANGEL

POEMS: COMPLETE EDITION

JOHN MASEFIELD

SELECTED POEMS

With a Preface by
JOHN BETJEMAN

ANNIVERSARY EDITION

MACMILLAN PUBLISHING CO., INC.
New York

The Selection of Poems
Copyright © 1978 by William Heinemann Ltd
Preface Copyright © 1978 by John Betjeman

All rights reserved. No part of this book may be reproduced or
transmitted in any form or by any means, electronic or mechanical,
including photocopying, recording or by any information storage and
retrieval system, without permission in writing from the Publisher.

Macmillan Publishing Co., Inc.
866 Third Avenue, New York, N.Y. 10022
Collier Macmillan Canada, Ltd.

Library of Congress Cataloging in Publication Data
Masefield, John, 1878-1967.
Selected poems.
"Anniversary edition."
PR6025.A77A6 1978   821'.9'12   78-10365
ISBN 0-02-581010-3

First American Edition 1978

Printed in the United States of America

CONTENTS

PREFACE BY JOHN BETJEMAN

John Masefield wrote two lyrics which will be remembered as long as the language lasts — "I must go down to the seas again" and "Quinquereme of Nineveh". His stories in verse, notably *The Widow in the Bye Street, The Everlasting Mercy* and *Reynard the Fox* sold in their thousands. My father who, despite his affection for me, was not given to reading poetry, certainly read all Masefield's long poems. When they had swear words in them, my father thought they proved how down to earth Masefield was. In his morning bath my father used to sing a Masefield lyric which had in it the lines, "Underneath her topsails, she trembled like a stag".

When I saw first this blood and thunder poet, he was not the tweedy, breezy sea-salt I had expected. He was spare, quiet and with luminous blue eyes. He read his poems on a warm summer evening in Faringdon Church in aid of the restoration of that handsome old building and his voice, though weak, high and a bit quavery, filled the whole church and thrilled the audience. He was a practised verse speaker and all his poems were written to be read aloud. He tells us in his autobiography *So Long To Learn* how much he enjoyed telling stories in verse. Inevitably he came in for a reaction against his wide-spread popularity, still more so when he was made Poet Laureate and submitted verses on topical events to *The Times*. He did not know he did not have to do this in his capacity as Poet Laureate; someone should have written to tell him, although I can see it would have been a difficult letter to write.

The Laureateship is now officially regarded not as a spur to further verse writing but as a reward, as Eric Gillett described it to me, for work already done. Nevertheless, his sense of duty caused Masefield to submit lyrics to *The Times*. There was no compulsion.

The appointment is in the gift of the Prime Minister who advises the Queen. Ramsay Macdonald advised the appointment of Masefield.

The large blue volume of Masefield's *Collected Poems*, first published in 1923, loaded the tables in school halls at prize giving, but the book is too unwieldy for modern flats and the poems are probably too long for modern tastes. Masefield did not specialise in brevity. He obtained his effects by direct, unadorned description. His canvas is as large as Brangwyn's. In fact there is a likeness between that ebullient and inventive Welshman and the shy Laureate from the borders of Herefordshire and Wales.

John Masefield was born at Ledbury in 1878. He was one of the numerous children of the solicitor in that still unspoilt country town, in a hilly country where there are many half-timbered old farms, small streams with alders and willow banks where daffodils still grow wild. This luxuriant orchard country near the Malvern Hills is a background to his inland verse. His solicitor father died young and the family had a struggle to make its way in a district which had, and still has, an old-fashioned social pattern. He was sent to King's School, Warwick, and while there, at the age of fourteen, he was accepted as a cadet by H.M.S. *Conway*, the merchant navy training ship at that time in the Mersey. Masefield had always had a longing to go to sea. His sea flowed westward and south from the English coast. He won prizes for seamanship when in *Conway* and on completion of his course he went as an apprentice aboard a sailing ship bound for Chile via Cape Horn. Poor fellow, he was appallingly seasick. The full terrors of his voyage are well described in *Dauber*, the story of an artist mocked at by the crew while he went on painting pictures despite discouragement.

> "Down in his bunk the Dauber lay awake
> Thinking of his unfitness for the sea . . . "

For Dauber one could substitute Masefield, and for artist one could substitute poet.

During the 1914-1918 war he was with the Red Cross in France and then in a hospital ship in the Gallipoli campaign in 1916. His every experience he put industriously to literary account. He was a most conscientious writer and was the obvious choice after the death of the too little appreciated Robert Bridges in 1930 as Poet Laureate. He fulfilled the task as might have been expected with a high sense of duty and awareness of the importance of his calling as a poet. He encouraged verse speaking and verse drama. His life, after his early struggles at sea and in a carpet factory in New York, seems to have been one long psalm of thanksgiving. His goodness shone out from him. I hope this book will gain him new readers.

from WONDERINGS

Out of a dateless darkness pictures gleam,
But are they memories or only dream?
One earliest image is a gorge of crags
Drenched in a spray, with rainbows among jags,
Fish-cruising ospreys gleaming, dipping, calling,
And thunder and majesty of water falling,
The endless onwards of a cataract
In terror and exultation of its act.

Over a precipice it streamed, and broke
To gliddery wool and after crashed to smoke,
Uptwisted, and creamed on, and where it drave
A path of wet stones led into a cave.
Within that cavern, sheltered from the gorge,
Men, stripped for effort, hammered at a forge;
At what their hammers beat I cannot tell,
With spurt of spark the fire rose and fell,
The craftsmen's bodies gleamed, as sparks were blown.
All this was shrewdly seen and inly known.
Cataract, cave and smithy were as clear
As things of home, as places once held dear.
Three strangenesses come next, of sight or thought.
High in the elms, the rooks their cradles wrought,
And there, in sunlight, in an April sky
Three immense floating giants passed me by;
Three figures, linked as one, as one, intent
Eastward, and staring east, at speed they went.
They were not clouds, as living things they fared,
I marvelled at their life, but was not scared.
Whatever purpose, impulse or design
Drove them, its splendour banished fear of mine.

Then, from behind a curtain, I beheld
The frosty, moonless Heaven, many-stelled,
And heard, that I was looking into Space,
An Everywhere unclosed in any place
But ever Somewhere, going on and on
On, into Nowhere that had never gone.
This caused the visions that I seemed to see
Streamings of fire flying over me
Rings and ellipses hurtling in their flame

1

A fire and beauty endlessly the same
Part of me, surely, and myself a part
(Perhaps) of it; a paint-dot in an art.

Then, from a time which happiness made tense,
Come memories of persons long gone hence:
A coachman pulling-up, to bid me mark
The mad-dog frenzy of a fox's bark:
An old man pointing where three vipers rose:
"They hissed at me, all standing on their toes".
Then, a most gentle friend, with silver hair,
At lunch, falling asleep upon her chair.
A little yellow chicken lying dead:
And then a gate through which a trackway led
Beside an apple-orchard to a boat
Wherein my pilgrim self went first afloat.

Great floods were out; the hedges in black lines
Wallowed like water-snakes with bony spines,
Within the channel, full of swirl in swill,
A six-mile current romped towards the mill.
I was then three; two half-remembered men
Launched with me forth and brought me back agen,
But half a century later, I was told
What risks beset us in that bliss of old.
The boat was crazy, like her merry crew,
And many drowned men's deaths that mill-race knew.
Life, looking on her lamb, postponed the slaughter
And stamped within my soul delight in water.

Beauty of water gave delight again:—
The earth was shining after winter rain,
Each little brook was shouting in its run
Each meadow was a jewel in the sun,
And in a midmost grass a foot-high fount
Throbbed and uptumbled its collapsing mount
Wonder, dissolved, resolved, upspringing, sped,
Beauty, yet never aught, yet never dead.

Terror of water followed, when I saw
The eddies of a flood in torrent draw
The wreckage under, as though hands were there
Hands, and the will to make a boy beware.
Even in summer when the pools were clear
The quiet depth was brooded-on by fear,

To be within its power was to die,
For all its still, reflected earth and sky.

But exquisite delight my spirit took
In many a roadside—many a meadow-brook,
One above all so beautiful a thing
I thought God had a cottage at its spring.
And by another once a partridge came
With chicks which I could stroke, they were so tame
Quick, pecking, peering, all the mottled clutch
Bright-eyed, unfearing, exquisite to touch.

One other water blessed me with her grace,
A deep, calm quiet in a sunny place,
Where yellow flags grew tall and reeds grew gray
As though all time would be a summer day.
Sometimes a ring would spread as a fish rose
Then, the ring spent, placidity would close,
A skating fly might skim, a shadow flit
As some exulting swallow stooped at it,
But save for these, no other aim there was
Than to be beauty and beauty's looking-glass.

Near by, within a little field there grew
Clover, dim white, with blushes glowing through,
Great-headed clover, exquisitely sweet,
Wherein the bees went fumbling for their meat
Wonder, that kept in poise life's dual thrust,
To red, to white, while being only dust.

Other intense delights of those glad hours
Were scents and colours of the fruits and flowers,
The perfume in the tulip's waxen shell
Whence the May Moon-Queen gather hydromel;
The pale blue chicory, with scrubby stalk,
(Uncommon there, that lover of the chalk),
And under dark green leaves, the first deep red
June strawberry with yellow speckles spread,
Each of the three too exquisite a prey
For hand to gather, save to give away,
For to a prodigal, the joy of living
Is not in having for oneself but giving,
For life is emptiness and Nature bare
Lacking the friend to have the larger share.

from LANDWORKERS

Long since, in England's pleasant lands
I used to see the farming-hands.
I need but shut my eyes, and fast
There come the pictures of the past,
Of men and women, long-since dead,
Who battled with the Earth for bread
(A daily bread they might but taste)
For Folly and his doll to waste.

And first, the whetstones making writhe
The screaming anguish of the scythe;
The hayfield, the moon-daisy-stelled,
Where the wet frog his hoppage held,
Where the just-blushing opal clover
Had the king bumble-bee for lover,
And many a blunt-tailed rusty mouse
Piped treble in his grassy house.

There at the swinging edges' scathe
The summer flowers fell in swathe;
Daisy and ragged-robbin drooped
Then tumbled, as the sharpness swooped.
A field-long grassy dragon snaked
Behind the scythes, where women raked;
And who, that looked on these, forgets
Their flapping lilac sun-bonnets?

Then, who forgets the bristled corn
When sloes are blue among the thorn?
The harvest-reapers stretched for luncheon
About the wooden cider-puncheon,
Backed on the sunburnt golden stooks
New-cutted by the fagging-hooks.
(For sickles did the reaping then
In those old days, when men were men.)

Each year the blue September comes
With wasps all sugar-drunk, in plums,
And crackling partridge-stubble twined
With trumpet-flowered bedëwind.
But those old harvesters uncouth
Are gone out of my world with youth,

4

Gone like the corn-crake, whose harsh word
So darling then is now not heard.

Then, like to maypoles set in lines,
The hopyards of the English vines:
The cribs, wherein I picked for hours
The resined, flakey, pungent flowers,
Whose gummage stained my fingers brown:
Then . . . all those rascallies from town,
The hoppers, cribbing deep, with hooting
New-comers, till they paid their footing,
Or crouching at the twilit meuse
Setting the brass hair-wire noose
That made the wide-eyed rabbit choke.
Or slinking quietly as smoke
Along the hedge till stick could reach
Apron or pinner set to bleach;
Or sudden hand could grab the wing
Of pullet come a-harvesting.
Or, at the inns on market-nights
Rousing the moon with songs and fights.
Where are they, thefts and songs and feuds?
The inns are shut and the moon broods
'These mad leaves that the man-tree bears
Are soon wisps blowing down the airs.'

With these, I well remember still
That miracle of strength and skill
The Cowman, who, with hook and heed,
Let forth the grim red bull to breed,
A ton of power surging by
With seven devils in his eye,
Lurching, like some ninth fatal wave
That a mad moon's compelling drave,
His soul a strength of hell in smoulder
The earthquake heaving in his shoulder,
His malice slanting from his look,
Yet ringed by Man and held by hook.
Man daunted him to please his Wife;
So Man will someday conquer Life.

Then, the grave man, who used to guide
The shire-stallion to his bride:
The stallion stalking, proud as Spain,

5

With ribbons in his tail and mane,
(It took two hours' work to do
That plaiting, red and white and blue.)
His fetlocks combed, his roller trim
And that grave man in charge of him,
The artist shewing forth his ware,
The might surmounted and made fair.

Then, more September memories
Of apples glowing on the trees,
Of men on ladders in the sun
Gathering apples by the ton,
Of heaps of red-fleshed cider-fruit
Wasp-pestered at each apple root
And smell of pommace warm in air
From cider-presses everywhere.

Then, the farm-carters, who could lash
The still air like a musket-crash,
Who strode ahead of waggons talking
To horses jingling in their stalking
From brasses at their collars hung.
The horses understood the tongue,
Of which Phoenician fragments stay
Still, in my memory today:—
"ZAKEEYA DAHBI WOOTA STAH".

Under the earth those heroes are;
Those Englishmen, slow, stubborn, kind,
Farm-labourers, time out of mind,
Who, with odd gurgles, growls and clicks,
Stacked the slain Summer into ricks
Who tamed the great beasts' strength, and beat
Earth's red rebellious clay to meat.

Each full of fancies, dark and odd
From when the devil had been god,
Knowing the rite, with seed or muck,
Without which "Twoulden have no luck":
Knowing how fatal 'twas to plough
Ere Earth and Heaven had said "Now";
And how the blood of bird or mouse
Would bring the crop or guard the house;
And how, unless you turned the penny,
The new moon rode you with her meyny.

Though Night's old terrors stayed, the Earth
Kept in them still the seeds of mirth,
Shrivelled, yet living, from a time
Before wild manhood became crime.

All helped the children to make gay
A maypole for the First of May,
For glory of the fragrant, green
Delightful Spring, the Meadow Queen;
All sang, (and after sixty years
The singing lingers in my ears)
From waggon-tops, while bearing back
The end of harvest to the stack;
The young men, with their swords, would dance
Our pagan blood's inheritance,
Or, strangely dressed, with helms and swords,
And uncouth, half-forgotten words,
(And bladders upon sticks, to beat
Spectators back) in market street
Would act that age-old play of Corn
Cut down by Death and then re-born.
And other touching graces stayed
From times ere pageant had decayed.

For sometimes still, when children died,
Women in white, each like a bride,
Would bear the body to its rest.
And when men died all did their best
To set a feast, however poor,
Of wine and sweetmeats at the door
Though God's recording angels knew
That in their life-times feasts were few.

I know, indeed, I knew of yore,
The bitter cross those heroes bore.
The pastoral those fellows played
Was piped beneath no beech-tree shade,
But fought by manhood grinded bare
Against starvation and despair.

What were they like to look at, say,
Those men who fed us yesterday?
Unlike us, clothing, gait and face,
That uncouth, ancient British race.
Their coats, cut in the antique shear,

7

Had stood the weather many a year,
With baggy pockets each a bin
To hide the wired rabbit in.
Brown corduroy their trews would be
Gartered with straps below the knee.
Their boots on stone struck sparks like steels
From iron on their soles and heels.
The oldest men still daily wore
The smocks of centuries before,
Each fairly needled on the chest
By loving hands long since gone west.
Alas, it's sixty years by clock
Since last I saw a man in smock.

Then, for their gait, their joints, sans oil,
All bent, from having stooped at toil,
Moved with a bow-legged shamble, slow
As the led bull or horse would go.
Since most had started work at seven
They had not quite the grace of Heaven.

Then, for their looks:—their air, their tinct,
(Like all that caused them) are extinct;
But in old photographs I see
Those lost leaves of the English tree,
And know, from seeing them, why Spain
That came to smite ran home again,
And why, at last, man's greed and knavery
Were forced to stop the trade of slavery,
And why, that deadly June day through
The red line stood at Waterloo,
And why all seas have felt the ploughs
Of England's island-builded bows.

Such, on the whole, my memory says
The farm-hands were, in ancient days.
But now, in topsy-turvy now,
Who tends the beasts and drives the plough?

Soon after dawn the other day
I saw a tractor rive the clay,
Sped by a girl of seventeen
With hair of gold and trowsers green,
With fag against her dainty tongue.
Her sister led a cart of dung

8

Beside the lane where she was going.
Boy-scouts in shorts were busy hoeing,
And as the leader of the band
The local parson bore a hand,
And further on, a girl apart
Was loading up a turnip-cart.

The same old work was being done
With pleasure, comradeship and fun;
And at the days-work-end for these
Even in war-time, there was ease,
And strength remaining for delight
In other joy than gin or fight,
In homes unlike the huts of old
Whose leaky thatch was green with mould,
Whose drink was from the brook beyond
Or scoopings from the seepage pond.
Then, from these minds, the fear was riddened
Of what would happen if you didn't
Observe some grimy rite or other
Due to the devil or his mother.
Quit, also, were they of the fear
Of that starvation ever near
The brave Victorians known to me
Twixt seventy eight and eighty three,
Who toiled from dawn till after dark,
And lodged like beasts in Noah's ark,
And brought up children food-bereft
Glad of the turnip sheep had left,
Who drank, if Fortune smiled, (who wouldn't
If Fortune mostly said you couldn't?)
Who poached a bit, and snared and fought
And most heroically wrought
The harvests by whose sap we stood.

I saw no change but for the good.

THE EVERLASTING MERCY

From '41 to '51
I was my folk's contrary son;
I bit my father's hand right through
And broke my mother's heart in two.

9

I sometimes go without my dinner
Now that I know the times I've gi'n her.

From '51 to '61
I cut my teeth and took to fun.
I learned what not to be afraid of
And what stuff women's lips are made of;
I learned with what a rosy feeling
Good ale makes floors seem like the ceiling,
And how the moon gives shiny light
To lads as roll home singing by't.
My blood did leap, my flesh did revel,
Saul Kane was tokened to the devil.

From '61 to '67
I lived in disbelief of heaven
I drunk, I fought, I poached, I whored,
I did despite unto the Lord,
I cursed, 'twould make a man look pale,
And nineteen times I went to jail.
    Now, friends, observe and look upon me,
    Mark how the Lord took pity on me.

By Dead Man's Thorn, while setting wires,
Who should come up but Billy Myers,
A friend of mine, who used to be
As black a sprig of hell as me,
With whom I'd planned, to save encroachin',
Which fields and coverts each should poach in.
Now when he saw me set my snare,
He tells me "Get to hell from there.
This field is mine," he says, "by right;
If you poach here, there'll be a fight.
Out now," he says, "and leave your wire;
It's mine."

                "It ain't."

                        "You put."

                                "You liar."

            "You closhy put."

                                "You bloody liar."

            "This is my field."

                        "This is my wire."

            "I'm ruler here."

                        "You ain't."

                                "I am."

"I'll fight you for it."

                "Right, by damn.
Not now, though, I've a-sprained my thumb,
We'll fight after the harvest hum.
And Silas Jones, that bookie wide,
Will make a purse five pounds a side."
Those were the words, that was the place
By which God brought me into grace.

On Wood Top Field the peewits go
Mewing and wheeling ever so;
And like the shaking of a timbrel
Cackles the laughter of the whimbrel.
In the old quarry-pit they say
Head-keeper Pike was made away.

He walks, head-keeper Pike, for harm.
He taps the windows of the farm;
The blood drips from his broken chin,
He taps and begs to be let in.
On Wood Top, nights, I've shaked to hark
The peewits wambling in the dark
Lest in the dark the old man might
Creep up to me to beg a light.

But Wood Top grass is short and sweet
And springy to a boxer's feet;
At harvest hum the moon so bright
Did shine on Wood Top for the fight.

When Bill was stripped down to his bends
I thought how long we two'd been friends,
And in my mind, about that wire,
I thought, "He's right, I am a liar.
As sure as skilly's made in prison
The right to poach that copse is his'n.
I'll have no luck to-night" thinks I.
"I'm fighting to defend a lie.
And this moonshiny evening's fun
Is worse than aught I ever done."
And thinking that way my heart bled so
I almost stept to Bill and said so.
And now Bill's dead I would be glad
If I could only think I had.

11

But no. I put the thought away
For fear of what my friends would say.
They'd backed me, see? O Lord, the sin
Done for the things there's money in.

The stakes were drove, the ropes were hitched
Into the ring my hat I pitched.
My corner faced the Squire's park
Just where the fir-trees make it dark;
The place where I begun poor Nell
Upon the woman's road to hell.
I thought of't, sitting in my corner
After the time-keep struck his warner
(Two brandy flasks, for fear of noise,
Clinked out the time to us two boys).
And while my seconds chafed and gloved me
I thought of Nell's eyes when she loved me,
And wondered how my tot would end,
First Nell cast off and now my friend;
And in the moonlight dim and wan
I knew quite well my luck was gone;
And looking round I felt a spite
At all who'd come to see me fight;
The five and forty human faces
Inflamed by drink and going to races,
Faces of men who'd never been
Merry or true or live or clean;
Who'd never felt the boxer's trim
Of brain divinely knit to limb,
Nor felt the whole live body go
One tingling health from top to toe;
Nor took a punch nor given a swing,
But just soaked deady round the ring
Until their brains and bloods were foul
Enough to make their throttles howl,
While we whom Jesus died to teach
Fought round on round, three minutes each.

And thinking that, you'll understand
I thought, "I'll go and take Bill's hand.
I'll up and say the fault was mine,
He sha'n't make play for these here swine."
And then I though that that was silly,
They'd think I was afraid of Billy:
They'd think (I thought it, God forgive me)

I funked the hiding Bill could give me.
And that thought made me mad and hot.
"Think that, will they? Well, they shall not.
They sha'n't think that. I will not. I'm
Damned if I will. I will not."
                                    Time!

From the beginning of the bout
My luck was gone, my hand was out.
Right from the start Bill called the play,
But I was quick and kept away
Till the fourth round, when work got mixed,
And then I knew Bill had me fixed.
My hand was out, why, Heaven knows;
Bill punched me when and where he chose.
Through two more rounds we quartered wide
And all the time my hands seemed tied;
Bill punched me when and where he pleased.
The cheering from my backers ceased,
But every punch I heard a yell
Of "That's the style, Bill, give him hell."
No one for me, but Jimmy's light
"Straight left! Straight left!" and "Watch his right."

   I don't know how a boxer goes
When all his body hums from blows;
I know I seemed to rock and spin,
I don't know how I saved my chin;
I know I thought my only friend
Was that clinked flask at each round's end
When my two seconds, Ed and Jimmy,
Had sixty seconds help to gimme.
But in the ninth, with pain and knocks
I stopped: I couldn't fight nor box.
Bill missed his swing, the light was tricky,
But I went down, and stayed down, dicky.
"Get up," cried Jim. I said, "I will."
Then all the gang yelled, "Out him, Bill.
Out him." Bill rushed . . . and Clink, Clink, Clink.
Time! and Jim's knee, and rum to drink.
And round the ring there ran a titter:
"Saved by the call, the bloody quitter."

They drove (a dodge that never fails)
A pin beneath my finger nails.

They poured what seemed a running beck
Of cold spring water down my neck;
Jim with a lancet quick as flies
Lowered the swellings round my eyes.
They sluiced my legs and fanned my face
Through all that blessed minute's grace;
They gave my calves a thorough kneading,
They salved my cuts and stopped the bleeding.
A gulp of liquor dulled the pain,
And then the two flasks clinked again.
Time!
    There was Bill as grim as death.
He rushed, I clinched, to get more breath
And breath I got, though Billy bats
Some stinging short-arms in my slats.
And when we broke, as I foresaw,
He swung his right in for the jaw.
I stopped it on my shoulder bone,
And at the shock I heard Bill groan—
A little groan or moan or grunt
As though I'd hit his wind a bunt.
At that, I clinched, and while we clinched,
His old-time right-arm dig was flinched,
And when we broke he hit me light
As though he didn't trust his right,
He flapped me somehow with his wrist
As though he couldn't use his fist,
And when he hit he winced with pain.
I thought, "Your sprained thumb's crocked again."
So I got strength and Bill gave ground,
And that round was an easy round.

During the wait my Jimmy said,
"What's making Billy fight so dead?
He's all to pieces. Is he blown?"
"His thumb's out."
               "No? Then it's your own.
It's all your own, but don't be rash—
He's got the goods if you've got cash,
And what one hand can do he'll do,
Be careful this next round or two."

Time! There was Bill, and I felt sick
That luck should play so mean a trick
And give me leave to knock him out

After he'd plainly won the bout.
But by the way the man came at me
He made it plain he meant to bat me;
If you'd a seen the way he come
You wouldn't think he'd crocked a thumb.
With all his skill and all his might
He clipped me dizzy left and right;
The Lord knows what the effort cost,
But he was mad to think he'd lost,
And knowing nothing else could save him
He didn't care what pain it gave him.
He called the music and the dance
For five rounds more and gave no chance.

Try to imagine if you can
The kind of manhood in the man,
And if you'd like to feel his pain,
You sprain your thumb and hit the sprain,
And hit it hard, with all your power
On something hard for half an hour,
While someone thumps you black and blue,
And then you'll know what Billy knew.
Bill took that pain without a sound
Till half-way through the eighteenth round,
And then I sent him down and out,
And Silas said, "Kane wins the bout."

When Bill came to, you understand,
I ripped the mitten from my hand
And went across to ask Bill shake.
My limbs were all one pain and ache,
I was so weary and so sore
I don't think I'd a stood much more.
Bill in his corner bathed his thumb,
Buttoned his short and glowered glum.
"I'll never shake you hand," he said.
"I'd rather see my children dead.
I've been about and had some fun with you.
But you're a liar and I've done with you.
You've knocked me out, you didn't beat me;
Look out the next time that you meet me,
There'll be no friend to watch the clock for you
And no convenient thumb to crock for you,
And I'll take care, with much delight,
You'll get what you'd a got to-night;

15

That puts my meaning clear, I guess.
Now get to hell; I want to dress."

I dressed. My backers one and all
Said, "Well done you," or "Good old Saul."
"Saul is a wonder and a fly 'un,
What'll you have, Saul, at the 'Lion'?"
With merry oaths they helped me down
The stony wood-path to the town.

The moonlight shone on Cabbage Walk,
It made the limestone look like chalk.
It was too late for any people,
Twelve struck as we went by the steeple.
A dog barked, and an owl was calling,
The Squire's brook was still a-falling,
The carved heads on the church looked down
On "Russell, Blacksmith of this Town,"
And all the graves of all the ghosts
Who rise on Christmas Eve in hosts
To dance and carol in festivity
For joy of Jesus Christ's Nativity
(Bell-ringer Dawe and his two sons
Beheld 'em from the bell-tower once)
Two and two about about
Singing the end of Advent out,
Dwindling down to windlestraws
When the glittering peacock craws,
As craw the glittering peacock should
When Christ's own star comes over the wood.
Lamb of the sky come out of fold
Wandering windy heavens cold.
So they shone and sang till twelve
When all the bells ring out of theirselve;
Rang a peal for Christmas morn,
Glory, men, for Christ is born.

All the old monks' singing places
Glimmered quick with flitting faces,
Singing anthems, singing hymns
Under carven cherubims.
Ringer Dawe aloft could mark
Faces at the window dark
Crowding, crowding, row on row,

Till all the church began to glow.
The chapel glowed, the nave, the choir,
All the faces became fire
Below the eastern window high
To see Christ's star come up the sky.
Then they lifted hands and turned,
And all their lifted fingers burned,
Burned like the golden altar tallows,
Burned like a troop of God's own Hallows,
Bringing to mind the burning time
When all the bells will rock and chime
And burning saints on burning horses
Will sweep the planets from their courses
And loose the stars to burn up night.
Lord, give us eyes to bear the light.

We all went quiet down the Scallenge
Lest Police Inspector Drew should challenge.
But 'Spector Drew was sleeping sweet,
His head upon a charges sheet,
Under the gas-jet flaring full,
Snorting and snoring like a bull,
His bull cheeks puffed, his bull lips blowing,
His ugly yellow front teeth showing.
Just as we peeped we saw him fumble
And scratch his head, and shift, and mumble.

Down in the lane so thin and dark
The tan-yards stank of bitter bark,
The curate's pigeons gave a flutter,
A cat went courting down the gutter,
And none else stirred a foot or feather.
The houses put their heads together,
Talking, perhaps, so dark and sly,
Of all the folk they'd seen go by,
Children, and men and women, merry all,
Who'd some day pass that way to burial.
It was all dark, but at the turning
The "Lion" had a window burning.
So in we went and up the stairs,
Treading as still as cats and hares.
The way the stairs creaked made you wonder
If dead men's bones were hidden under.
At head of stairs upon the landing
A woman with a lamp was standing;

She greet each gent at head of stairs
With "Step in, gents, and take your chairs.
The punch'll come when kettle bubble,
But don't make noise or there'll be trouble."
'Twas Doxy Jane, a bouncing girl
With eyes all sparks and hair all curl,
And cheeks all red and lips all coal,
And thirst for men instead of soul.
She's trod her pathway to the fire.
Old Rivers had his nephew by her.

I step aside from Tom and Jimmy
To find if she'd a kiss to gimme.
I blew out lamp 'fore she could speak.
She said, "If you ain't got a cheek,"
And then beside me in the dim,
"Did he beat you or you beat him?"
"Why, I beat him" (though that was wrong),
She said, "You must be turble strong.
I'd be afraid you'd beat me, too."
"You'd not," I said, "I wouldn't do."
"Never?"
                    "No, never."
                              "Never?"
                                        "No."
"O Saul. Here's missus. Let me go."
It wasn't missus, so I didn't,
Whether I mid do or I midn't,
Until she'd promised we should meet
Next evening, six, at top of street,
When we could have a quiet talk
On that low wall up Worcester Walk.
And while we whispered there together
I give her silver for a feather
And felt a drunkenness like wine
And shut out Christ in husks and swine,
I felt the dart strike through my liver.
God punish me for't and forgive her.

Each one could be a Jesus mild,
Each one has been a little child,
A little child with laughing look,
A lovely white unwritten book;
A book that God will take, my friend,
As each goes out at journey's end.

The Lord who gave us Earth and Heaven
Takes that as thanks for all He's given.
The book He lent is given back
All blotted red and smutted black.

"Open the door," said Jim, "and call."
Jane gasped, "They'll see me. Loose me, Saul."
She pushed me by, and ducked downstair
With half the pins out of her hair.
I went inside the lit room rollin',
Her scented handkerchief I'd stolen.
"What would you fancy, Saul?" they said.
"A gin punch hot and then to bed."
"Jane, fetch the punch bowl to the gemmen;
And mind you don't put too much lemon.
Our good friend Saul has had a fight of it,
Now smoke up, boys, and make a night of it."

The room was full of men and stink
Of bad cigars and heavy drink.
Riley was nodding to the floor
And gurgling as he wanted more.
His mouth was wide, his face was pale,
His swollen face was sweating ale;
And one of those assembled Greeks
Had corked black crosses on his cheeks.
Thomas was having words with Goss,
He "wouldn't pay, the fight was cross."
And Goss told Tom that "cross or no,
The bets go as the verdicts go,
By all I've ever heard or read of.
So pay, or else I'll knock your head off."
Jim Gurvil said his smutty say
About a girl down Bye Street way.
And how the girl from Frogatt's circus
Died giving birth in Newent work'us.
And Dick told how the Dymock wench
Bore twins, poor thing, on Dog Hill bench;
And how he'd owned to one in court
And how Judge made him sorry for 't.
Jock set a jew's harp twanging drily;
"Gimme another cup," said Riley.
A dozen more were in their glories
With laughs and smokes and smutty stories;

And Jimmy joked and took his sup
And sang his song of "Up, come up."

Jane brought the bowl of stewing gin
And poured the egg and lemon in,
And whisked it up and served it out
While bawdy questions went about.
Jack chucked her chin, and Jim accost her
With bits out of the "Maid of Gloster."
And fifteen arms went round her waist.
(And then men ask, Are Barmaids chaste?)

O young men, pray to be kept whole
From bringing down a weaker soul.
Your minute's joy so meet in doin'
May be the woman's door to ruin;
The door to wandering up and down,
A painted whore at half a crown.
The bright mind fouled, the beauty gay
All eaten out and fallen away,
By drunken days and weary tramps
From pub to pub by city lamps,
Till men despise the game they started,
Till health and beauty are departed,
And in a slum the reeking hag
Mumbles a crust with toothy jag,
Or gets the river's help to end
The life too wrecked for man to mend.

We spat and smoked and took our swipe
Till Silas up and tap his pipe,
And begged us all to pay attention
Because he'd several things to mention.
We'd seen the fight (Hear, hear. That's you);
But still one task remained to do;
That task was his, he didn't shun it,
To give the purse to him as won it;
With this remark, from start to out
He'd never seen a brisker bout.
There was the purse. At that he'd leave it.
Let Kane come forward to receive it.

I took the purse and hemmed and bowed,
And called for gin punch for the crowd,
And when the second bowl was done,

I called, "Let's have another one."
Si's wife come in and sipped and sipped
(As women will) till she was pipped.
And Si hit Dicky Twot a clouter
Because he put his arm about her;
But after Si got overtasked
She sat and kissed whoever asked.
My Doxy Jane was splashed by this,
I took her on my knee to kiss.
And Tom cried out, "O damn the gin;
Why can't we all have women in?
Bess Evans, now, or Sister Polly,
Or those two housemaids at the Folly?
Let some one nip to Biddy Price's,
They'd all come in a brace of trices.
Rose Davies, Sue, and Betsy Perks;
One man, one girl, and damn all Turks."
But, no. "More gin," they cried; "Come on,
We'll have the girls in when it's gone."
So round the gin went, hot and heady,
Hot Hollands punch on top of deady.

Hot Hollands punch on top of stout
Puts madness in and wisdom out.
From drunken man to drunken man
The drunken madness raged and ran.
"I'm climber Joe who climbed the spire."
"You're climber Joe the bloody liar."
"Who say I lie?"
                    "I do."
                            "You lie,
I climbed the spire and had a fly."
"I'm French Suzanne, the Circus Dancer,
I'm going to dance a bloody Lancer."
"If I'd my rights I'm Squire's heir."
"By rights I'd be a millionaire."
"By rights I'd be the lord of you,
But Farmer Scriggins had his do,
He done me, so I've had to hoove it,
I've got it all wrote down to prove it.
And one of these dark winter nights
He'll learn I mean to have my rights;
I'll bloody him a bloody fix,
I'll bloody burn his bloody ricks."

From three long hours of gin and smokes,
And two girls' breath and fifteen blokes',
A warmish night, and windows shut,
The room stank like a fox's gut.
The heat and smell and drinking deep
Began to stun the gang to sleep.
Some fell downstairs to sleep on the mat,
Some snored it sodden where they sat.
Dick Twot had lost a tooth and wept,
But all the drunken others slept.
Jane slept beside me in the chair,
And I got up; I wanted air.

I opened window wide and leaned
Out of that pigstye of the fiend
And felt a cool wind go like grace
About the sleeping market-place.
The clock struck three, and sweetly, slowly,
The bells chimed Holy, Holy, Holy;
And in a second's pause there fell
The cold note of the chapel bell,
And then a cock crew, flapping wings,
And summat made me think of things.
How long those ticking clocks had gone
From church and chapel, on and on,
Ticking the time out, ticking slow
To men and girls who'd come and go,
And how they ticked in belfry dark
When half the town was bishop's park,
And how they'd rung a chime full tilt
The night after the church was built,
And how that night was Lambert's Feast,
The night I'd fought and been a beast.
And how a change had come. And then
I thought, "You tick to different men."
What with the fight and what with drinking
And being awake alone there thinking,
My mind began to carp and tetter,
"If this life's all, the beasts are better"
And then I thought, "I wish I'd seen
The many towns this town has been;
I wish I knew if they'd a-got
A kind of summat we've a-not,
If them as built the church so fair
Were half the chaps folk say they were;

For they'd the skill to draw their plan,
And skill's a joy to any man;
And they'd the strength, not skill alone,
To build it beautiful in stone;
And strength and skill together thus . . .
O, they were happier men than us.

"But if they were, they had to die
The same as every one and I.
And no one lives again, but dies,
And all the bright goes out of eyes,
And all the skill goes out of hands,
And all the wise brain understands,
And all the beauty, all the power
Is cut down like a withered flower.
In all the show from birth to rest
I give the poor dumb cattle best."

I wondered, then, why life should be,
And what would be the end of me
When youth and health and strength were gone
And cold old age came creeping on?
A keeper's gun? The Union ward?
Or that new quod at Hereford?
And looking round I felt disgust
At all my nights of drink and lust,
And all the looks of all the swine
Who'd said that they were friends of mine;
And yet I knew, when morning came,
The morning would be just the same,
For I'd have drinks and Jane would meet me
And drunken Silas Jones would greet me,
And I'd risk quod and keeper's gun
Till all the silly game was done.
"For parson chaps are mad supposin'
A chap can change the road he's chosen."

And then the Devil whispered "Saul,
Why should you want to live at all?
Why fret and sweat and try to mend?
It's all the same thing in the end.
But when it's done," he said, "it's ended.
Why stand it, since it can't be mended?"
And in my heart I heard him plain,
"Throw yourself down and end it, Kane."

"Why not?" said I. "Why not? But no,
I won't. I've never had my go.
I've not had all the world can give.
Death by and by, but first I'll live.
The world owes me my time of times,
And that time's coming now, by crimes."
A madness took me then. I felt
I'd like to hit the world a belt.
I felt that I could fly through air,
A screaming star with blazing hair,
A rushing comet, crackling, numbing
The folk with fear of judgment coming,
A 'Lijah in a fiery car
Coming to tell folk what they are.

"That's what I'll do," I shouted loud,
"I'll tell this sanctimonious crowd,
This town of window-peeping, prying,
Maligning, peering, hinting, lying,
Male and female human blots
Who would, but daren't be, whores and sots,
That they're so steeped in petty vice
That they're less excellent than lice,
That they're so soaked in petty virtue
That touching one of them will dirt you,
Dirt you with the stain of mean
Cheating trade and going between,
Pinching, starving, scraping, hoarding,
Spying through the chinks of boarding
To see if Sue the prentice lean
Dares to touch the margarine.
Fawning, cringing, oiling boots,
Raging in the crowd's pursuits,
Flinging stones at all the Stephens,
Standing firm with all the evens,
Making hell for all the odd,
All the lonely ones of God,
Those poor lonely ones who find
Dogs more mild than human kind.
For dogs," I said, "are nobles born
To most of you, you cockled corn.
I've known dogs to leave their dinner,
Nosing a kind heart in a sinner.
Poor old Crafty wagged his tail
The day I first came home from jail,

24

When all my folk, so primly clad,
Glowered black and thought me mad,
And muttered how they'd been respected,
While I was what they'd all expected.
(I've thought of that old dog for years,
And of how near I come to tears.)

"But you, you minds of bread and cheese,
Are less divine than that dog's fleas.
You suck blood from kindly friends,
And kill them when it serves your ends.
Double traitors, double black,
Stabbing only in the back,
Stabbing with the knives you borrow
From the friends you bring to sorrow.
You stab all that's true and strong;
Truth and strength you say are wrong;
Meek and mild, and sweet and creeping,
Repeating, canting, cadging, peeping,
That's the art and that's the life
To win a man his neighbour's wife.
All that's good and all that's true,
You kill that, so I'll kill you."

At that I tore my clothes in shreds
And hurled them on the window leads;
I flung my boots through both the winders
And knocked the glass to little flinders;
The punch bowl and the tumblers followed,
And then I seized the lamps and holloed
And down the stairs, and tore back bolts,
As mad as twenty blooded colts;
And out into the street I pass,
As mad as two-year-olds at grass,
A naked madman waving grand
A blazing lamp in either hand.
I yelled like twenty drunken sailors,
"The devil's come among the tailors."
A blaze of flame behind me streamed,
And then I clashed the lamps and screamed
"I'm Satan, newly come from hell."
And then I spied the fire-bell.

I've been a ringer, so I know
How best to make a big bell go.

25

So on to bell-rope swift I swoop,
And stick my one foot in the loop
And heave a down-swig till I groan
"Awake, you swine, you devil's own."
I made the fire-bell awake,
I felt the bell-rope throb and shake;
I felt the air mingle and clang
And beat the walls a muffled bang,
And stifle back and boom and bay
Like muffled peals on Boxing Day,
And then surge up and gather shape,
And spread great pinions and escape;
And each great bird of clanging shrieks
O Fire, Fire! from iron beaks.
My shoulders cracked to send around
Those shrieking birds made out of sound
With news of fire in their bills.
(They heard 'em plain beyond Wall Hills.)

Up go the winders, out come heads,
I heard the springs go creak in beds;
But still I heave and sweat and tire,
And still the clang goes "Fire, Fire!"
"Where is it, then? Who is it, there?
You ringer, stop, and tell us where."
"Run round and let the Captain know."
"It must be bad, he's ringing so."
"It's in the town, I see the flame;
Look there! Look there, how red it came."
"Where is it, then? O stop the bell."
I stopped and called: "It's fire of hell;
And this is Sodom and Gomorrah,
And now I'll burn you up, begorra."

By this the firemen were mustering,
The half-dressed stable men were flustering,
Backing the horses out of stalls
While this man swears and that man bawls,
"Don't take th' old mare. Back, Toby, back.
Back, Lincoln. Where's the fire, Jack?"
"Damned if I know. Out Preston way."
"No. It's at Chancey's Pitch, they say."
"It's sixteen ricks at Pauntley burnt."
"You back old Darby out, I durn't."

They ran the big red engine out,
And put 'em to with damn and shout.
And then they start to raise the shire,
"Who brought the news, and where's the fire?"
They'd moonlight, lamps, and gas to light 'em,
I give a screech-owl's screech to fright 'em,
And snatch from underneath their noses
The nozzles of the fire hoses.
"I am the fire. Back, stand back,
Or else I'll fetch your skulls a crack;
D'you see these copper nozzles here?
They weigh ten pounds apiece, my dear;
I'm fire of hell come up this minute
To burn this town, and all that's in it.
To burn you dead and burn you clean,
You cogwheels in a stopped machine,
You hearts of snakes, and brains of pigeons.
You dead devout of dead religions,
You offspring of the hen and ass.
By pirate ruled, and Caiaphas.
Now your account is totted. Learn
Hell's flames are loose and you shall burn."

At that I leaped and screamed and ran,
I heard their cries go "Catch him, man."
"Who was it?" "Down him." "Out him, Ern."
"Duck him at pump, we'll see who'll burn."
A policeman clutched, a fireman clutched,
A dozen others snatched and touched.
"By God, he's stripped down to his buff."
"By God, we'll make him warm enough."
"After him." "Catch him," "Out him," "Scrob him."
"We'll give him hell." "By God, we'll mob him."
"We'll duck him, scrout him, flog him, fratch him."
"All right," I said. "But first you'll catch him."

The men who don't know to the root
The joy of being swift of foot,
Have never known divine and fresh
The glory of the gift of flesh,
Nor felt the feet exult, nor gone
Along a dim road, on and on,
Knowing again the bursting glows
The mating hare in April knows,

Who tingles to the pads with mirth
At being the swiftest thing on earth.
O, if you want to know delight,
Run naked in an autumn night,
And laugh, as I laughed then, to find
A running rabble drop behind,
And whang, on every door you pass,
Two copper nozzles, tipped with brass,
And doubly whang at every turning,
And yell, "All hell's let loose, and burning."

I beat my brass and shouted fire
At doors of parson, lawyer, squire,
At all three doors I threshed and slammed
And yelled aloud that they were damned.
I clodded squire's glass with turves
Because he spring-gunned his preserves.
Through parson's glass my nozzle swishes
Because he stood for loaves and fishes,
But parson's glass I spared a tittle.
He give me an orange once when little,
And he who gives a child a treat
Makes joy-bells ring in Heaven's street.

And he who gives a child a home
Builds palaces in Kingdom come,
And she who gives a baby birth
Brings Saviour Christ again to Earth,
For life is joy, and mind is fruit,
And body's precious earth and root.
But lawyer's glass—well, never mind,
Th' old Adam's strong in me, I find.
God pardon man, and may God's son
Forgive the evil things I've done.

What more? By Dirty Lane I crept
Back to the "Lion," where I slept.
The raging madness hot and floodin'
Boiled itself out and left me sudden,
Left me worn out and sick and cold,
Aching as though I'd all grown old;
So there I lay, and there they found me
On door-mat, with a curtain round me.
Si took my heels and Jane my head
And laughed, and carried me to bed.

28

And from the neighbouring street they reskied
My boots and trousers, coat and weskit;
They bath-bricked both the nozzles bright
To be mementoes of the night,
And knowing what I should awake with
They flannelled me a quart to slake with,
And sat and shook till half-past two
Expecting Police Inspector Drew.

I woke and drank, and went to meat
In clothes still dirty from the street.
Down in the bar I heard 'em tell
How someone rang the fire-bell,
And how th' Inspector's search had thriven,
And how five pounds reward was given.
And Shepherd Boyce, of Marley, glad us
By saying it was blokes from mad'us,
Or two young rips lodged at the "Prince"
Whom none had seen nor heard of since,
Or that young blade from Worcester Walk
(You know how country people talk).

Young Joe the ostler come in sad,
He said th' old mare had bit his dad.
He said there'd come a blazing screeching
Daft Bible-prophet chap a-preaching,
Had put th' old mare in such a taking
She'd thought the bloody earth was quaking.
And others come and spread a tale
Of cut-throats out of Gloucester jail,
And how we needed extra cops
With all them Welsh come picking hops;
With drunken Welsh in all our sheds
We might be murdered in our beds.
By all accounts, both men and wives
Had had the scare up of their lives.

I ate and drank and gathered strength,
And stretched along the bench full length,
Or crossed to window seat to pat
Black Silas Jones's little cat.
At four I called, "You devil's own,
The second trumpet shall be blown.
The second trump, the second blast;
Hell's flames are loosed, and judgment's passed

Too late for mercy now. Take warning
I'm death and hell and Judgment morning."
I hurled the bench into the settle,
I banged the table on the kettle,
I sent Joe's quart of cider spinning.
"Lo, here begins my second inning."
Each bottle, mug, and jug and pot
I smashed to crocks in half a tot;
And Joe, and Si, and Nick, and Percy
I rolled together topsy versy.
And as I ran I heard 'em call,
"Now damn to hell, what's gone with Saul?"

Out into street I ran uproarious,
The devil dancing in me glorious.
And as I ran I yell and shriek
"Come on, now, turn the other cheek."
Across the way by almshouse pump
I see old puffing parson stump.

Old parson, red-eyed as a ferret
From nightly wrestlings with the spirit;
I ran across, and barred his path.
His turkey gills went red as wrath
And then he froze, as parsons can.
"The police will deal with you, my man."
"Not yet," said I, "not yet they won't;
And now you'll hear me, like or don't.
The English Church both is and was
A subsidy of Caiaphas.
I don't believe in Prayer nor Bible,
They're lies all through, and you're a libel,
A libel on the Devil's plan
When first he miscreated man.
You mumble through a formal code
To get which martyrs burned and glowed.
I look on martyrs as mistakes,
But still they burned for it at stakes;
Your only fire's the jolly fire
Where you can guzzle port with Squire,
And back and praise his damned opinions
About his temporal dominions.
You let him give the man who digs,
A filthy hut unfit for pigs,
Without a well, without a drain,

With mossy thatch that lets in rain,
Without a 'lotment, 'less he rent it,
And never meat, unless he scent it,
But weekly doles of 'leven shilling
To make a grown man strong and willing
To do the hardest work on earth
And feed his wife when she gives birth,
And feed his little children's bones.
I tell you, man, the Devil groans.
With all your main and all your might
You back what is against what's right;
You let the Squire do things like these,
You back him in't and give him ease,
You take his hand, and drink his wine,
And he's a hog, but you're a swine.
For you take gold to teach God's ways
And teach man how to sing God's praise.
And now I'll tell you what you teach
In downright honest English speech.

"You teach the ground-down starving man
That Squire's greed 's Jehovah's plan.
You get his learning circumvented
Lest it should make him discontented
(Better a brutal, starving nation
Than men with thoughts above their station),
You let him neither read nor think,
You goad his wretched soul to drink
And then to jail, the drunken boor;
O sad intemperance of the poor.
You starve his soul till it's rapscallion,
Then blame his flesh for being stallion.
You send your wife around to paint
The golden glories of 'restraint.'
How moral exercise bewild'rin'
Would soon result in fewer children.
You work a day in Squire's fields
And see what sweet restraint it yields;
A woman's day at turnip picking,
Your heart's too fat for plough or ricking.

"And you whom luck taught French and Greek
Have purple flaps on either cheek,
A stately house, and time for knowledge,
And gold to send your sons to college,

That pleasant place, where getting learning
Is also key to money earning,
But quite your damn'dest want of grace
Is what you do to save your face;
The way you sit astride the gates
By padding wages out of rates;
Your Christmas gifts of shoddy blankets
That every working soul may thank its
Loving parson, loving squire
Through whom he can't afford a fire.
Your well-packed bench, your prison pen,
To keep them something less than men;
You friendly clubs to help 'em bury,
Your charities of midwifery.
Your bidding children duck and cap
To them who give them workhouse pap.
O, what you are, and what you preach,
And what you do, and what you teach
Is not God's Word, nor honest schism,
But Devil's cant and pauperism."

By this time many folk had gathered
To listen to me while I blathered;
I said my piece, and when I'd said it,
I'll do old purple parson credit,
He sunk (as sometimes parsons can)
His coat's excuses in the man.
"You think that Squire and I are kings
Who made the existing state of things,
And made it ill. I answer, No,
States are not made, nor patched; they grow,
Grow slow through centuries of pain
And grow correctly in the main,
But only grow by certain laws
Of certain bits in certain jaws.
You want to doctor that. Let be.
You cannot patch a growing tree.
Put these two words beneath your hat,
These two: securus judicat.
The social states of human kinds
Are made by multitudes of minds,
And after multitudes of years
A little human growth appears
Worth having, even to the soul
Who sees most plain it's not the whole.

32

This state is dull and evil, both,
I keep it in the path of growth;
You think the Church an outworn retter;
Kane, keep it, till you've built a better.
And keep the existing social state;
I quite agree it's out of date,
One does too much, another shirks,
Unjust, I grant; but still . . . it works.
To get the whole world out of bed
And washed, and dressed, and warmed, and fed,
To work, and back to bed again
Believe me, Saul, costs worlds of pain.
Then, as to whether true or sham
That book of Christ, Whose priest I am;
The Bible is a lie, say you,
Where do you stand, suppose it true?
Good-bye. But if you've more to say,
My doors are open night and day.
Meanwhile, my friend, 'twould be no sin
To mix more water in your gin.
We're neither saints nor Philip Sidneys,
But mortal men with mortal kidneys."
He took his snuff, and wheezed a greeting,
And waddled off to mothers' meeting;
I hung my head upon my chest,
I give old purple parson best,
For while the Plough tips round the Pole
The trained mind outs the upright soul,
As Jesus said the trained mind might,
Being wiser than the sons of light,
But trained men's minds are spread so thin
They let all sorts of darkness in;
Whatever light man finds they doubt it,
They love not light, but talk about it.

But parson'd proved to people's eyes
That I was drunk, and he was wise;
And people grinned and women tittered,
And little children mocked and twittered,
So blazing mad, I stalked to bar
To show how noble drunkards are,
And guzzled spirits like a beast,
To show contempt for Church and priest,
Until, by six, my wits went round
Like hungry pigs in parish pound.

At half-past six, rememb'ring Jane,
I staggered into street again
With mind made up (or primed with gin)
To bash the cop who'd run me in;
For well I knew I'd have to cock up
My legs that night inside the lock-up,
And it was my most fixed intent
To have a fight before I went.
Our Fates are strange, and no one knows his;
Our lovely Saviour Christ disposes.

Jane wasn't where we'd planned, the jade,
She'd thought me drunk and hadn't stayed.
So I went up the Walk to look for her
And lingered by the little brook for her,
And dowsed my face, and drank at spring,
And watched two wild duck on the wing.
The moon come pale, the wind come cool,
A big pike leaps in Lower Pool,
The peacock screamed, the clouds were straking,
My cut cheek felt the weather breaking;
An orange sunset waned and thinned
Foretelling rain and western wind,
And while I watched I heard distinct
The metals on the railway clinked.
The blood-edged clouds were all in tatters,
The sky and earth seemed mad as hatters;
They had a death look, wild and odd,
Of something dark foretold by God.
And seeing it so, I felt so shaken
I wouldn't keep the road I'd taken,
But wandered back towards the inn
Resolved to brace myself with gin.
And as I walked, I said, "It's strange,
There's Death let loose to-night, and Change."

In Cabbage Walk I made a haul
Of two big pears from lawyer's wall,
And, munching one, I took the lane
Back into Market-place again.
Lamp-lighter Dick had passed the turning
And all the Homend lamps were burning,
The windows shone, the shops were busy,
But that strange Heaven made me dizzy.
The sky had all God's warning writ

In bloody marks all over it,
And over all I though there was
A ghastly light beside the gas.
The Devil's tasks and Devil's rages
Were giving me the Devil's wages.

In Market-place it's always light,
The big shop windows make it bright;
And in the press of people buying
I spied a little fellow crying
Because his mother'd gone inside
And left him there, and so he cried.
And mother'd beat him when she found him,
And mother's whip would curl right round him,
And mother'd say he'd done't to crost her,
Though there being crowds about he'd lost her.

Lord, give to men who are old and rougher
The things that little children suffer,
And let keep bright and undefiled
The young years of the little child.
I pat his head at edge of street
And gi'm my second pear to eat.
Right under lamp, I pat his head,
"I'll stay till mother come," I said,
And stay I did, and joked and talked,
And shoppers wondered as they walked.
"There's that Saul Kane, the drunken blaggard,
Talking to little Jimmy Jaggard.
The drunken blaggard reeks of drink."
"Whatever will his mother think?"
"Wherever has his mother gone?
Nip round to Mrs. Jaggard's, John,
And say her Jimmy's out again,
In Market-place, with boozer Kane."
"When he come out to-day he staggered.
O, Jimmy Jaggard, Jimmy Jaggard."
"His mother's gone inside to bargain,
Run in and tell her, Polly Margin,
And tell her poacher Kane is tipsy
And selling Jimmy to a gipsy."
"Run in to Mrs Jaggard, Ellen,
Or else, dear knows, there'll be no tellin',
And don't dare leave yer till you've fount her,
You'll find her at the linen counter."

I told a tale, to Jim's delight,
Of where the tom-cats go by night,
And how when moonlight come they went
Among the chimneys black and bent,
From roof to roof, from house to house,
With little baskets full of mouse
All red and white, both joint and chop
Like meat out of a butcher's shop;
Then all along the wall they creep
And everyone is fast asleep,
And honey-hunting moths go by,
And by the bread-batch crickets cry;
Then on they hurry, never waiting,
To lawyer's backyard cellar grating,
Where Jaggard's cat, with clever paw,
Unhooks a broke-brick's secret door:
Then down into the cellar black,
Across the wood slug's slimy track,
Into an old cask's quiet hollow,
Where they've got seats for what's to follow;
Then each tom-cat lights little candles,
And O, the stories and the scandals,
And O, the songs and Christmas carols,
And O, the milk from little barrels.
They light a fire fit for roasting
(And how good mouse-meat smells when toasting),
Then down they sit to merry feast
While moon goes west and sun comes east.

Sometimes they make so merry there
Old lawyer come to head of stair
To 'fend with fist and poker took firm
His parchments channelled by the bookworm,
And all his deeds, and all his packs
Of withered ink and sealing wax;
And there he stands, with candle raised,
And listens like a man amazed,
Or like a ghost a man stands dumb at,
He says, "Hush! Hush! I'm sure there's summat!"
He hears outside the brown owl call,
He hears the death-tick tap the wall,
The gnawing of the wainscot mouse,
The creaking up and down the house,
The unhooked window's hinges ranging,
The sounds that say the wind is changing.

As last he turns, and shakes his head,
"It's nothing, I'll go back to bed."

And just then Mrs. Jaggard came
To view and end her Jimmy's shame.

She made one rush and gi'm a bat
And shook him like a dog a rat.
"I can't turn round but what you're straying,
I'll give you tales and gipsy playing.
I'll give you wand'ring off like this
And listening to whatever't is,
You'll laugh the little side of the can,
You'll have the whip for this, my man;
And not a bite of meat nor bread
You'll touch before you go to bed.
Some day you'll break your mother's heart,
After God knows she's done her part,
Working her arms off day and night
Trying to keep your collars white.
Look at your face, too, in the street.
What dirty filth've you found to cat?
Now don't you blubber here, boy, or
I'll give you sum't to blubber for."
She snatched him off from where we stand
And knocked the pear-core from his hand,
And looked at me, "You Devil's limb,
How dare you talk to Jaggard's Jim;
You drunken, poaching, boozing brute, you,
If Jaggard was a man he'd shoot you."
She glared all this, but didn't speak,
She gasped, white hollows in her cheek;
Jimmy was writhing, screaming wild,
The shoppers thought I'd killed the child.

I had to speak, so I begun,
"You'd oughtn't beat your little son;
He did no harm, but seeing him there
I talked to him and gi'm a pear;
I'm sure the poor child meant no wrong,
It's all my fault he stayed so long,
He'd not have stayed, mum, I'll be bound
If I'd not chanced to come around.
It's all my fault he stayed, not his.

I kept him here, that's how it is."
"Oh! And how dare you, then?" says she,
"How dare you tempt my boy from me?
How dare you do 't, you drunken swine,
Is he your child or is he mine?
A drunken sot they've had the beak to,
Has got his dirty whores to speak to,
His dirty mates with whom he drink,
Not little children, one would think.
Look on him there." she says, "look on him
And smell the stinking gin upon him,
The lowest sot, the drunk'nest liar,
The dirtiest dog in all the shire:
Nice friends for any woman's son
After ten years, and all she'd done.

"For I've had eight, and buried five,
And only three are left alive.
I've given them all we could afford,
I've taught them all to fear the Lord.
They've had the best we had to give,
The only three the Lord let live.

"For Minnie whom I loved the worst
Died mad in childbed with her first.
And John and Mary died of measles,
And Rob was drownded at the Teasels
And little Nan, dear little sweet,
A cart run over in the street;
Her little shift was all one stain,
I prayed God put her out of pain.
And all the rest are gone or going
The road to hell, and there's no knowing
For all I've done and all I've made them
I'd better not have overlaid them.
For Susan went the ways of shame
The time the 'till'ry regiment came,
And t'have her child without a father
I think I'd have her buried rather.
And Dicky boozes, God forgimme,
And now't's to be the same with Jimmy
And all I've done and all I've bore
Has made a drunkard and a whore,
A bastard boy who wasn't meant,
And Jimmy gwine where Dicky went;

38

For Dick began the self-same way
And my old hairs are going gray,
And my poor man's a withered knee,
And all the burden falls on me.

"I've washed eight little children's limbs,
I've taught eight little souls their hymns,
I've risen sick and lain down pinched
And borne it all and never flinched;
But to see him, the town's disgrace,
With God's commandments broke in's face,
Who never worked, not he, nor earned,
Nor will do till the seas are burned,
Who never did since he was whole
A hand's turn for a human soul,
But poached and stole and gone with women,
And swilled down gin enough to swim in;
To see him only lift one finger
To make my little Jimmy linger.
In spite of all his mother's prayers,
And all her ten long years of cares,
And all her broken spirit's cry
That drunkard's finger puts them by,
And Jimmy turns. And now I see
That just as Dick was, Jim will be,
And all my life will have been vain.
I might have spared myself the pain,
And done the world a blessed riddance
If I'd a drowned 'em all like kittens.
And he the sot, so strong and proud,
Who'd make white shirts of 's mother's shroud,
He laughs now, it's a joke to him,
Though it's the gates of hell to Jim.

"I've had my heart burnt out like coal,
And drops of blood wrung from my soul
Day in, day out, in pain and tears,
For five and twenty wretched years;
And he, he's ate the fat and sweet,
And loafed and spat at top of street,
And drunk and leched from day till morrow,
And never known a moment's sorrow.
He come out drunk from th' inn to look
The day my little Ann was took;
He sat there drinking, glad and gay,

The night my girl was led astray;
He praised my Dick for singing well,
The night Dick took the road to hell;
And when my corpse goes stiff and blind,
Leaving four helpless souls behind,
He will be there still, drunk and strong.
It do seem hard. It do seem wrong.
But 'Woe to him by whom the offence,'
Says our Lord Jesus' Testaments.
Whatever seems, God doth not slumber,
Though He lets pass times without number
He'll come with trump to call His own,
And this world's way'll be overthrown.
He'll come with glory and with fire
To cast great darkness on the liar,
To burn the drunkard and the treacher,
And do His judgment on the lecher,
To glorify the spirits' faces
Of those whose ways were stony places,
Who chose with Ruth the better part;
O Lord, I see Thee as Thou art,
O God, the fiery four-edged sword,
The thunder of the wrath outpoured,
The fiery four-faced creatures burning,
And all the four-faced wheels all turning,
Coming with trump and fiery saint.
Jim, take me home, I'm turning faint."

They went, and some cried, "Good old sod.
She put it to him straight, by God."
Summat she was, or looked, or said,
Went home and made me hang my head.
I slunk away into the night
Knowing deep down that she was right.
I'd often heard religious ranters,
And put them down as windy canters,
But this old mother made me see
The harm I done by being me,
Being both strong and given to sin
I 'tracted weaker vessels in.
So back to bar to get more drink,
I didn't dare begin to think,
And there were drinks and drunken singing,
As though this life were dice for flinging;
Dice to be flung, and nothing furder,

And Christ's blood just another murder.
"Come on, drinks round, salue, drink hearty.
Now, Jane, the punch-bowl for the party.
If any here won't drink with me
I'll knock his bloody eyes out. See?
Come on, cigars round, rum for mine,
Sing us a smutty song, some swine."
But though the drinks and songs went round
That thought remained it was not drowned.
And when I'd rise to get a light
I'd think, "What's come to me to-night?"

There's always crowd when drinks are standing.
The house doors slammed along the landing,
The rising wind was gusty yet,
And those who came in late were wet;
And all my body's nerves were snappin'
With sense of summat 'bout to happen.
And music seemed to come and go
And seven lights danced in a row.

There used to be a custom then,
Miss Bourne, the Friend, went round at ten
To all the pubs in all the place
To bring the drunkard's soul to grace;
Some sulked, of course, and some were stirred,
But none gave her a dirty word.
A tall pale woman, grey and bent,
Folk said of her that she was sent.
She wore Friend's clothes, and women smiled,
But she'd a heart just like a child.
She come to us near closing time
When we were at some smutty rhyme,
And I was mad and ripe for fun;
I wouldn't a minded what I done,
So when she come so prim and grey
I pound the bar and sing, "Hooray,
Here's Quaker come to bless and kiss us,
Come, have a gin and bitters, missus.
Or maybe Quaker girls so prim
Would rather start a bloody hymn.
Now, Dick, oblige. A hymn, you swine,
Pipe up the 'Officer of the Line,'
A song to make one's belly ache,
Or 'Nell and Roger at the Wake,'

41

Or that sweet song, the talk in town,
'The lady fair and Abel Brown.'
'O, who's that knocking at the door.'
Miss Bourne'll pay the music score."
The men stood dumb as cattle are,
They grinned, but thought I'd gone too far,
There come a hush and no one break it,
They wondered how Miss Bourne would take it,
She up to me with black eyes wide,
She looked as though her spirit cried;
She took my tumbler from the bar
Beside where all the matches are
And poured it out upon the floor dust,
Among the fag-ends, spit and sawdust.

"Saul Kane," she said, "when next you drink,
Do me the gentleness to think
That every drop of drink accursed
Makes Christ within you die of thirst,
That every dirty word you say
Is one more flint upon His way.
Another thorn about His head,
Another mock by where He tread,
Another nail, another cross.
All that you are is that Christ's loss."
The clock run down and struck a chime
And Mrs. Si said, "Closing time."

The wet was pelting on the pane
And something broke inside my brain,
I heard the rain drip from the gutters
And Silas putting up the shutters,
While one by one the drinkers went;
I got a glimpse of what it meant,
How she and I had stood before
In some old town by some old door
Waiting intent while someone knocked
Before the door for ever locked;
She was so white that I was scared,
A gas-jet, turned the wrong way, flared,
And Silas snapped the bars in place.
Miss Bourne stood white and searched my face.
When Silas done, with ends of tunes
He 'gan a-gathering the spittoons,
His wife primmed lips and took the till.

Miss Bourne stood still and I stood still,
And "Tick. Slow. Tick. Slow" went the clock.
She said, "He waits until you knock."
She turned as that and went out swift,
Si grinned and winked, his missus sniffed.

I heard her clang the "Lion" door,
I marked a drink-drop roll to floor;
It took up scraps of sawdust, furry,
And crinkled on, a half inch, blurry;
A drop from my last glass of gin;
And someone waiting to come in,
A hand upon the door latch gropin'
Knocking the man inside to open.
I know the very words I said,
They bayed like bloodhounds in my head.
"The water's going out to sea
And there's a great moon calling me;
But there's a great sun calls the moon,
And all God's bells will carol soon
For joy and glory and delight
Of someone coming home to-night."
Out into darkness, out to night,
My flaring heart gave plenty light,
So wild it was there was no knowing
Whether the clouds or stars were blowing;
Blown chimney pots and folk blown blind
And puddles glimmering like my mind,
And chinking glass from windows hanging,
And inn signs swung like people hanging,
And in my heart the drink unpriced,
The burning cataracts of Christ.

I did not think, I did not strive,
The deep peace burnt my me alive;
The bolted door had broken in,
I knew that I had done with sin.
I knew that Christ had given me birth
To brother all the souls on earth,
And every bird and every beast
Should share the crumbs broke at the feast.

O glory of the lighted mind.
How dead I'd been, how dumb, how blind.

The station brook, to my new eyes,
Was babbling out of Paradise;
The waters rushing from the rain
Were singing Christ has risen again.
I thought all earthly creatures knelt
From rapture of the joy I felt.
The narrow station-wall's brick ledge,
The wild hop withering in the hedge.
The lights in huntsman's upper storey
Were parts of an eternal glory,
Were God's eternal garden flowers.
I stood in bliss at this for hours.

O glory of the lighted soul.
The dawn came up on Bradlow Knoll,
The dawn with glittering on the grasses
The dawn which pass and never passes.
"It's dawn," I said, "and chimney's smoking,
And all the blessed fields are soaking.
It's dawn, and there's an engine shunting;
And hounds, for huntsman's going hunting.
It's dawn, and I must wander north
Along the road Christ led me forth."

So up the road I wander slow
Past where the snowdrops used to grow
With celandines in early springs,
When rainbows were triumphant things
And dew so bright and flowers to glad,
Eternal joy to lass and lad.
And past the lovely brook I paced,
The brook whose source I never traced,
The brook, the one of two which rise
In my green dream in Paradise,
In wells where heavenly buckets clink
To give God's wandering thirsty drink
By those clean cots of carven stone
Where the clear water sings alone.
Then down, past that white-blossomed pond,
And past the chestnut trees beyond,
And past the bridge the fishers knew,
Where yellow flag flowers once grew,
Where we'd go gathering cops of clover,
In sunny June times long since over.
O clover-cops half white, half red,

O beauty from beyond the dead.
O blossom, key to earth and heaven,
O souls that Christ has new forgiven.

Then down the hill to gipsies' pitch
By where the brook clucks in the ditch.
A gipsy's camp was in the copse,
Three felted tents, with beehive tops,
And round black marks where fires had been,
And one old waggon painted green,
And three ribbed horses wrenching grass,
And three wild boys to watch me pass,
And one old woman by the fire
Hulking a rabbit warm from wire.

I loved to see the horses bait.
I felt I walked at Heaven's gate,
That Heaven's gate was opened wide
Yet still the gipsies camped outside.
The waste souls will prefer the wild,
Long after life is meek and mild.
Perhaps when man has entered in
His perfect city free from sin,
The campers will come past the walls
With old lame horses full of galls,
And waggons hung about with withies,
And burning coke in tinkers' stithies,
And see the golden town, and choose,
And think the wild too good to lose.
And camp outside, as these camped then,
With wonder at the entering men.
So past, and past the stone-heap white
That dewberry trailers hid from sight,
And down the field so full of springs,
Where mewing peewits clap their wings,
And past the trap made for the mill
Into the field below the hill.
There was a mist along the stream,
A wet mist, dim, like in a dream;
I heard the heavy breath of cows,
And waterdrops from th' alder boughs;
And eels, or snakes, in dripping grass
Whipping aside to let me pass.
The gate was backed against the ryme
To pass the cows at milking time.

And by the gate as I went out
A moldwarp rooted earth wi 's snout.
A few steps up the Callows' Lane
Brought me above the mist again;
The two great fields arose like death
Above the mists of human breath.

All earthly things that blessèd morning
Were everlasting joy and warning.
The gate was Jesus' way made plain
The mole was Satan foiled again,
Black blinded Satan snouting way
Along the red of Adam's clay;
The mist was error and damnation,
The lane the road unto salvation,
Out of the mist into the light;
O blessed gift of inner sight.
The past was faded like a dream;
There come the jingling of a team,
A ploughman's voice, a clink of chain,
Slow hoofs, and harness under strain.
Up the slow slope a team came bowing,
Old Callow at his autumn ploughing,
Old Callow, stooped above the hales,
Ploughing the stubble into wales;
His grave eyes looking straight ahead,
Shearing a long straight furrow red;
His plough-foot high to give it earth
To bring new food for men to birth.

O wet red swathe of earth laid bare,
O truth, O strength, O gleaming share,
O patient eyes that watch the goal,
O ploughman of the sinner's soul.
O Jesus, drive the coulter deep
To plough my living man from sleep.

Slow up the hill the plough team plod,
Old Callow at the task of God,
Helped by man's wit, helped by the brute
Turning a stubborn clay to fruit,
His eyes for ever on some sign
To help him plough a perfect line.
At top of rise the plough team stopped,
The fore-horse bent his head and cropped.

Then the chains chack, the brasses jingle,
The lean reins gather through the cringle,
The figures move against the sky,
The clay wave breaks as they go by.
I kneeled there in the muddy fallow,
I knew that Christ was there with Callow,
That Christ was standing there with me,
That Christ had taught me what to be,
That I should plough, and as I ploughed
My Saviour Christ would sing aloud,
And as I drove the clods apart
Christ would be ploughing in my heart,
Through rest-harrow and bitter roots,
Through all my bad life's rotten fruits.

O Christ who holds the open gate,
O Christ who drives the furrow straight,
O Christ, the plough, O Christ, the laughter
Of holy white birds flying after,
Lo, all my heart's field red and torn,
And Thou wilt bring the young green corn
The young green corn divinely springing,
The young green corn for ever singing;
And when the field is fresh and fair
Thy blessèd feet shall glitter there.
And we will walk the weeded field,
And tell the golden harvest's yield,
The corn that makes the holy bread
By which the soul of man is fed,
The holy bread, the food unpriced,
Thy everlasting mercy, Christ.

The share will jar on many a stone,
Thou wilt not let me stand alone;
And I shall feel (Thou wilt not fail),
Thy hand on mine upon the hale.

Near Bullen Bank, on Gloucester Road,
Thy everlasting mercy showed
The ploughman patient on the hill
For ever there, for ever still,
Ploughing the hill with steady yoke
Of pine-trees lightning-struck and broke.
I've marked the May Hill ploughman stay
There on his hill, day after day

Driving his team against the sky,
While men and women live and die.
And now and then he seems to stoop
To clear the coulter with the scoop,
Or touch an ox to haw or gee
While Severn stream goes out to sea.
The sea with all her ships and sails,
And that great smoky port in Wales,
And Gloucester tower bright i' the sun,
All know that patient wandering one.
And sometimes when they burn the leaves
The bonfires' smoking trails and heaves,
And girt red flamës twink and twire
As though he ploughed the hill afire.
And in men's hearts in many lands
A spiritual ploughman stands
For ever waiting, waiting now,
The heart's "Put in, man, zook, the plough."

By this the sun was all one glitter,
The little birds were all in twitter;
Our of a tuft a little lark
Went higher up than I could mark,
His little throat was all one thirst
To sing until his heart should burst,
To sing aloft in golden light
His song from blue air out of sight.
The mist drove by, and now the cows
Came plodding up to milking house,
Followed by Frank, the Callows' cowman,
Who whistled "Adam was a ploughman."
There come such cawing from the rooks,
Such running chuck from little brooks,
One thought it March, just budding green
With hedgerows full of celandine.
An otter 'out of stream and played,
Two hares come loping up and stayed;
Wide-eyed and tender-eared but bold.
Sheep bleated up by Penny's fold.
I heard a partridge covey call;
The morning sun was bright on all.

Down the long slope the plough team drove,
The tossing rooks arose and hove.
A stone struck on the share. A word

Came to the team. The red earth stirred.
I crossed the hedge by shooter's gap,
I hitched my boxer's belt a strap,
I jumped the ditch and crossed the fallow,
I took the hales from farmer Callow.

How swift the summer goes,
Forget-me-not, pink, rose.
The young grass when I started
And now the hay is carted,
And now my song is ended,
And all the summer spended;
The blackbird's second brood
Routs beech-leaves in the wood,
The pink and rose have speeded,
Forget-me-not has seeded.
Only the winds that blew,
The rain that makes things new,
The earth that hides things old,
And blessings manifold.

O lovely lily clean,
O lily springing green,
O lily bursting white,
Dear lily of delight,
Spring in my heart agen
That I may flower to men.

THE WIDOW IN THE BYE STREET

I

Down Bye Street, in a little Shropshire town,
There lived a widow with her only son:
She had no wealth nor title to renown,
Nor any joyous hours, never one.
She rose from ragged mattress before sun
And stitched all day until her eyes were red,
And had to stitch, because her man was dead.

Sometimes she fell asleep, she stitched so hard,
Letting the linen fall upon the floor;
And hungry cats would steal in from the yard,
And mangy chickens pecked about the door
Craning their necks so ragged and so sore

To search the room for bread-crumbs, or for mouse,
But they got nothing in the widow's house.

Mostly she made her bread by hemming shrouds
For one rich undertaker in the High Street,
Who used to pray that folks might die in crowds
And that their friends might pay to let them lie sweet;
And when one died the widow in the Bye Street
Stitched night and day to give the worm his dole.
The dead were better dressed than that poor soul.

Her little son was all her life's delight,
For in his little features she could find
A glimpse of that dead husband out of sight,
Where out of sight is never out of mind.
And so she stitched till she was nearly blind,
Or till the tallow candle end was done,
To get a living for her little son.

Her love for him being such she would not rest,
It was a want which ate her out and in,
Another hunger in her withered breast
Pressing her woman's bones against the skin.
To make him plump she starved her body thin.
And he, he ate the food, and never knew,
He laughed and played as little children do.

When there was little sickness in the place
She took what God would send, and what God sent
Never brought any colour to her face
Nor life into her footsteps when she went.
Going, she trembled always withered and bent
For all went to her son, always the same,
He was first served whatever blessing came.

Sometimes she wandered out to gather sticks,
For it was bitter cold there when it snowed.
And she stole hay out of the farmer's ricks
For bands to wrap her feet in while she sewed,
And when her feet were warm and the grate glowed
She hugged her little son, her heart's desire,
With "Jimmy, ain't it snug beside the fire?"

So years went on till Jimmy was a lad
And went to work as poor lads have to do,

50

And then the widow's loving heart was glad
To know that all the pains she had gone through
And all the years of putting on the screw,
Down to the sharpest turn a mortal can,
Had borne their fruit, and made her child a man.

He got a job at working on the line
Tipping the earth down, trolley after truck,
From daylight till the evening, wet or fine,
With arms all red from wallowing in the muck,
And spitting, as the trolly tipped, for luck,
And singing "Binger" as he swung the pick
Because the red blood ran in him so quick.

So there was bacon then, at night, for supper
In Bye Street there, where he and mother stay;
And boots they had, not leaky in the upper,
And room rent ready on the settling day;
And beer for poor old mother, worn and grey,
And fire in frost; and in the widow's eyes
It seemed the Lord had made earth paradise.

And there they sat of evenings after dark
Singing their song of "Binger," he and she,
Her poor old cackle made the mongrels bark,
And "You sing Binger, mother," carols he;
By crimes, but that's a good song, that her be."
And then they slept there in the room they shared,
And all the time Fate had his end prepared.

One thing alone made life not perfect sweet:
The mother's daily fear of what would come
When woman and her lovely boy should meet,
When the new wife would break up the old home.
Fear of that unborn evil struck her dumb,
And when her darling and a woman met,
She shook and prayed, "Not her, O God; not yet."

"Not yet, dear God, my Jimmy go from me."
Then she would subtly question with her son.
"Not very handsome, I don't think her be?"
"God help the man who marries such an one."
Her red eyes peered to spy the mischief done.
She took great care to keep the girls away,
And all her trouble made him easier prey.

51

There was a woman out at Plaister's End,
Light of her body, fifty to the pound,
A copper coin for any man to spend,
Lovely to look on when the wits were drowned.
Her husband's skeleton was never found,
It lay among the rocks at Glydyr Mor
Where he drank poison, finding her a whore.

She was not native there, for she belonged
Out Milford way, or Swansea; no one knew.
She had the piteous look of someone wronged,
"Anna," her name, a widow, last of Triw.
She had lived at Plaister's End a year or two;
At Callow's cottage, renting half an acre;
She was a henwife and a perfume-maker.

Secret she was; she lived in reputation
But secret unseen threads went floating out;
Her smile, her voice, her face, were all temptation,
All subtle flies to trouble man the trout;
Man to entice, entrap, entangle, flout . . .
To take and spoil, and then to cast aside:
Gain without giving was the craft she plied.

And she complained, poor lonely widowed soul,
How no one cared, and men were rutters all;
While true love is an ever-burning goal
Burning the brighter as the shadows fall.
And all love's dogs went hunting at the call,
Married or not she took them by the brain,
Sucked at their hearts and tossed them back again.

Like the straw fires lit on Saint John's Eve,
She burned and dwindled in her fickle heart;
For if she wept when Harry took his leave,
Her tears were lures to beckon Bob to start.
And if, while loving Bob, a tinker's cart
Came by, she opened window with a smile
And gave the tinker hints to wait a while.

She passed for pure; but, years before, in Wales,
Living at Mountain Ash with different men,
Her less discretion had inspired tales
Of certain things she did, and how, and when,
Those seven years of youth; we are frantic then.

She had been frantic in her years of youth,
The tales were not more evil than the truth.

She had two children as the fruits of trade
Though she drank bitter herbs to kill the curse,
Both of them sons, and one she overlaid,
The other one the parish had to nurse.
Now she grew plump with money in her purse,
Passing for pure a hundred miles, I guess,
From where her little son wore workhouse dress.

There with the Union boys he came and went,
A parish bastard fed on bread and tea,
Wearing a bright tin badge in furthest Gwent,
And no one knowing who his folk could be.
His mother never knew his new name: she,—
She touched the lust of those who served her turn,
And chief among her men was Shepherd Ern.

A moody, treacherous man of bawdy mind,
Married to that mild girl from Ercal Hill,
Whose gentle goodness made him more inclined
To hotter sauces sharper on the bill.
The new lust gives the lecher the new thrill,
The new wine scratches as it slips the throat,
The new flag is so bright by the old boat.

Ern was her man to buy her bread and meat,
Half of his weekly wage was hers to spend,
She used to mock "How is your wife, my sweet?"
Or wail, "O, Ernie, how is this to end?"
Or coo, "My Ernie is without a friend,
She cannot understand my precious life,"
And Ernie would go home and beat his wife.

So the four souls are ranged, the chess-board set.
The dark, invisible hand of secret Fate
Brought it to come to being that they met
After so many years of lying in wait.
While we least think it he prepares his Mate.
Mate, and the King's pawn played, it never ceases,
Though all the earth is dust of taken pieces.

II

October Fair-time is the time for fun
For all the street is hurdled into rows
Of pens of heifers blinking at the sun,
And Lemster sheep which pant and seem to doze,
And stalls of hardbake and galanty shows,
And cheapjacks smashing crocks, and trumpets blowing,
And the loud organ of the horses going.

There you can buy blue ribbons for your girl
Or take her in a swing-boat tossing high,
Or hold her fast when all the horses whirl
Round to the steam pipe whanging at the sky,
Or stand her cockshies at the cocoa-shy,
Or buy her brooches with her name in red,
Or Queen Victoria done in gingerbread.

Then there are rifle shots at tossing balls,
"And if you hit you get a good cigar."
And strength-whackers for lads to lamm with mauls,
And Cheshire cheeses on a greasy spar.
The country folk flock in from near and far,
Women and men, like blow-flies to the roast,
All love the fair; but Anna loved it most.

Anna was all agog to see the fair;
She made Ern promise to be there to meet her,
To arm her round to all the pleasures there,
And buy her ribbons for her neck, and treat her,
So that no woman at the fair should beat her
In having pleasure at a man's expense.
She planned to meet him at the chapel fence.

So Ernie went; and Jimmy took his mother,
Dressed in her finest with a Monmouth shawl,
And there was such a crowd she thought she'd smother,
And O, she loved a pep'mint above all.
Clash go the crockeries where the cheapjacks bawl,
Baa go the sheep, thud goes the waxwork's drum,
And Ernie cursed for Anna hadn't come.

He hunted for her up and down the place,
Raging and snapping like a working brew.
"If you're with someone else I'll smash his face,

And when I've done for him I'll go for you."
He bought no fairings as he'd vowed to do
For his poor little children back at home
Stuck at the glass "to see till father come."

Not finding her, he went into an inn,
Busy with ringing till and scratching matches.
Where thirsty drovers mingled stout with gin
And three or four Welsh herds were singing catches.
    The swing-doors clattered, letting in in snatches
The noises of the fair, now low, now loud.
Ern called for beer and glowered at the crowd.

While he was glowering at his drinking there
In came the gipsy Bessie, hawking toys;
A bold-eyed strapping harlot with black hair,
One of the tribe which camped at Shepherd's Bois.
She lured him out of inn into the noise
Of the steam-organ where the horses spun,
And so the end of all things was begun.

Newness in lust, always the old in love.
"Put up your toys," he said, "and come along,
We'll have a turn of swing-boats up above,
And see the murder when they strike the gong."
"Don't 'ee," she giggled. "My, but ain't you strong.
And where's your proper girl? You don't know me."
"I do." "You don't." "Why, then, I will," said he.

Anna was late because the cart which drove her
Called for her late (the horse had broke a trace),
She was all dressed and scented for her lover,
Her bright blue blouse had imitation lace,
The paint was red as roses on her face,
She hummed a song, because she thought to see
How envious all the other girls would be.

When she arrived and found her Ernie gone,
Her bitter heart thought, "This is how it is.
Keeping me waiting while the sports are on:
Promising faithful, too, and then to miss.
O, Ernie, won't I give it you for this."
And looking up she saw a couple cling,
Ern with his arm round Bessie in the swing.

Ern caught her eye and spat, and cut her dead,
Bessie laughed hardly, in the gipsy way.
Anna, though blind with fury, tossed her head,
Biting her lips until the red was grey,
For bitter moments given, bitter pay,
The time for payment comes, early or late,
No earthly debtor but accounts to Fate.

She turned aside, telling with bitter oaths
What Ern should suffer if he turned agen,
And there was Jimmy stripping off his clothes
Within a little ring of farming men.
'Now, Jimmy, put the old tup into pen.'
His mother, watching, thought her heart would curdle,
To see Jim drag the old ram to the hurdle.

Then the ram butted and the game began,
Till Jimmy's muscles cracked and the ram grunted.
The good old wrestling game of Ram and Man,
At which none knows the hunter from the hunted.
"Come and see Jimmy have his belly bunted."
"Good tup. Good Jim. Good Jimmy. Sick him, Rover,
By dang, but Jimmy's got him fairly over."

Then there was clap of hands and Jimmy grinned
And took five silver shillings from his backers,
And said th' old tup had put him out of wind
Or else he'd take all comers at the Whackers.
And some made rude remarks of rams and knackers,
And mother shook to get her son alone,
So's to be sure he hadn't broke a bone.

None but the lucky man deserves the fair,
For lucky men have money and success,
Things that a whore is very glad to share,
Or dip, at least, a finger in the mess.
Anne, with her raddled cheeks and Sunday dress,
Smiled upon Jimmy, seeing him succeed,
As though to say, "You are a man, indeed."

All the great things of life are swiftly done,
Creation, death, and love the double gate.
However much we dawdle in the sun
We have to hurry at the touch of Fate;
When Life knocks at the door no one can wait,

When Death makes his arrest we have to go.
And so with Love, and Jimmy found it so.

Love, the sharp spear, went pricking to the bone,
In that one look, desire and bitter aching,
Longing to have that woman all alone
For her dear beauty's sake all else forsaking;
And sudden agony that set him shaking
Lest she, whose beauty made his heart's blood cruddle,
Should be another man's to kiss and cuddle.

She was beside him when he left the ring,
Her soft dress brushed against him as he passed her;
He thought her penny scent a sweeter thing
Than precious ointment out of alabaster;
Love, the mild servant, makes a drunken master.
She smiled, half sadly, out of thoughtful eyes,
And all the strong young man was easy prize.

She spoke, to take him, seeing him a sheep,
"How beautiful you wrastled with the ram,
It made me all go tremble just to peep,
I am that fond of wrastling, that I am.
Why, here's your mother, too. Good-evening, ma'am.
I was just telling Jim how well he done
How proud you must be of so fine a son."

Old mother blinked, while Jimmy hardly knew
Whether he knew the woman there or not;
But well he knew, if not, he wanted to,
Joy of her beauty ran in him so hot,
Old trembling mother by him was forgot,
While Anna searched the mother's face, to know
Whether she took her for a whore or no.

The woman's maxim, "Win the woman first,"
Made her be gracious to the withered thing.
"This being in crowds do give one such a thirst,
I wonder if they've tea going at 'The King'?
My throat's that dry my very tongue do cling,
Perhaps you'd take my arm, we'd wander up
(If you'd agree) and try and get a cup.

"Come, ma'am, a cup of tea would do you good;
There's nothing like a nice hot cup of tea
After the crowd and all the time you've stood;
And 'The King' 's strict, it isn't like 'The Key.'
Now, take my arm, my dear, and lean on me."
And Jimmy's mother, being nearly blind,
Took Anna's arm, and only thought her kind.

So off they set, with Anna talking to her,
How nice the tea would be after the crowd,
And mother thinking half the time she knew her,
And Jimmy's heart's blood ticking quick and loud,
And Death beside him knitting at his shroud,
And all the High Street babbling with the fair,
And white October clouds in the blue air.

So tea was made and down they sat to drink;
O the pale beauty sitting at the board!
There is more death in women than we think,
There is much danger in the soul adored,
The white hands bring the poison and the cord;
Death has a lodge in lips as red as cherries,
Death has a mansion in the yew-tree berries.

They sat there talking after tea was done,
And Jimmy blushed at Anna's sparkling looks,
And Anna flattered mother on her son,
Catching both fishes on her subtle hooks.
With twilight, tea and talk in ingle-nooks,
And music coming up from the dim street,
Mother had never known a fair so sweet.

No cow-bells clink, for milking time is come,
The drovers stack the hurdles into carts,
New masters drive the straying cattle home,
Many a young calf from his mother parts,
Hogs straggle back to sty by fits and starts;
The farmers take a last glass at the inns,
And now the frolic of the fair begins.

All of the side shows of the fair are lighted,
Flares and bright lights, and brassy cymbals clanging,
"Beginning now" and "Everyone's invited,"
Shatter the pauses of the organ's whanging,
The Oldest Show on Earth and the Last Hanging,

"The Murder in the Red Barn," with real blood,
The rifles crack, the Sally shy-sticks thud.

Anna walked slowly homewards with her prey,
Holding old tottering mother's weight upon her,
And pouring in sweet poison on the way
Of "Such a pleasure, ma'am, and such an honour,"
And "One's so safe with such a son to con her
Through all the noises and through all the press,
Boys daredn't squirt tormentors on her dress."

At mother's door they stop to say "Good-night."
And mother must go in to set the table.
Anna pretended that she felt a fright
To go alone through all the merry babel:
"My friends are waiting at 'The Cain and Abel,'
Just down the other side of Market Square,
It'd be a mercy if you'd set me there."

So Jimmy came, while mother went inside;
Anna has got her victim in her clutch.
Jimmy, all blushing, glad to be her guide,
Thrilled by her scent, and trembling at her touch.
She was all white and dark, and said not much;
She sighed, to hint that pleasure's grave was dug,
And smiled within to see him such a mug.

They passed the doctor's house among the trees,
She sighed so deep that Jimmy asked her why.
"I'm too unhappy upon nights like these,
When everyone has happiness but I!"
"Then, aren't you happy?" She appeared to cry,
Blinked with her eyes and turned away her head:
"Not much; but some men understand," she said.

Her voice caught lightly on a broken note,
Jimmy half-dared but dared not touch her hand,
Yet all his blood went pumping in his throat
Beside the beauty he could understand,
And Death stopped knitting at the muffling band.
"The shroud is done," he muttered, "toe to chin."
He snapped the ends, and tucked his needles in.

Jimmy, half stammering, choked, "Has any man—"
He stopped, she shook her head to answer "No."

59

"Then tell me." "No. P'raps some day, if I can.
It hurts to talk of some things ever so.
But you're so different. There, come, we must go.
None but unhappy women know how good
It is to meet a soul who's understood."

"No. Wait a moment. May I call you Anna?"
"Perhaps. There must be nearness 'twixt us two."
Love in her face hung out his bloody banner,
And all love's clanging trumpets shocked and blew.
"When we got up to-day we never knew."
"I'm sure I didn't think, nor you did." "Never."
"And now this friendship's come to us for ever."

"Now, Anna, take my arm, dear." "Not to-night,
That must come later when we know our minds,
We must agree to keep this evening white,
We'll eat the fruit to-night and save the rinds."
And all the folk whose shadows darked the blinds,
And all the dancers whirling in the fair,
Were wretched worms to Jim and Anna there.

"How wonderful life is," said Anna, lowly,
"But it begins again with you for friend."
In the dim lamplight Jimmy thought her holy,
A lovely fragile thing for him to tend,
Grace beyond measure, beauty without end.
"Anna," he said; "Good-night. This is the door.
I never knew what people meant before."

"Good-night, my friend. Good-bye." "But, O my sweet,
The night's quite early yet, don't say good-bye,
Come just another short turn down the street,
The whole life's bubbling up for you and I.
Somehow I feel to-morrow we may die.
Come just as far as to the blacksmith's light."
But "No," said Anna; "Not to-night. Good-night."

All the tides triumph when the white moon fills.
Down in the race the toppling waters shout,
The breakers shake the bases of the hills,
There is a thundering where the streams go out.
And the wise shipman puts his ship about
Seeing the gathering of those waters wan,
But what when love makes high tide in a man?

Jimmy walked home with all his mind on fire,
One lovely face for ever set in flame.
He shivered as he went, like tautened wire,
Surge after surge of shuddering in him came
And then swept out repeating one sweet name,
"Anna, O Anna," to the evening star.
Anna was sipping whiskey in the bar.

So back to home and mother Jimmy wandered,
Thinking of Plaister's End and Anna's lips.
He ate no supper worth the name, but pondered
On Plaister's End hedge, scarlet with ripe hips,
And of the lovely moon there in eclipse,
And how she must be shining in the house
Behind the hedge of those old dog-rose boughs.

Old mother cleared away. The clock struck eight.
"Why, boy, you've left your bacon, lawks a me,
So that's what comes of having tea so late,
Another time you'll go without your tea.
Your father liked his cup, too, didn't he,
Always 'another cup' he used to say,
He never went without on any day.

"How nice the lady was and how she talked,
I've never had a nicer fair, not ever."
"She said she'd like to see us if we walked
To Plaister's End, beyond by Watersever.
Nice-looking woman, too, and that, and clever;
We might go round one evening, p'raps, we two;
Or I might go, if it's too far for you."

"No," said the mother, "we're not folk for that;
Meet at the fair and that, and there an end.
Rake out the fire and put out the cat,
These fairs are sinful, tempting folk to spend.
Of course she spoke polite and like a friend;
Of course she had to do, and so I let her,
But now it's done and past, so I forget her."

"I don't see why forget her. Why forget her?
She treat us kind. She weren't like everyone.
I never saw a woman I liked better,
And he's not easy pleased, my father's son.
So I'll go round some night when work is done."

"Now, Jim, my dear, trust mother, there's a dear."
"Well, so I do, but sometimes you're so queer."

She blinked at him out of her withered eyes
Below her lashless eyelids red and bleared.
Her months of sacrifice had won the prize,
Her Jim had come to what she always feared.
And yet she doubted, so she shook and peered
And begged her God not let a woman take
The lovely son whom she had starved to make.

Doubting, she stood the dishes in the rack,
"We'll ask her in some evening, then," she said.
"How nice her hair looked in the bit of black."
And still she peered from eyes all dim and red
To note at once if Jimmy drooped his head,
Or if his ears blushed when he heard her praised,
And Jimmy blushed and hung his head and gazed.

"This is the end," she thought. "This is the end.
I'll have to sew again for Mr. Jones,
Do hems when I can hardly see to mend,
And have the old ache in my marrow-bones.
And when his wife's in child-bed, when she groans,
She'll send for me until the pains have ceased,
And give me leavings at the christening feast.

"And sit aslant to eye me as I eat,
'You're only wanted here, ma'am, for today,
Just for the christ'ning party, for the treat,
Don't ever think I mean to let you stay;
Two's company, three's none, that's what I say.'"
Life can be bitter to the very bone
When one is poor, and woman, and alone.

"Jimmy," she said, still doubting, "Come, my dear,
Let's have our 'Binger' 'fore we go to bed."
And then "The parson's dog," she cackled clear,
"Lep over stile," she sang, nodding her head,
"His name was little Binger." "Jim," she said,
"Binger, now, chorus" . . . Jimmy kicked the hob,
The sacrament of song died in a sob.

Jimmy went out into the night to think
Under the moon so steady in the blue.

The woman's beauty ran in him like drink,
The fear that men had loved her burnt him through;
The fear that even then another knew
All the deep mystery which women make
To hide the inner nothing made him shake.

"Anna, I love you, and I always shall."
He looked towards Plaister's End beyond Cot Hills.
A white star glimmered in the long canal,
A droning from the music came in thrills.
Love is a flame to burn out human wills,
Love is a flame to set the will on fire,
Love is a flame to cheat men into mire.

One of the three, we make Love what we choose,
But Jimmy did not know, he only thought
That Anna was too beautiful to lose,
That she was all the world and he was naught,
That it was sweet, though bitter, to be caught.
"Anna, I love you." Underneath the moon,
"I shall go mad unless I see you soon."

The fair's lights threw aloft a misty glow.
The organ whangs, the giddy horses reel,
The rifles cease, the folk begin to go,
The hands unclamp the swing-boats from the wheel
There is a smell of trodden orange peel;
The organ drones and dies, the horses stop.
And then the tent collapses from the top.

The fair is over, let the people troop,
The drunkards stagger homewards down the gutters,
The showmen heave in an excited group,
The poles tilt slowly down, the canvas flutters,
The mauls knock out the pins, the last flare sputters.
"Lower away," "Go easy." "Lower, lower."
"You've dang near knock my skull in. Loose it slower."

"Back in the horses." "Are the swing-boats loaded?"
"All right to start." "Bill, where's the cushion gone?
The red one for the Queen?" "I think I stowed it."
"You think you think. Lord, where's that cushion, John?"
"It's in that bloody box you're sitting on,
What more d'you want?" A concertina plays
Far off as wandering lovers go their ways.

63

Up the dim Bye Street to the market-place
The dead bones of the fair are borne in carts,
Horses and swing-boats at a funeral pace
After triumphant hours quickening hearts;
A policeman eyes each waggon as it starts,
The drowsy showmen stumble half asleep,
One of them catcalls, having drunken deep.

So out, over the pass, into the plain,
And the dawn finds them filling empty cans
In some sweet-smelling dusty country lane,
Where a brook chatters over rusty pans.
The iron chimneys of the caravans
Smoke as they go. And now the fair has gone
To find a new pitch somewhere further on.

But as the fair moved out two lovers came,
Ernie and Bessie loitering out together;
Bessie with wild eyes, hungry as a flame,
Ern like a stallion tugging at a tether.
It was calm moonlight, and October weather,
So still, so lovely, as they topped the ridge,
They brushed by Jimmy standing on the bridge.

And, as they passed, they gravely eyed each other,
And the blood burned in each heart beating there;
And out into the Bye Street tottered mother,
Without her shawl, in the October air.
"Jimmy," she cried, "Jimmy." and Bessie's hair
Drooped on the instant over Ernie's face,
And the two lovers clung in an embrace.

"O, Ern." "My own, my Bessie." As they kissed
Jimmy was envious of the thing unknown.
So this was Love, the something he had missed.
Woman and man athirst, aflame, alone.
Envy went knocking at his marrow-bone,
And Anna's face swam up so dim, so fair,
Shining and sweet, with poppies in her hair.

III

After the fair, the gang began again.
Tipping the trollies down the banks of earth.
The truck of stone clanks on the endless chain,

64

A clever pony guides it to its berth.
"Let go." It tips, the navvies shout for mirth
To see the pony step aside, so wise,
But Jimmy sighed, thinking of Anna's eyes.

And when he stopped his shovelling he looked
Over the junipers towards Plaister way,
The beauty of his darling had him hooked,
He had no heart for wrastling with the clay.
"O Lord Almighty, I must get away;
O Lord, I must. I must just see my flower,
Why, I could run there in the dinner hour."

The whistle on the pilot engine blew,
The men knocked off, and Jimmy slipped aside
Over the fence, over the bridge, and through,
And then ahead along the water-side,
Under the red-brick rail-bridge, arching wide,
Over the hedge, across the fields and on;
The foreman asked: "Where's Jimmy Gurney gone?"

It is a mile and more to Plaister's End,
But Jimmy ran the short way by the stream,
And there was Anna's cottage at the bend,
With blue smoke on the chimney, faint as steam.
"God, she's at home," and up his heart a gleam
Leapt like a rocket on November nights,
And shattered slowly in a burst of lights.

Anna was singing at her kitchen fire,
She was surprised, and not well pleased to see
A sweating navvy, red with heat and mire,
Come to her door, whoever he might be.
But when she saw that it was Jimmy, she
Smiled at his eyes upon her, full of pain,
And thought, "But, still, he mustn't come again.

"People will talk; boys are such crazy things;
But he's a dear boy though he is so green."
So, hurriedly, she slipped her apron strings,
And dabbed her hair, and wiped her fingers clean,
And came to greet him languid as a queen,
Looking as sweet, as fair, as pure, as sad,
As when she drove her loving husband mad.

"Poor boy," she said, "poor boy, how hot you are."
She laid a cool hand to his sweating face.
"How kind to come. Have you been running far?
I'm just going out; come up the road a pace.
O dear, these hens; they're all about the place."
So Jimmy shooed the hens at her command,
And got outside the gate as she had planned.

"Anna, my dear, I love you; love you, true;
I had to come—I don't know—I can't rest—
I lay awake all night, thinking of you.
Many must love you, but I love you best."
"Many have loved me, yes, dear," she confessed,
She smiled upon him with a tender pride,
"But my love ended when my husband died.

"Still, we'll be friends, dear friends, dear, tender friends.
Love with its fever's at an end for me.
Be by me gently now the fever ends,
Life is a lovelier thing than lovers see,
I'd like to trust a man, Jimmy," said she,
"May I trust you?" "Oh, Anna dear, my dear—"
"Don't come so close," she said, "with people near."

"Dear, don't be vexed, it's very sweet to find
One who will understand; but life is life,
And those who do not know are so unkind.
But you'll be by me, Jimmy, in the strife,
I love you though I cannot be your wife;
And now be off, before the whistle goes,
Or else you'll lose your quarter, goodness knows."

"When can I see you, Anna? Tell me, dear.
To-night? To-morrow? Shall I come to-night?"
"Jimmy, my friend, I cannot have you here;
But when I come to town perhaps we might.
Dear, you must go; no kissing; you can write,
And I'll arrange a meeting when I learn
What friends are doing" (meaning Shepherd Ern).

"Good-bye, my own." "Dear Jim, you understand.
If we were only free, dear, free to meet,
Dear, I would take you by your big, strong hand
And kiss your dear boy eyes so blue and sweet;

But my dead husband lies under the sheet,
Dead in my heart, dear, lovely, lonely one,
So, Jim, my dear, my loving days are done.

"But though my heart is buried in his grave
Something might be—friendship and utter trust—
And you, my dear starved little Jim shall have
Flowers of friendship from my dead heart's dust;
Life would be sweet if men would never lust.
Why do you, Jimmy? Tell me sometime, dear,
Why men are always what we women fear.

"Not now. Good-bye; we understand, we two,
And life, O Jim, how glorious life is;
This sunshine in my heart is due to you;
I was so sad, and life has given this.
I think 'I wish I had something of his,'
Do give me something, will you be so kind?
Something to keep you always in my mind."

"I will," he said "Now go, or you'll be late."
He broke from her and ran, and never dreamt
That as she stood to watch him from the gate
Her heart was half amusement, half contempt,
Comparing Jim the squab, red and unkempt,
In sweaty corduroys, with Shepherd Ern.
She blew him kisses till he passed the turn.

The whistle blew before he reached the line;
The foreman asked him what the hell he meant,
Whether a duke had asked him out to dine,
Or if he thought the bag would pay his rent?
And Jim was fined before the foreman went.
But still his spirit glowed from Anna's words,
Cooed in the voice so like a singing bird's.

"O Anna, darling, you shall have a present;
I'd give you golden gems if I were rich,
And everything that's sweet and all that's pleasant."
He dropped his pick as though he had a stitch,
And stared tow'rds Plaister's End, past Bushe's Pitch.
"O beauty, what I have to give I'll give,
All mine is yours, beloved, while I live."

All through the afternoon his pick was slacking,
His eyes were always turning west and south,
The foreman was inclined to send him packing,
But put it down to after fair-day drouth;
He looked at Jimmy with an ugly mouth,
And Jimmy slacked, and muttered in a moan,
"My love, my beautiful, my very own."

So she had loved. Another man had had her;
She had been his with passion in the night;
An agony of envy made him sadder,
Yet stabbed a pang of bitter-sweet delight—
O he would keep his image of her white.
The foreman cursed, stepped up, and asked him flat
What kind of gum-tree he was gaping at.

It was Jim's custom, when the pay day came,
To take his weekly five and twenty shilling
Back in the little packet to his dame;
Not taking out a farthing for a filling,
Nor twopence for a pot, for he was willing
That she should have it all to save or spend.
But love makes many lovely customs end.

Next pay day came and Jimmy took the money,
But not to mother, for he meant to buy
A thirteen-shilling locket for his honey,
Whatever bellies hungered and went dry,
A silver heart-shape with a ruby eye.
He bought the thing and paid the shopman's price,
And hurried off to make the sacrifice.

"Is it for me? You dear, dear generous boy.
How sweet of you. I'll wear it in my dress.
When you're beside me life is such a joy,
You bring the sun to solitariness."
She brushed his jacket with a light caress,
His arms went round her fast, she yielded meek;
He had the happiness to kiss her cheek.

"My dear, my dear." "My very dear, my Jim,
How very kind my Jimmy is to me;
I ache to think that some are harsh to him;
Not like my Jimmy, beautiful and free.
My darling boy, how lovely it would be

It all would trust as we two trust each other."
And Jimmy's heart grew hard against his mother.

She, poor old soul, was waiting in the gloom
For Jimmy's pay, that she could do the shopping.
The clock ticked out a solemn tale of doom;
Clogs on the bricks outside went clippa-clopping,
The owls were coming out and dew was dropping.
The bacon burnt, and Jimmy not yet home.
The clock was ticking dooms out like a gnome.

"What can have kept him that he doesn't come?
O God, they'd tell me if he'd come to hurt."
The unknown, unseen evil struck her numb,
She saw his body bloody in the dirt,
She saw the life blood pumping through the shirt,
She saw him tipsy in the navvies' booth,
She saw all forms of evil but the truth.

At last she hurried up the line to ask
If Jim were hurt or why he wasn't back.
She found the watchman wearing through his task;
Over the fire basket in his shack;
Behind, the new embankment rose up black.
"Gurney?" he said. "He'd got to see a friend."
"Where?" "I dunno. I think out Plaister's End."

Thanking the man, she tottered down the hill,
The long-feared fang had bitten to the bone.
The brook beside her talked as water will
That it was lonely singing all alone,
The night was lonely with the water's tone,
And she was lonely to the very marrow.
Love puts such bitter poison on Fate's arrow.

She went the long way to them by the mills,
She told herself that she must find her son.
The night was ominous of many ills;
The soughing larch-clump almost made her run,
Her boots hurt (she had got a stone in one)
And bitter beaks were tearing at her liver
That her boy's heart was turned from her forever.

She kept the lane, past Spindle's, past the Callows'.
Her lips still muttering prayers against the worst,

69

And there were people coming from the sallows,
Along the wild duck patch by Beggar's Hurst.
Being in moonlight mother saw them first,
She saw them moving in the moonlight dim,
A woman with a sweet voice saying "Jim."

Trembling she grovelled down into the ditch,
They wandered past her pressing side to side,
"O Anna, my belov'd, if I were rich."
It was her son, and Anna's voice replied,
"Dear boy, dear beauty boy, my love and pride."
And he: "It's but a silver thing, but I
Will earn you better lockets by and by."

"Dear boy, you mustn't." "But I mean to do."
"What was that funny sort of noise I heard?"
"Where?" "In the hedge, a sort of sob or coo.
Listen. It's gone." "It may have been a bird."
Jim tossed a stone but mother never stirred.
She hugged the hedgerow, choking down her pain
While the hot tears were blinding in her brain.

The two passed on, the withered woman rose,
For many minutes she could only shake,
Staring ahead with trembling little "Oh's,"
The noise a very frightened child might make.
"O God, dear God, don't let the woman take
My little son, God, not my little Jim.
O God, I'll have to starve if I lose him."

So back she trembled, nodding with her head,
Laughing and trembling in the bursts of tears,
Her ditch-filled boots both squelching in the tread,
Her shopping-bonnet sagging to her ears,
Her heart too dumb with brokenness for fears.
The nightmare whickering with the laugh of death
Could not have added terror to her breath.

She reached the house, and: "I'm all right," said she.
"I'll just take off my things; but I'm all right,
I'd be all right with just a cup of tea,
If I could only get this grate to light,
The paper's damp and Jimmy's late to-night.
'Belov'd, if I was rich,' was what he said,
O Jim, I wish that God would kill me dead."

While she was blinking at the unlit grate,
Scratching the moistened match-heads off the wood,
She heard Jim coming, so she reached his plate,
And forked the over-frizzled scraps of food.
"You're late," she said, "and this yer isn't good,
Whatever makes you come in late like this?"
"I've been to Plaister's End, that's how it is."

"You've been to Plaister's End?"
                                    "Yes."
                                          "I've been staying
For money for the shopping ever so.
Down here we can't get victuals without paying,
There's no trust down the Bye Street, as you know.
And now it's dark and it's too late to go.
You've been to Plaister's End. What took you there?"
"The lady who was with us at the fair."

'The lady, eh? The lady?"
                              "Yes, the lady."
"You've been to see her?"
                              "Yes."
                                    "What happened then?"
"I saw her."
              "Yes. And what filth did she trade ye?
Or d'you expect your locket back agen?
I know the rotten ways of whores with men.
What did it cost ye?"
                        "What did what cost?"
                                                "It
Your devil's penny for the devil's bit."

"I don't know what you mean."
                                "Jimmy, my own,
Don't lie to mother, boy, for mother knows.
I know you and that lady to the bone,
And she's a whore, that thing you call a rose,
A whore who takes whatever male thing goes;
A harlot with the devil's skill to tell
The special key of each man's door to hell."

"She's not. She's nothing of the kind, I tell 'ee."
"You can't tell women like a woman can;
A beggar tells a lie to fill his belly,
A strumpet tells a lie to win a man,

71

Women were liars since the world began;
And she's a liar, branded in the eyes,
A rotten liar, who inspires lies."

"I say she's not."

          "No, don't 'ee Jim, my dearie,
You've seen her often in the last few days,
She's given a love as makes you come in weary
To lie to me before going out to laze.
She's tempted you into the devil's ways,
She's robbing you, full fist, of what you earn,
In God's name, what's she giving in return?"

"Her faith, my dear, and that's enough for me."
"Her faith. Her faith. O Jimmy, listen, dear;
Love doesn't ask for faith, my son, not he;
He asks for life throughout the live-long year,
And life's a test for any plough to ere.
Life tests a plough in meadows made of stones,
Love takes a toll of spirit, mind and bones.

"I know a woman's portion when she loves,
It's hers to give, my darling, not to take;
It isn't lockets, dear, nor pairs of gloves,
It isn't marriage bells nor wedding cake,
It's up and cook, although the belly ache;
And bear the child, and up and work again,
And count a sick man's grumble worth the pain.

"Will she do this, and fifty times as much?"
"No. I don't ask her."

          "No. I warrant, no.
She's one to get a young fool in her clutch,
And you're a fool to let her trap you so.
She love you? She? O Jimmy, let her go;
I was so happy, dear, before she came,
And now I'm going to the grave in shame.

"I bore you, Jimmy, in this very room.
For fifteen years I got you all you had,
You were my little son, made in my womb,
Left all to me, for God had took your dad,
You were a good son, doing all I bade,
Until this strumpet came from God knows where,
And now you lie, and I am in despair.

"Jimmy, I won't say more. I know you think
That I don't know, being just a withered old,
With chaps all fallen in and eyes that blink,
And hands that tremble so they cannot hold.
A bag of bones to put in churchyard mould,
A red-eyed hag beside your evening star."
And Jimmy gulped, and thought "By God, you are."

"Well, if I am, my dear, I don't pretend.
I got my eyes red, Jimmy, making you.
My dear, before our love time's at an end
Think just a minute what it is you do.
If this were right, my dear, you'd tell me true;
You don't, and so it's wrong; you lie; and she
Lies too, or else you wouldn' lie to me.

"Women and men have only got one way
And that way's marriage; other ways are lust.
If you must marry this one, then you may,
If not you'll drop her."
                "No." "I say you must.
Or bring my hairs with sorrow to the dust.
Marry your whore, you'll pay, and there an end.
My God, you shall not have a whore for friend.

"By God, you shall not, not while I'm alive.
Never, so help me God, shall that thing be.
If she's a woman fit to touch she'll wive,
If not she's whore, and she shall deal with me.
And may God's blessed mercy help us see
And may He make my Jimmy count the cost,
My little boy who's lost, as I am lost."

People in love cannot be won by kindness,
And opposition makes them feel like martyrs.
When folk are crazy with a drunken blindness,
It's best to flog them with each other's garters,
And have the flogging done by Shropshire carters,
Born under Ercall where the white stones lie;
Ercall that smells of honey in July.

Jimmy said nothing in reply, but thought
That mother was an old, hard jealous thing.
"I'll love my girl through good and ill report,
I shall be true whatever grief it bring."

And in his heart he heard the death-bell ring
For mother's death, and thought what it would be
To bury her in churchyard and be free.

He saw the narrow grave under the wall,
Home without mother nagging at his dear,
And Anna there with him at evenfall,
Bidding him dry his eyes and be of cheer.
"The death that took poor mother brings me near,
Nearer than we have ever been before,
Near as the dead one came, but dearer, more."

"Good-night, my son," said mother. "Night," he said.
He dabbed her brow wi's lips and blew the light,
She lay quite silent crying on the bed,
Stirring no limb, but crying through the night.
He slept, convinced that he was Anna's knight.
And when he went to work he left behind
Money for mother crying herself blind.

After that night he came to Anna's call,
He was a fly in Anna's subtle weavings,
Mother had no more share in him at all;
All that the mother had was Anna's leavings.
There were more lies, more lockets, more deceivings,
Taunts from the proud old woman, lies from him,
And Anna's coo of "Cruel. Leave her, Jim."

Also the foreman spoke: "You make me sick,
You come-day-go-day-God-send-plenty-beer.
You put less mizzle on your bit of Dick,
Or get you time, I'll have no slackers here,
I've had my eye on you too long, my dear."
And Jimmy pondered while the man attacked.
"I'd see her all day long if I were sacked."

And trembling mother thought, "I'll go to see 'r.
She'd give me back my boy if she were told
Just what he is to me, my pretty dear:
She wouldn't leave me starving in the cold,
Like what I am." But she was weak and old.
She thought, "But if I ast her, I'm afraid
He'd hate me ever after," so she stayed.

IV

Bessie, the gipsy, got with child by Ern,
She joined her tribe again at Shepherd's Meen,
In that old quarry overgrown with fern,
Where goats are tethered on the patch of green.
There she reflected on the fool she'd been,
And plaited kipes and waited for the bastard,
And thought that love was glorious while it lasted.

And Ern the moody man went moody home,
To that most gentle girl from Ercall Hill,
And bade her take a heed now he had come,
Or else, by cripes, he'd put her through the mill.
He didn't want her love, he'd had his fill,
Thank you, of her, the bread and butter sack.
And Anna heard that Shepherd Ern was back

"Back. And I'll have him back to me," she muttered.
"This lovesick boy of twenty, green as grass,
Has made me wonder if my brains are buttered,
He, and his lockets, and his love, the ass.
I don't know why he comes. Alas! alas!
God knows I want no love; but every sun
I bolt my doors on some poor loving one.

"It breaks my heart to turn them out of doors,
I hear them crying to me in the rain;
One, with a white face, curses, one implores,
'Anna, for God's sake, let me in again,
Anna, belov'd, I cannot bear the pain.'
Live hoovey sheep bleating outside a fold
'Anna, belov'd, I'm in the wind and cold.'

"I want no men. I'm weary to the soul
Of men like moths about a candle flame,
Of men like flies about a sugar bowl,
Acting alike, and all wanting the same.
My dreamed-of swirl of passion never came,
No man has given me the love I dreamed,
But in the best of each one something gleamed.

"If my dear darling were alive, but he . . .
He was the same; he didn't understand.
The eyes of that dead child are haunting me,

I only turned the blanket with my hand.
It didn't hurt, he died as I had planned.
A little skinny creature, weak and red;
It looked so peaceful after it was dead.

"I have been all alone, in spite of all.
Never a light to help me place my feet:
I have had many a pain and many a fall.
Life's a long headache in a noisy street,
Love at the budding looks so very sweet,
Men put such bright disguises on their lust,
And then it all goes crumble into dust.

"Jimmy the same, dear, lovely Jimmy, too,
He goes the self-same way the others went,
I shall bring sorrow to those eyes of blue.
He asks the love I'm sure I never meant.
Am I to blame? And all his money spent.
Men make this shutting doors such cruel pain,
O, Ern, I want you in my life again."

On Sunday afternoons the lovers walk
Arm within arm, dressed in their Sunday best,
The man with the blue necktie sucks a stalk,
The woman answers when she is addressed.
On quiet country stiles they sit to rest,
And after fifty years of wear and tear
They think how beautiful their courtships were.

Jimmy and Anna met to walk together
The Sunday after Shepherd Ern returned;
And Anna's hat was lovely with a feather
Bought and dyed blue with money Jimmy earned.
They walked towards Callow's Farm, and Anna yearned:
"Dear boy," she said, "this road is dull to-day,
Suppose we turn and walk the other way."

They turned, she sighed. "What makes you sigh?" he asked,
"Thinking," she said, "thinking and grieving, too.
Perhaps some wicked woman will come masked
Into your life, my dear, to ruin you.
And trusting every woman as you do

It might mean death to love and be deceived;
You'd take it hard, I thought, and so I grieved."

"Dear one, dear Anna." "O my lovely boy,
Life is all golden to the finger tips.
What will be must be: but to-day's a joy.
Reach me that lovely branch of scarlet hips."
He reached and gave; she put it to her lips.
"And here," she said, "we come to Plaister Turns,"
And then she chose the road to Shepherd Ern's.

As the deft angler, when the fishes rise,
Flicks on the broadening circle over each
The delicatest touch of dropping flies,
Then pulls more line and whips a longer reach,
Longing to feel the rod bend, the reel screech,
And the quick comrade net the monster out,
So Anna played the fly over her trout.

Twice she passed, thrice, she with the boy beside her,
A lovely fly, hooked for a human heart,
She passed his little gate, while Jimmy eyed her,
Feeling her beauty tear his soul apart:
Then did the great trout rise, the great pike dart,
The gate went clack, a man came up the hill,
The lucky strike had hooked him through the gill.

Her breath comes quick, her tired beauty glows.
She would not look behind, she looked ahead.
It seemed to Jimmy she was like a rose,
A golden white rose faintly flushed with red.
Her eyes danced quicker at the approaching tread,
Her finger nails dug sharp into her palm.
She yearned to Jimmy's shoulder, and kept calm.

"Evening," said Shepherd Ern. She turned and eyed him
Cold and surprised, but interested too,
To see how much he felt the hook inside him,
And how much he surmised, and Jimmy knew,
And if her beauty still could make him do
The love tricks he had gambolled in the past.
A glow shot through her that her fish was grassed.

"Evening," she said. "Good evening." Jimmy felt
Jealous and angry at the shepherd's tone;

He longed to hit the fellow's nose a belt,
He wanted his beloved his alone.
A fellow's girl should be a fellow's own.
Ern gave the lad a glance and turned to Anna,
Jim might have been in China by his manner.

"Still walking out?" "As you are." "I'll be bound"
"Can you talk gipsy yet, or plait a kipe?"
"I'll teach you if I can when I come round."
"And when will that be?" "When the time is ripe."
And Jimmy longed to hit the man a swipe
Under the chin to knock him out of time,
But Anna stayed: she still had twigs to lime.

"Come, Anna, come, my dear," he muttered low.
She frowned, and blinked and spoke again to Ern.
"I hear the gipsy has a row to hoe."
"The more you hear," he said "the less you'll learn."
"We've just come out," she said, "to take a turn;
Suppose you come along; the more the merrier."
"All right," he said, "but how about the terrier?"

He cocked an eye at Jimmy. "Does he bite?"
Jimmy blushed scarlet. "He's a dear," said she.
Ern walked a step, "Will you be in to-night?"
She shook her head, "I doubt if that may be.
Jim, here's a friend who wants to talk to me,
So will you go and come another day?"
"By crimes, I won't!" said Jimmy, "I shall stay."

"I thought he bit," said Ern, and Anna smiled,
And Jimmy saw the smile and watched her face
While all the jealous devils made him wild;
A third in love is always out of place;
And then her gentle body full of grace
Leaned to him sweetly as she tossed her head,
"Perhaps we two'll be getting on," she said.

They walked, but Jimmy turned to watch the third.
"I'm here, not you," he said; the shepherd grinned:
Anna was smiling sweet without a word;
She got the scarlet berry branch unpinned.
"It's cold," she said, "this evening, in the wind."

A quick glance showed that Jimmy didn't mind her,
She beckoned with the berry branch behind her.

Then dropped it gently on the broken stones,
Preoccupied, unheeding, walking straight,
Saying "You jealous boy," in even tones,
Looking so beautiful, so delicate,
Being so very sweet: but at her gate
She felt her shoe unlaced and looked to know
If Ern had taken up the sprig or no.

He had, she smiled. "Anna," said Jimmy sadly,
"That man's not fit to be a friend of yourn,
He's nobbut just an oaf; I love you madly,
And hearing you speak kind to 'm made me burn.
Who is he then?" She answered "Shepherd Ern,
A pleasant man, an old, old friend of mine."
"By cripes, then, Anna, drop him, he's a swine."

"Jimmy," she said, "you must have faith in me,
Faith's all the battle in a love like ours.
You must believe, my darling, don't you see,
That life to have its sweets must have its sours.
Love isn't always two souls picking flowers.
You must have faith. I give you all I can.
What, can't I say 'Good evening' to a man?"

"Yes," he replied, "but not a man like him."
"Why not a man like him?" she said. "What next?"
By this they'd reached her cottage in the dim,
Among the daisies that the cold had kexed.
"Because I say. Now Anna, don't be vexed."
"I'm more than vexed," she said, "with words like these.
'You say,' indeed! How dare you! Leave me, please."

"Anna, my Anna." "Leave me." She was cold,
Proud and imperious with a lifting lip,
Blazing within, but outwardly controlled;
He had a colt's first instant of the whip.
The long lash curled to cut a second strip.
"You to presume to teach! Of course, I know.
You're mother's Sunday scholar, aren't you? Go."

She slammed the door behind her, clutching skirts.
"Anna." He heard her bedroom latches thud.

He learned at last how bitterly love hurts;
He longed to cut her throat and see her blood,
To stamp her blinking eyeballs into mud.
"Anna, by God!" Love's many torments make
That tune soon change to "Dear, for Jesus' sake."

He beat the door for her. She never stirred,
But, primming bitter lips before her glass,
Admired her hat as though she hadn't heard,
And tried her front hair parted, and in mass.
She heard her lover's hasty footsteps pass.
"He's gone," she thought. She crouched below the pane,
And heard him cursing as he tramped the lane.

Rage ran in Jimmy as he tramped the night;
Rage, strongly mingled with a youth's disgust
At finding a beloved woman light,
And all her precious beauty dirty dust;
A tinsel-varnish gilded over lust.
Nothing but that. He sat him down to rage,
Beside the stream whose waters never age.

Plashing, it slithered down the tiny fall
To eddy wrinkles in the trembling pool
With that light voice whose music cannot pall,
Always the note of solace, flute-like, cool.
And when hot-headed man has been a fool,
He could not do a wiser thing than go
To that dim pool where purple teazles grow.

He glowered there until suspicion came,
Suspicion, anger's bastard, with mean tongue,
To mutter to him till his heart was flame,
And every fibre of his soul was wrung,
That even then Ern and his Anna clung
Mouth against mouth in passionate embrace.
There was no peace for Jimmy in the place.

Raging he hurried back to learn the truth.
The little swinging wicket glimmered white,
The chimney jagged the skyline like a tooth,
Bells came in swoons for it was Sunday night.
The garden was all dark, but there was light
Up in the little room where Anna slept:
The hot blood beat his brain; he crept, he crept,

Clutching himself to hear, clutching to know,
Along the path, rustling with withered leaves,
Up to the apple, too decayed to blow,
Which crooked a palsied finger at the eaves,
And up the lichened trunk his body heaves.
Dust blinded him, twigs snapped, the branches shook,
He leaned along a mossy bough to look.

Nothing at first, except a guttering candle
Shaking amazing shadows on the ceiling,
Then Anna's voice upon a bar of "Randal,
Where have you been?" and voice and music reeling,
Trembling, as though she sang with flooding feeling.
The singing stopped midway upon the stair,
Then Anna showed in white with loosened hair.

Her back was towards him, and she stood awhile,
Like a wild creature tossing back her mane,
And then her head went back, he saw a smile
On the half face half turned towards the pane;
Her eyes closed, and her arms went out again.
Jim gritted teeth, and called upon his Maker,
She drooped into a man's arms there to take her.

Agony first, sharp, sudden, like a knife,
Then down the tree to batter at the door;
"Open there. Let me in. I'll have your life.
You Jezebel of hell, you painted whore,
Talk about faith, I'll give you faith galore."
The window creaked, a jug of water came
Over his head and neck with certain aim.

"Clear out," said Ern; "I'm here, not you, to-night,
Clear out. We whip young puppies when they yap."
"If you're a man," said Jim, "come down and fight,
I'll put a stopper on your ugly chap."
"Go home," said Ern; "go home and get your pap.
To kennel, pup, and bid you mother bake
Some soothing syrup in your puppy cake."

There was a dibble sticking in the bed,
Jim wrenched it out and swung it swiftly round,
And sent it flying at the shepherd's head:
"I'll give you puppy cake. Take that, you hound."
The broken glass went clinking to the ground,

The dibble balanced, checked, and followed flat.
"My God," said Ern, "I'll give you hell for that."

He flung the door ajar with "Now, my pup—
Hold up the candle, Anna—now, we'll see."
"By crimes, come on," said Jimmy; "put them up.
Come, put them up, you coward, here I be."
And Jim, eleven stone, what chance had he
Against fourteen? but what he could he did;
Ern swung his right: "That settle you, my kid."

Jimmy went down and out: "The kid," said Ern.
"A kid, a sucking puppy; hold the light."
And Anna smiled: "It gave me such a turn,
You look so splendid, Ernie, when you fight."
She looked at Jim with: "Ern, is he all right?"
"He's coming to." She shuddered, "Pah, the brute,
What things he said"; she stirred him with her foot.

"You go inside," said Ern, "and bolt the door,
I'll deal with him." She went and Jimmy stood.
"Now, pup," said Ern, "don't come round here no more.
I'm here, not you, let that be understood.
I tell you frankly, pup, for your own good."
"Give me my hat," said Jim. He passed the gate,
And as he tottered off he called, "You wait."

"Thanks, I don't have to," Shepherd Ern replied;
"You'll do whatever waiting's being done."
The door closed gently as he went inside,
The bolts jarred in the channels one by one.
"I'll give you throwing bats about, my son.
Anna." "My dear?" "Where are you?" "Come and find."
The light went out, the windows stared out blind—

Blind as blind eyes forever seeing dark.
And in the dim the lovers went upstairs,
Her eyes fast closed, the shepherd's burning stark,
His lips entangled in her straying hairs,
Breath coming short as in a convert's prayers,
Her stealthy face all drowsy in the dim
And full of shudders as she yearned to him.

Jim crossed the water, cursing in his tears,
"By cripes, you wait. My God, he's with her now

And all her hair pulled down over her ears;
Loving the blaggard like a filthy sow,
I saw her kiss him from the apple bough.
They say a whore is always full of wiles.
O God, how sweet her eyes are when she smiles!

"Curse her and curse her. No, my God, she's sweet
It's all a helly nightmare. I shall wake.
If it were all a dream I'd kiss her feet.
I wish it were a dream for Jesus' sake.
One thing: I bet I made his guzzle ache,
I cop it fair before he sent me down,
I'll cop him yet some evening on the crown.

"O God, O God, what pretty ways she had!
He's kissing all her skin, so white and soft.
She's kissing back. I think I'm going mad.
Like rutting rattens in the apple loft.
She held that light she carried high aloft
Full in the eyes for him to hit me by.
I had the light all dazzling in my eye.

"She had her dress all clutched up to her shoulder,
And all her naked arm was all one gleam.
It's going to freeze to-night, it's turning colder.
I wish there was more water in the stream,
I'd drownd myself. Perhaps it's all a dream,
And by and by I'll wake and find it stuff;
By crimes, the pain I suffer's real enough."

About two hundred yards from Gunder Loss
He stopped to shudder, leaning on the gate,
He bit the touchwood underneath the moss;
"Rotten, like her," he muttered in his hate;
He spat it out again with "But, you wait,
We'll see again, before to-morrow's past,
In this life he laughs longest who laughs last."

All through the night the stream ran to the sea,
The different water always saying the same,
Cat-like, and then a tinkle, never glee,
A lonely little child alone in shame.
An otter snapped a thorn twig when he came,
If drifted down, it passed the Hazel Mill,
It passed the Springs; but Jimmy stayed there still.

83

Over the pointed hill-top came the light,
Out of the mists on Ercall came the sun,
Red like a huntsman hallowing after night,
Blowing a horn to rouse up everyone;
Through many glittering cities he had run,
Splashing the wind vanes on the dewy roofs
With golden sparks struck by his horses' hoofs.

The watchman rose, rubbing his rusty eyes,
He stirred the pot of cocoa for his mate;
The fireman watched his head of power rise.
"What time?" he asked. "You haven't long to wait."
"Now, is it time?" "Yes. Let her ripple." Straight
The whistle shrieked its message, "Up to work!
Up, or be fined a quarter if you shirk."

Hearing the whistle, Jimmy raised his head,
"The warning call, and me in Sunday clo'es;
I'd better go; I've time. The sun looks red,
I feel so stiff I'm very nearly froze."
So over brook and through the fields he goes,
And up the line among the navvies' smiles,
"Young Jimmy Gurney's been upon the tiles."

The second whistle blew and work began,
Jimmy worked too, not knowing what he did,
He tripped and stumbled like a drunken man;
He muddled all, whatever he was bid,
The foreman cursed, "Good God, what ails the kid?
Hi! Gurney. You. We'll have you crocking soon,
You take a lie down till the afternoon."

"I won't," he answered. "Why the devil should I?
I'm here, I mean to work. I do my piece,
Or would do if a man could, but how could I
When you come nagging round and never cease?
Well, take the job and give me my release.
I want the sack, now give it, there's my pick;
Give me the sack." The sack was given quick.

V

Dully he got his time-check from the keeper.
"Curse her," he said; "and that's the end of whores"—
He stumbled drunkenly across a sleeper—
"Give all you have and get kicked out a-doors."

84

He cashed his time-check at the station stores.
"Bett'ring yourself, I hope, Jim," said the master;
"That's it," said Jim; "and so I will do, blast her."

Beyond the bridge, a sharp turn to the right
Leads to "The Bull and Boar," the carters' rest;
An inn so hidden it is out of sight
To anyone not coming from the west,
The high embankment hides it with its crest.
Far up above the Chester trains go by,
The drinkers see them sweep against the sky.

Canal men used it when the barges came,
The navvies used it when the line was making;
The pigeons strut and sidle, ruffling, tame,
The chuckling brook in front sets shadows shaking.
Cider and beer for thirsty workers' slaking,
A quiet house; like all that God controls,
It is Fate's instrument on human souls.

Thither Jim turned. "And now I'll drink," he said.
"I'll drink and drink—I never did before—
I'll drink and drink until I'm mad or dead,
For that's what comes of meddling with a whore."
He called for liquor at "The Bull and Boar";
Moody he drank; the woman asked him why:
"Have you had trouble?" "No, he said, "I'm dry.

"Dry and burnt up, so give's another drink;
That's better, that's much better, that's the sort."
And then he sang, so that he should not think,
His Binger-Bopper song, but cut it short.
His wits were working like a brewer's wort
Until among them came the vision gleaming
Of Ern with bloody nose and Anna screaming.

"That's what I'll do," he muttered; "knock him out
And kick his face in with a running jump.
I'll not have dazzled eyes this second bout,
And she can wash the fragments under pump."
It was his ace; but Death had played a trump.
Death the blind beggar chuckled, nodding dumb,
"My game; the shroud is ready, Jimmy—come."

Meanwhile, the mother, waiting for her child,
Had tottered out a dozen times to search.
"Jimmy," she said, "you'll drive your mother wild.
Your father's name's too good a name to smirch,
Come home, my dear, she'll leave you in the lurch;
He was so good, my little Jim, so clever;
He never stops a night away, not ever.

"He never slept a night away till now,
Never, not once, in all the time he's been;
It's the Lord's will, they say, and we must bow,
But O it's like a knife, it cuts so keen!
He'll work in's Sunday clothes, it'll be seen,
And then they'll laugh, and say 'It isn't strange;
He slept with her, and so he couldn't change.'

"Perhaps," she thought, "I'm wrong; perhaps he's dead;
Killed himself like; folk do in love, they say.
He never tells what passes in his head,
And he's been looking late so old and grey.
A railway train has cut his head away,
Like the poor hare we found at Maylow's shack.
O God have pity, bring my darling back!"

All the high stars went sweeping through the sky,
The sun made all the orient clean, clear gold,
"O blessed God," she prayed, "do let me die,
Or bring my wand'ring lamb back into fold.
The whistle's gone, and all the bacon's cold;
I must know somehow if he's on the line,
He could have bacon sandwich when he dine."

She cut the bread, and started, short of breath,
Up the canal now draining for the rail;
A poor old woman pitted against death,
Bringing her pennyworth of love for bail.
Wisdom, beauty, and love may not avail.
She was too late; "Yes, he was here; oh, yes.
He chucked his job and went." "Where?" "Home, I guess."

"Home, but he hasn't been home." "Well, he went.
Perhaps you missed him, mother." "Or perhaps
He took the field path yonder through the bent.
He very likely done that, don't he, chaps?"
The speaker tested both his trouser straps

And took his pick. "He's in the town," he said.
"He'll be all right, after a bit in bed."

She trembled down the high embankment's ridge
Glad, though too late; not yet too late, indeed.
For forty yards away, beyond the bridge,
Jimmy still drank, the devil still sowed seed.
"A bit in bed," she thought, "Is what I need.
I'll go to 'Bull and Boar' and rest a bit,
They've got a bench outside; they'd let me sit."

Even as two soldiers on a fortress wall
See the bright fire streak of a coming shell,
Catch breath, and wonder "Which way will it fall?
To you? to me? or will it all be well?"
Ev'n so stood life and death, and could not tell
Whether she'd go to th' inn and find her son,
Or take the field and let the doom be done.

"No, not the inn," she thought. "People would talk.
I couldn't in the open daytime; no.
I'll just sit here upon the timber balk,
I'll rest for just a minute and then go."
Resting, her old tired heart began to glow,
Glowed and gave thanks, and thought itself in clover,
"He's lost his job, so now she'll throw him over."

Sitting, she saw the rustling thistle-kex,
The picks flash bright above, the trollies tip,
The bridge-stone shining, full of silver specks,
And three swift children running down the dip.
A Stoke Saint Michael carter cracked his whip,
The water in the runway made its din.
She half heard singing coming from the inn.

She turned, and left the inn, and took the path,
And "Brother Life, you lose," said Brother Death,
"Even as the Lord of all appointed hath
In this great miracle of blood and breath."
He doeth all things well as the book saith,
He bids the changing stars fulfil their turn,
His hand is on us when we least discern.

Slowly she tottered, stopping with the stitch,
Catching her breath, "O lawks, a dear, a dear.

How the poor tubings in my heart do twitch,
It hurts like the rheumatics very near."
And every painful footstep drew her clear
From that young life she bore with so much pain.
She hever had him to herself again.

Out of the inn came Jimmy, red with drink,
Crying: "I'll show her. Wait a bit. I'll show her.
You wait a bit. I'm not the kid you think.
I'm Jimmy Gurney, champion tupper-thrower,
When I get done with her you'll never know her,
Nor him you won't. Out of my way, you fowls,
Or else I'll rip the red things off your jowls."

He went across the fields to Plaister's End.
There was a lot of water in the brook,
Sun and white cloud and weather on the mend
For any man with any eyes to look.
He found old Callow's plough-bat, which he took,
"My innings now, my pretty dear," said he.
"You wait a bit, I'll show you. Now you'll see."

Her chimney smoke was blowing blue and faint,
The wise duck shook a tail across the pool,
The blacksmith's shanty smelt of burning paint,
Four newly-tired cartwheels hung to cool.
He had loved the place when under Anna's rule.
Now he clenched teeth and flung aside the gate,
There at the door they stood. He grinned. "Now wait."

Ern had just brought her in a wired hare,
She stood beside him stroking down the fur.
"Oh, Ern, poor thing, look how its eyes do stare,"
"It isn't *it*" he answered. "It's a her."
She stroked the breast and plucked away a bur,
She kissed the pads, and leapt back with a shout,
"My God, he's got the spudder. Ern. Look out."

Ern clenched his fists. Too late. He felt no pain,
Only incredible haste in something swift,
A shock that made the sky black on his brain,
Then stillness, while a little cloud went drift.
The weight upon his thigh bones wouldn't lift;
Then poultry in a long procession came,
Grey-legged, doing the goose-step, eyes like flame.

Grey-legged old cocks and hens sedate in age,
Marching with jerks as though they moved on springs,
With sidelong hate in round eyes red with rage,
And shouldered muskets clipped by jealous wings,
Then an array of horns and stupid things:
Sheep on a hill with harebells, hare for dinner.
"Hare." A slow darkness covered up the sinner.

"But little time is right hand fain of blow."
Only a second changes life to death;
Hate ends before the pulses cease to go,
There is great power in the stop of breath.
There's too great truth in what the dumb thing saith,
Hate never goes so far as that, nor can.
"I am what life becomes. D'you hate me, man?"

Hate with his babbling instant, red and damning,
Passed with his instant, having drunken red.
"You've killed him."
                        "No, I've not, he's only shamming.
Get up." "He can't." "O God, he isn't dead."
"O God." "Here. Get a basin. Bathe his head.
Ernie, for God's sake, what are you playing at?
I only give him one like, with the bat."

Man cannot call the brimming instant back;
Time's an affair of instants spun to days;
If man must make an instant gold, or black,
Let him, he may, but Time must go his ways.
Life may be duller for an instant's blaze.
Life's an affair of instants spun to years,
Instants are only cause of all these tears.

Then Anna screamed aloud. "Help. Murder. Murder."
"By God, it is," he said. "Through you, you slut."
Backing, she screamed, until the blacksmith heard her.
"Hurry," they cried, "the woman's throat's being cut."
Jim had his coat off by the water butt.
"He might come to," he said, "with wine or soup.
I only hit him once, like, with the scoop.

"Splash water on him, chaps. I only meant
To hit him just a clip, like, nothing more.
There. Look. He isn't dead, his eyelids went.
And he went down. O God, his head's all tore.

I've washed and washed: it's all one gob of gore.
He don't look dead to you? What? Nor to you?
Not kill, the clip I give him couldn't do."

"God send: he looks damn bad," the blacksmith said.
"Py Cot," his mate said, "she wass altogether;
She hass an illness look of peing ted."
"Here. Get a glass," the smith said, "and a feather."
"Wass you at fightings or at playings whether?"
"Here, get a glass and feather. Quick's the word."
The glass was clear. The feather never stirred.

"By God, I'm sorry, Jim. That settles it."
"By God. I've killed him then." "The doctor might."
"Try, if you like; but that's a nasty hit."
"Doctor's gone by. He won't be back till night."
"Py Cot, the feather was not looking right."
"By Jesus, chaps, I never meant to kill 'un.
Only to bat. I'll go to p'leece and tell 'un.

"O Ern, for God's sake speak, for God's sake speak."
No answer followed: Ern had done with dust,
"The p'leece is best," the smith said, "or a beak.
I'll come along; and so the lady must.
Evans, you bring the lady, will you just?
Tell 'em just how it come, lad. Come your ways;
And Joe, you watch the body where is lays."

They walked to town, Jim on the blacksmith's arm.
Jimmy was crying like a child, and saying,
"I never meant to do him any harm."
His teeth went clack, like bones at murmurs playing,
And then he trembled hard and broke out praying,
"God help my poor old mother. If he's dead,
I've brought her my last wages home," he said.

He trod his last free journey down the street;
Treading the middle road, and seeing both sides,
The school, the inns, the butchers selling meat,
The busy market where the town divides.
Then past the tanpits full of stinking hides,
And up the lane to death, as weak as pith.
"By God, I hate this, Jimmy," said the smith.

VI

Anna in black, the judge in scarlet robes,
A fuss of lawyers' people coming, going,
The windows shut, the gas alight in globes,
Evening outside, and pleasant weather blowing.
"They'll hang him?" "I suppose so; there's no knowing."
"A pretty piece, the woman, ain't she, John?
He killed the fellow just for carrying on."

"She give her piece to counsel pretty clear."
"Ah, that she did, and when she stop she smiled."
"She's had a-many men, that pretty dear;
She's drove a-many pretty fellows wild."
"More silly idiots they to be beguiled."
"Well, I don't know." "Well, I do. See her eyes?
Mystery, eh? A woman's mystery's lies."

"Perhaps." "No p'raps about it, that's the truth.
I know these women; they're a rotten lot."
"You didn't use to think so in your youth."
"No; but I'm wiser now, and not so hot.
Married or buried, *I* say, wives or shot,
These unmanned, unattached Maries and Susans
Make life no better than a proper nuisance."

"Well, I don't know." "Well, if you don't you will."
"I look on women as as good as men."
"Now, that's the kind of talk that makes me ill.
When have they been as good? I ask you when?"
"Always they have." "They haven't. Now and then
P'raps one or two was neither hen nor fury."
"One for your mother, that. Here comes the jury."

Guilty. Thumbs down. No hope. The judge passed sentence;
"A frantic passionate youth, unfit for life,
A fitting time afforded for repentance,
Then certain justice with a pitiless knife.
For her his wretched victim's widowed wife,
Pity. For her who bore him, pity. (Cheers.)
The jury were exempt for seven years."

All bowed; the Judge passed to the robing room,
Dismissed his clerks, disrobed, and knelt and prayed
As was his custom after passing doom,

Doom upon life, upon the thing not made.
"O God, who made us out of dust, and laid
Thee in us bright, to lead us to the truth,
O God, have pity upon this poor youth.

"Show him Thy grace, O God, before he die;
Shine in his heart; have mercy upon me,
Who deal the laws men make to travel by
Under the sun upon the path to Thee;
O God, Thou knowest I'm as blind as he,
As blind, as frantic, not so single, worse,
Only Thy pity spared me from the curse.

"Thy pity, and Thy mercy, God, did save,
Thy bounteous gifts, not any grace of mine,
From all the pitfalls leading to the grave,
From all the death-feasts with the husks and swine.
God, who hast given me all things, now make shine
Bright in this sinner's heart that he may see.
God, take this poor boy's spirit back to Thee."

Then trembling with his hands, for he was old,
He went to meet his college friend, the Dean,
The loiterers watched him as his carriage rolled.
"There goes the Judge," said one, and one was keen:
"Hanging that wretched boy, that's where he's been."
A policeman spat, two lawyers talked statistics,
" 'Crime passionel' in Agricultural Districts."

"They'd oughtn't hang a boy": but one said "Stuff.
This sentimental talk is rotten, rotten.
The law's the law and not half strict enough,
Forgers and murderers are misbegotten,
Let them be hanged and let them be forgotten.
A rotten fool should have a rotten end;
Mend them, you say? The rotten never mend."

And one "Not mend? The rotten not, perhaps.
The rotting would; so would the just infected.
A week in quod has ruined lots of chaps
Who'd all got good in them till prison wrecked it."
And one, "Society must be protected."
"He's just a kid. She trapped him" "No, she didden.
"He'll be reprieved." "He mid be and he midden."

92

So the talk went; and Anna took the train,
Too sad for tears, and pale; a lady spoke
Asking if she were ill or suffering pain?
"Neither," she said; but sorrow made her choke,
"I'm only sick because my heart is broke,
My friend, a man, my oldest friend here, died.
I had to see the man who killed him, tried.

"He's to be hanged. Only a boy. My friend.
I thought him just a boy; I didn't know.
And Ern was killed, and now the boy's to end,
And all because he thought he loved me so."
"My dear," the lady said; and Anna, "Oh.
It's very hard to bear the ills men make,
He thought he loved, and it was all mistake."

"My dear," the lady said; "you poor, poor woman,
Have you no friends to go to?" "I'm alone.
I've parents living, but they're both inhuman,
And none can cure what pierces to the bone.
I'll have to leave and go where I'm not known.
Begin my life again." Her friend said "Yes.
Certainly that. But leave me your address.

"For I might hear of something; I'll enquire,
Perhaps the boy might be reprieved or pardoned.
Couldn't we ask the rector or the squire
To write and ask the Judge? He can't be hardened.
What do you do? Is it housework? Have you gardened?
Your hands are very white and soft to touch."
"Lately I've not had heart for doing much."

So the talk passes as the train descends
Into the vale and halts and starts to climb
To where the apple-bearing country ends
And pleasant-pastured hills rise sweet with thyme,
Where clinking sheepbells make a broken chime
And sunwarm gorses rich the air with scent
And kestrels poise for mice, there Anna went.

There, in the April, in the garden-close,
One heard her in the morning singing sweet,
Calling the birds from the unbudded rose,
Offering her lips with grains for them to eat.

The red breasts come with little wiry feet,
Sparrows and tits and all wild feathery things,
Brushing her lifted face with quivering wings.

Jimmy was taken down into a cell,
He did not need a hand, he made no fuss.
The men were kind "for what the kid done . . . well
The same might come to any one of us."
They brought him bits of cake at tea time: thus
The love that fashioned all in human ken,
Works in the marvellous hearts of simple men.

And in the nights (they watched him night and day)
They told him bits of stories through the grating,
Of how the game went at the football play,
And how the rooks outside had started mating.
And all the time they knew the rope was waiting,
And every evening friend would say to friend,
"I hope we've not to drag him at the end."

And poor old mother came to see her son,
"The Lord has gave," she said, "the Lord has took;
I loved you very dear, my darling one,
And now there's none but God where we can look.
We've got God's promise written in His Book,
He will not fail; but oh, it do seem hard."
She hired a room outside the prison yard.

"Where did you get the money for the room?
And how are you living, mother; how'll you live?"
"It's what I'd saved to put me in the tomb,
I'll want no tomb but what the parish give."
"Mother, I lied to you that time, O forgive,
I brought home half my wages, half I spent,
And you went short that week to pay the rent.

"I went to see 'r, I spent my money on her,
And you who bore me paid the cost in pain.
You went without to buy the clothes upon her:
A hat, a locket, and a silver chain.
O mother dear, if all might be again,
Only from last October, you and me;
O mother dear, how different it would be.

"We were so happy in the room together,
Singing at 'Binger-Bopper,' weren't us just?
And going a-hopping in the summer weather,
And all the hedges covered white with dust,
And blackberries, and that, and traveller's trust.
I thought her wronged, and true, and sweet, and wise,
The devil takes sweet shapes when he tells lies.

"Mother, my dear, will you forgive your son?"
"God knows I do, Jim, I forgive you, dear;
You didn't know, and couldn't, what you done.
God pity all poor people suffering here,
And may His Mercy shine upon us clear,
And may we have His Holy Word for mark,
To lead us to His Kingdom through the dark."

"Amen." "Amen," said Jimmy; then they kissed.
The warders watched, the little larks were singing,
A plough team jangled, turning at the rist;
Beyond the mild cathedral bells were ringing,
The elm-tree rooks were cawing at the springing:
O beauty of the time when winter's done,
And all the fields are laughing at the sun!

"I s'pose they've brought the line beyond the Knapp?"
"Ah, and beyond the Barcle, so they say."
"Hearing the rooks begin reminds a chap.
Look queer, the street will, with the lock away;
O God, I'll never see it." "Let us pray.
Don't think of that, but think," the mother said,
"Of men going on long after we are dead."

"Red helpless little things will come to birth,
And hear the whistles going down the line,
And grow up strong and go about the earth,
And have much happier times than yours and mine;
And some day one of them will get a sign,
And talk to folk, and put an end to sin,
And then God's blessed kingdom will begin.

"God dropped a spark down into everyone,
And if we find and fan it to a blaze
It'll spring up and glow like—like the sun,
And light the wandering out of stony ways.
God warms His hands at man's heart when he prays.

And light of prayer is spreading heart to heart;
It'll light all where now it lights a part.

"And God who gave His mercies takes His mercies,
And God who gives beginning gives the end.
I dread my death; but it's the end of curses,
A rest for broken things too broke to mend.
O Captain Christ, our blessed Lord and Friend,
We are two wandered sinners in the mire,
Burn our dead hearts with love out of Thy fire.

"And when thy death comes, Master, let us bear it
As of Thy will, however hard to go;
Thy Cross is infinite for us to share it,
They help is infinite for us to know.
And when the long trumpets of the Judgment blow
May our poor souls be glad and meet agen,
And rest in Thee." "Say, 'Amen,' Jim." "Amen."

*   *   *   *

There was a group outside the prison gate,
Waiting to hear them ring the passing bell,
Waiting as empty people always wait
For the strong toxic of another's hell.
And mother stood there, too, not seeing well,
Praying through tears to let His will be done,
And not to hide His mercy from her son.

Talk in the little group was passing quick.
"It's nothing now to what it was, to watch."
"Poor wretched kid, I bet he's feeling sick."
"Eh? What d'you say, chaps? Someone got a match?"
"They draw a bolt and drop you down a hatch
And break you neck, whereas they used to strangle
In olden times, when you could see them dangle."

Someone said "Off hats" when the bell began.
Mother was whimpering now upon her knees.
A broken ringing like a beaten pan
It sent the sparrows wavering to the trees.
The wall-top grasses whickered in the breeze,
The broken ringing clanged, clattered and clanged
As though men's bees were swarming, not men hanged.

Now certain Justice was the pitiless knife.
The white sick chaplain snuffling at the nose,
"I am the resurrection and the life."
The bell still clangs, the small procession goes,
The prison warders ready ranged in rows.
"Now, Gurney, come, my dear; it's time," they said.
And ninety seconds later he was dead.

Some of life's sad ones are too strong to die,
Grief doesn't kill them as it kills the weak,
Sorrow is not for those who sit and cry
Lapped in the love of turning t'other cheek,
But for the noble souls austere and bleak
Who have had the bitter dose and drained the cup
And wait for Death face fronted, standing up.

As the last man upon the sinking ship,
Seeing the brine creep brightly on the deck,
Hearing aloft the slatting topsails rip,
Ripping to rags among the topmast's wreck,
Yet hoists the new red ensign without speck,
That she, so fair, may sink with colours flying,
So the old widowed mother kept from dying.

She tottered home, back to the little room,
It was all over for her, but for life;
She drew the blinds, and trembled in the gloom;
"I sat here thus when I was wedded wife;
Sorrow sometimes, and joy; but always strife,
Struggle to live except just at the last.
O God, I thank Thee for the mercies past.

"Harry, my man, when we were courting; eh . . .
The April morning up the Cony-gree.
How grand he looked upon our wedding day.
'I wish we'd had the bells,' he said to me;
And we'd the moon that evening, I and he,
And dew come wet, oh, I remember how,
And we come home to where I'm sitting now.

"And he lay dead here, and his son was born here;
He never saw his son, his little Jim.
And now I'm all alone here, left to mourn here,
And there are all his clothes, but never him.

He's down under the prison in the dim,
With quicklime working on him to the bone,
The flesh I made with many and many a groan.

"Oh, how his little face come, with bright hair,
Dear little face. We made this room so snug;
He sit beside me in his little chair,
I give him real tea sometimes in his mug.
He liked the velvet in the patchwork rug.
He used to stroke it, did my pretty son,
He called it Bunny, little Jimmie done.

"And then he ran so, he was strong at running,
Always a strong one, like his dad at that.
In summertimes I done my sewing sunning,
And he'd be sprawling, playing with the cat.
And neighbours brought their knitting out to chat
Till five o'clock; he had his tea at five;
How sweet life was when Jimmy was alive!"

      *   *   *   *

Darkness and midnight, and the midnight chimes.
Another four-and-twenty hours begin,
Darkness again, and many, many times,
The alternating light and darkness spin
Until the face so thin is still more thin,
Gazing each earthly evening wet or fine
For Jimmy coming from work along the line.

Over her head the Chester wires hum,
Under the bridge the rocking engines flash.
"He's very late this evening, but he'll come
And bring his little packet full of cash
(Always he does) and supper's cracker hash,
That is his favourite food excepting bacon.
They say my boy was hanged; but they're mistaken."

And sometimes she will walk the cindery mile,
Singing, as she and Jimmy used to do,
Singing, "The parson's dog lep over a stile."
Along the path where water lilies grew.
The stars are placid on the evening's blue,
Burning like eyes so calm, so unafraid,
On all that God has given and man has made.

Burning they watch, and mothlike owls come out,
The redbreast warbles shrilly once and stops;
The homing cowman gives his dog a shout,
The lamps are lighted in the village shops.
Silence; the last bird passes; in the copse
The hazels cross the moon, a nightjar spins,
Dew wets the grass, the nightingale begins.

Singing her crazy song the mother goes,
Singing as though her heart were full of peace,
Moths knock the petals from the dropping rose,
Stars make the glimmering pool a golden fleece,
The moon droops west, but still she does not cease,
The little mice peep out to hear her sing,
Until the inn-man's cockerel shakes his wing.

And in the sunny dawns of hot Julys,
The labourers going to meadow see her there.
Rubbing the sleep out of their heavy eyes,
They lean upon the parapet to stare;
They see her plaiting basil in her hair,
Basil, the dark red wound-wort, cops of clover,
The blue self-heal and golden Jacks of Dover.

Dully they watch her, then they turn to go
To that high Shropshire upland of late hay;
Her singing lingers with them as they mow,
And many times they try it, now grave, now gay,
'Till, with full throat over the hills away,
They lift it clear; oh, very clear it towers
Mixed with the swish of many falling flowers.

DAUBER

I

Four bells were struck, the watch was called on deck
All work aboard was over for the hour.
And some men sang and others played at check,
Or mended clothes or watched the sunset glower.
The bursting west was like an opening flower,
And one man watched it till the light was dim,
But no one went across to talk to him.

He was the painter in that swift ship's crew—
Lampman and painter—tall, a slight-built man,
Young for his years, and not yet twenty-two;
Sickly, and not yet brown with the sea's tan.
Bullied and damned at since the voyage began,
"Being neither man nor seaman by his tally,"
He bunked with the idlers just abaft the galley.

His work began at five; he worked all day,
Keeping no watch and having all night in.
His work was what the mate might care to say;
He mixed red lead in many a bouilli tin;
His dungarees were smeared with paraffin.
"Go drown himself" his round-house mates advised him,
And all hands called him "Dauber" and despised him.

Si, the apprentice, stood beside the spar,
Stripped to the waist, a basin at his side,
Slushing his hands to get away the tar,
And then he washed himself and rinsed and dried;
Towelling his face, hair-towzelled, eager-eyed,
He crossed the spar to Dauber, and there stood
Watching the gold of heaven turn to blood.

They stood there by the rail while the swift ship
Tore on out of the tropics, straining her sheets,
Whitening her trackway to a milky strip,
Dim with green bubbles and twisted water-meets,
Her clacking tackle tugged at pins and cleats,
Her great sails bellied stiff, her great masts leaned:
They watched how the seas struck and burst and greened.

Si talked with Dauber, standing by the side.
"Why did you come to sea, painter?" he said.
"I want to be a painter," he replied,
"And know the sea and ships from A to Z,
And paint great ships at sea before I'm dead;
Ships under skysails running down the Trade—
Ships and the sea; there's nothing finer made.

"But there's so much to learn, with sails and ropes,
And how the sails look, full or being furled,
And how the lights change in the troughs and slopes,
And the sea's colours up and down the world,
And how a storm looks when the sprays are hurled

High as the yard (they say) I want to see;
There's none ashore can teach such things to me.

"And then the men and rigging, and the way
Ships move, running or beating, and the poise
At the roll's end, the checking in the sway—
I want to paint them perfect, short of the noise;
And then the life, the half-decks full of boys,
The fo'c's'les with the men there, dripping wet.
I know the subjects that I want to get.

"It's not been done, the sea, not yet been done,
From the inside, by one who really knows;
I'd give up all if I could be the one,
But art comes dear the way the money goes.
So I have come to sea, and I suppose
Three years will teach me all I want to learn
And make enough to keep me till I earn."

Even as he spoke his busy pencil moved,
Drawing the leap of water off the side
Where the great clipper trampled iron-hooved,
Making the blue hills of the sea divide,
Shearing a glittering scatter in her stride,
And leaping on full tilt with all sails drawing,
Proud as a war-horse, snuffing battle, pawing.

"I cannot get it yet—not yet," he said;
"That leap and light, and sudden change to green,
And all the glitter from the sunset's red,
And the milky colours where the bursts have been,
And then the clipper striding like a queen
Over it all, all beauty to the crown.
I see it all, I cannot put it down.

"It's hard not to be able. There, look there!
I cannot get the movement nor the light;
Sometimes it almost makes a man despair
To try and try and never get it right.
Oh, if I could—oh, if I only might,
I wouldn't mind what hells I'd have to pass,
Not if the whole world called me fool and ass."

Down sank the crimson sun into the sea,
The wind cut chill at once, the west grew dun.

"Out sidelights!" called the mate. "Hi, where is he?"
The Boatswain called, "Out sidelights, damn you! Run!"
"He's always late or lazing," murmured one—
"The Dauber, with his sketching." Soon the tints
Of red and green passed on dark water-glints.

Darker it grew, still darker, and the stars
Burned golden, and the fiery fishes came.
The wire-note loudened from the straining spars;
The sheet-blocks clacked together always the same;
The rushing fishes streaked the seas with flame,
Racing the one speed noble as their own:
What unknown joy was in those fish unknown!

Just by the round-house door, as it grew dark,
The Boatswain caught the Dauber with, "Now, you;
Till now I've spared you, damn you! now you hark:
I've just had hell for what you didn't do;
I'll have you broke and sent among the crew
If you get me more trouble by a particle.
Don't you forget, you daubing, useless article!

"You thing, you twice-laid thing from Port Mahon!"
Then came the Cook's "Is that the Dauber there?
Why don't you leave them stinking paints alone?
They stink the house out, poisoning all the air.
Just take them out." "Where to?" "I don't care where.
I won't have stinking paint here." From their plates:
"That's right; wet paint breeds fever," growled his mates.

He took his still wet drawings from the berth
And climbed the ladder to the deck-house top;
Beneath, the noisy half-deck rang with mirth,
For two ship's boys were putting on the strop;
One, clambering up to let the skylight drop,
Saw him bend down beneath a boat and lay
His drawings there, till all were hid away.

And stand there silent, leaning on the boat,
Watching the constellations rise and burn,
Until the beauty took him by the throat,
So stately is their glittering overturn;
Armies of marching eyes, armies that yearn
With banners rising and falling, and passing by
Over the empty silence of the sky.

The Dauber sighed there looking at the sails,
Wind-steadied arches leaning on the night,
The high trucks traced on heaven and left no trails;
The moonlight made the topsails almost white,
The passing sidelight seemed to drip green light.
And on the clipper rushed with fire-bright bows;
He sighed, "I'll never do 't," and left the house.

"Now," said the reefer, "up! Come, Sam; come, Si,
Dauber's been hiding something." Up they slid,
Treading on naked tiptoe stealthily
To grope for treasure at the long-boat skid.
"Drawings!" said Sam. "Is that what Dauber hid?
Lord! I expected pudding, not this rot.
Still, come, we'll have some fun with what we've got."

They smeared the paint with turpentine until
They could remove with mess-clouts every trace
Of quick perception caught by patient skill,
And lines that had brought blood into his face.
They wiped the pigments off, and did erase,
With knives, all sticking clots. When they had done,
Under the boat they laid them every one.

All he had drawn since first he came to sea,
His six weeks' leisure's fruits, they laid them there.
They chuckled then to think how mad he'd be
Finding his paintings vanished into air.
Eight bells were struck, and feet from everywhere
Went shuffling aft to muster in the dark;
The mate's pipe glowed above, a dim red spark.

Names in the darkness passed and voices cried;
The red spark glowed and died, the faces seemed
As things remembered when a brain has died,
To all but high intenseness deeply dreamed.
Like hissing spears the fishes' fire streamed,
And on the clipper rushed with tossing mast,
A bath of flame broke round her as she passed.

The watch was set, the night came, and the men
Hid from the moon in shadowed nooks to sleep,
Bunched like the dead; still, like the dead, as when
Plague in a city leaves none even to weep.
The ship's track brightened to a mile-broad sweep;

The mate there felt her pulse, and eyed the spars;
South-west by south she staggered under the stars.

Down in his bunk the Dauber lay awake
Thinking of his unfitness for the sea.
Each failure, each derision, each mistake,
There in the life not made for such as he;
A morning grim with trouble sure to be,
A noon of pain from failure, and a night
Bitter with men's contemning and despite.

This is the first beginning, the green leaf,
Still in the Trades before bad weather fell;
What harvest would he reap of hate and grief
When the loud Horn made every life a hell?
When the sick ship lay over, clanging her bell,
And no time came for painting or for drawing,
But all hands fought, and icy death came clawing?

Hell, he expected,—hell. His eyes grew blind;
The snoring from his messmates droned and snuffled,
And then a gush of pity calmed his mind.
The cruel torment of his thought was muffled,
Without, on deck, an old, old seaman shuffled,
Humming his song, and through the open door
A moonbeam moved and thrust along the floor.

The green bunk curtains moved, the brass rings clicked,
The Cook cursed in his sleep, turning and turning,
The moonbeam's moving finger touched and picked,
And all the stars in all the sky were burning.
"This is the art I've come for, and am learning,
The sea and ships and men and travelling things.
It is most proud, whatever pain it brings."

He leaned upon his arm and watched the light
Sliding and fading to the steady roll;
This he would some day paint, the ship at night
And sleeping seamen tired to the soul;
The space below the bunks as black as coal,
Gleams upon chests, upon the unlit lamp,
The ranging door-hook, and the locker clamp.

This he would paint, and that, and all these scenes,
And proud ships carrying on, and men their minds,

104

And blues of rollers toppling into greens,
And shattering into white that bursts and blinds,
And scattering ships running erect like hinds,
And men in oilskins beating down a sail
High on the yellow yard, in snow, in hail.

With faces ducked down from the slanting drive
Of half-thawed hail mixed with half-frozen spray,
The roaring canvas, like a thing alive,
Shaking the mast, knocking their hands away
The foot-ropes jerking to the tug and sway,
The savage eyes salt-reddened at the rims,
And icicles on the south-wester brims.

And sunnier scenes would grow under his brush,
The tropic dawn with all things dropping dew,
The darkness and the wonder and the hush,
The insensate grey before the marvel grew;
Then the veil lifted from the trembling blue,
The walls of sky burst in, the flower, the rose,
All the expanse of heaven a mind that glows.

He turned out of his bunk; the Cook still tossed,
One of the other two spoke in his sleep,
A cockroach scuttled where the moonbeam crossed;
Outside there was the ship, the night, the deep.
"It is worth while," the youth said; "I will keep
To my resolve, I'll learn to paint all this.
My Lord, my God, how beautiful it is!"

Outside was the ship's rush to the wind's hurry
A resonant wire-hum from every rope,
The broadening bow-wash in a fiery flurry,
The leaning masts in their majestic slope,
And all things strange with moonlight: filled with hope
By all that beauty going as man bade,
He turned and slept in peace. Eight bells were made.

II

Next day was Sunday, his free painting day,
While the fine weather held, from eight till eight.
He rose when called at five, and did array
The round-house gear, and set the kit-bags straight
Then kneeling down, like housemaid at a grate,

He scrubbed the deck with sand until his knees
Were blue with dye from his wet dungarees.

Soon all was clean, his Sunday tasks were done;
His day was clear for painting as he chose.
The wetted decks were drying in the sun,
The men coiled up, or swabbed, or sought repose.
The drifts of silver arrows fell and rose
As flying fish took wing; the breakfast passed,
Wasting good time, but he was free at last.

Free for two hours and more to tingle deep,
Catching a likeness in a line or tint,
The canvas running up in a proud sweep,
Wind-wrinkled at the clews, and white like lint,
The glittering of the blue waves into glint;
Free to attempt it all, the proud ship's pawings.
The sea, the sky—he went to fetch his drawings.

Up to the deck-house top he quickly climbed,
He stooped to find them underneath the boat.
He found them all obliterated, slimed,
Blotted, erased, gone from him line and note.
They were all spoiled: a lump came in his throat,
Being vain of his attempts, and tender skinned—
Beneath the skylight watching reefers grinned.

He clambered down, holding the ruined things.
"Bosun," he called, "look here, did you do these:
Wipe off my paints and cut them into strings,
And smear them till you can't tell chalk from cheese?
Don't stare, but did you do it? Answer, please."
The Bosun turned: "I'll give you a thick ear!
Do it? I didn't. Get to hell from here!

"I touch your stinking daubs? The Dauber's daft."
A crowd was gathering now to hear the fun;
The reefers tumbled out, the men laid aft,
The Cook blinked, cleaning a mess-kid in the sun.
"What's up with Dauber now?" said everyone.
"Someone has spoiled my drawings—look at this!"
"Well, that's a dirty trick, by God, it is!"

"It is," said Sam, "a low-down dirty trick,
To spoil a fellow's work in such a way,

And if you catch him, Dauber, punch him sick,
For he deserves it, be he who he may."
A seaman shook his old head wise and grey.
"It seems to me," he said, "who ain't no judge,
Them drawings look much better now they're smudge."

"Where were they, Dauber? On the deck-house? Where?"
"Under the long-boat, in a secret place."
"The blackguard must have seen you put them there.
He is a swine! I tell him to his face:
I didn't think we'd anyone so base."
"Nor I," said Dauber. "There was six weeks' time
Just wasted in these drawings: it's a crime!"

"Well, don't you say we did it," growled his mates,
"And as for crime, be damned! the things were smears—
Best overboard, like you, with shot for weights;
Thank God they're gone, and now go shake your ears."
The Dauber listened, very near to tears.
"Dauber, if I were you," said Sam again,
"I'd aft, and see the Captain and complain."

A sigh came from the assembled seamen there.
Would he be such a fool for their delight
As go to tell the Captain? Would he dare?
And would the thunder roar, the lightning smite?
There was the Captain come to take a sight,
Handling his sextant by the chart-house aft.
The Dauber turned, the seamen thought him daft.

The Captain took his sights—a mate below
Noted the times; they shouted to each other,
The Captain quick with "Stop," the answer slow,
Repeating slowly one height then another.
The swooping clipper stumbled through the smother,
The ladder brasses in the sunlight burned,
The Dauber waited till the Captain turned.

There stood the Dauber, humbled to the bone,
Waiting to speak. The Captain let him wait,
Glanced at the course, and called in even tone,
"What is the man there wanting, Mr. Mate?"
The logship clattered on the grating straight,
The reel rolled to the scuppers with a clatter,
The Mate came grim: "Well, Dauber, what's the matter?"

107

"Please, sir, they spoiled my drawings." "Who did?"
  "They."
"Who's they?" "I don't quite know, sir."
"Don't quite know, sir?
Then why are you aft to talk about it, hey?
Whom d'you complain of?" "No one." "No one?" "No, Sir."
"Well, then, go forward till you've found them. Go, sir.
If you complain of someone, then I'll see.
Now get to hell! and don't come bothering me."

"But, sir, they washed them off, and some they cut.
Look here, sir, how they spoiled them." "Never mind.
Go shove your head inside the scuttle butt,
And that will make you cooler. You will find
Nothing like water when you're mad and blind.
Where were the drawings? in your chest, or where?"
"Under the long-boat, sir; I put them there."

"Under the long-boat, hey? Now mind your tip.
I'll have the skids kept clear with nothing round them;
The long-boat ain't a store in this here ship.
Lucky for you it wasn't I who found them.
If I had seen them, Dauber, I'd have drowned them.
Now you be warned by this. I tell you plain—
Don't stow your brass-rags under boats again.

"Go forward to your berth." The Dauber turned.
The listeners down below them winked and smiled,
Knowing how red the Dauber's temples burned,
Having lost the case about his only child.
His work was done to nothing and defiled,
And there was no redress: the Captain's voice
Spoke, and called, "Painter," making his rejoice.

The Captain and the Mate conversed together.
"Drawings, you tell me, Mister?" "Yes, sir; views
Wiped off with turps, I gather that's his blether.
He says they're things he can't afford to lose.
He's Dick, who came to sea in dancing shoes,
And found the dance a bear dance. They were hidden
Under the long-boat's chocks, which I've forbidden."

"Wiped off with turps?" The Captain sucked his lip.
"Who did it, Mister?" "Reefers, I suppose;
Them devils do the most pranks in a ship;

The round-house might have done it, Cook or Bose."
"I can't take notice of it till he knows.
How does he do his work?" "Well, no offence;
He tries: he does his best. He's got no sense."

"Painter," the Captain called; the Dauber came.
"What's all this talk of drawings? What's the matter?"
"They spoiled my drawings, sir." "Well, who's to blame?
The long-boat's there for no one to get at her;
You broke the rules, and if you choose to scatter
Gear up and down where it's no right to be,
And suffer as result, don't come to me.

"Your place is in the round-house, and your gear
Belongs where you belong. Who spoiled your things?
Find out who spoiled your things and fetch him here."
"But, sir, they cut the canvas into strings."
"I want no argument nor questionings.
Go back where you belong and say no more,
And please remember that you're not on shore."

The Dauber touched his brow and slunk away—
They eyed his going with a bitter eye.
"Dauber," said Sam, "what did the Captain say?"
The Dauber drooped his head without reply.
"Go forward, Dauber, and enjoy your cry."
The Mate limped to the rail; like little feet
Over his head the drumming reef-points beat.

The Dauber reached the berth and entered in.
Much mockery followed after as he went,
And each face seemed to greet him with the grin
Of hounds hot following on a creature spent.
"Aren't you a fool?" each mocking visage meant.
"Who did it, Dauber? What did Captain say?
It is a crime, and there'll be hell to pay."

He bowed his head, the house was full of smoke;
The Sails was pointing shackles on his chest.
"Lord, Dauber, be a man and take a joke"—
He puffed his pipe—"and let the matter rest.
Spit brown, my son, and get a hairy breast;
Get shoulders on you at the crojick braces,
And let this painting business go to blazes.

"What good can painting do to anyone?
I don't say never do it; far from that—
No harm in sometimes painting just for fun.
Keep it for fun, and stick to what you're at.
Your job's to fill your bones up and get fat;
Rib up like Barney's Bull, and thick your neck.
Throw paints to hell, boy; you belong on deck."

"That's right," said Chips; "it's downright good advice.
Painting's no good; what good can painting do
Up on a lower topsail stiff with ice,
With all your little fish-hooks frozen blue?
Painting won't help you at the weather clew,
Nor pass your gaskets for you, nor make sail.
Painting's a balmy job not worth a nail."

The Dauber did not answer; time was passing.
He pulled his easel out, his paints, his stool.
The wind was dropping, and the sea was glassing—
New realms of beauty waited for his rule;
The draught out of the crojick kept him cool.
He sat to paint, alone and melancholy.
"No turning fools," the Chips said, "from their folly."

He dipped his brush and tried to fix a line,
And then came peace, and gentle beauty came,
Turning his spirit's water into wine,
Lightening his darkness with a touch of flame.
O, joy of trying for beauty, ever the same,
You never fail, your comforts never end;
O, balm of this world's way; O, perfect friend!

III

They lost the Trades soon after; then came calm,
Light little gusts and rain, which soon increased
To glorious northers shouting out a psalm
At seeing the bright blue water silver fleeced;
Hornwards she rushed, trampling the seas to yeast.
There fell a rain-squall in a blind day's end
When for an hour the Dauber found a friend.

Out of the rain the voices called and passed,
The staysails flogged, the tackle yanked and shook.
Inside the harness-room a lantern cast

Light and wild shadows as it ranged its hook.
The watch on deck was gathered in the nook,
They had taken shelter in that secret place,
Wild light gave wild emotions to each face.

One beat the beef-cask, and the others sang
A song that had brought anchors out of seas
In ports where bells of Christians never rang,
Nor any sea mark blazed among the trees.
By forlorn swamps, in ice, by windy keys,
That song had sounded; now it shook the air
From these eight wanderers brought together there.

Under the poop-break, sheltering from the rain,
The Dauber sketched some likeness of the room,
A note to be a prompting to his brain,
A spark to make old memory reillume.
"Dauber," said someone near him in the gloom,
"How goes it, Dauber?" It was reefer Si.
"There's not much use in trying to keep dry."

They sat upon the sail-room doorway coaming,
The lad held forth like youth, the Dauber listened
To how the boy had had a taste for roaming,
And what the sea is said to be and isn't.
Where the dim lamplight fell the wet deck glistened,
Si said the Horn was still some weeks away,
"But tell me, Dauber, where d'you hail from? Eh?"

The rain blew past and let the stars appear;
The seas grew larger as the moonlight grew
For half an hour the ring of heaven was clear,
Dusty with moonlight, grey rather than blue;
In that great moon the showing stars were few.
The sleepy time-boy's feet passed overhead.
"I come from out past Gloucester," Dauber said;

"Not far from Pauntley, if you know those parts;
The place is Spital Farm, near Silver Hill,
Above a trap-hatch where a mill-stream starts.
We had a mill once, but we've stopped the mill,
My dad and sister keep the farm on still.
We're only tenants, but we've rented there,
Father and son, for over eighty year.

111

"Father has worked the farm since grandfer went;
It means the world to him; I can't think why
They bleed him to the last half-crown for rent,
And this and that have almost milked him dry.
The land's all starved, if he'd put money by,
And corn was up, and rent was down two-thirds. . .
But then they aren't, so what's the use of words.

"Yet still he couldn't bear to see it pass
To strangers, or to think a time would come
When other men than us would mow the grass,
And other names than ours have the home.
Some sorrows come from evil thought, but some
Comes when two men are near, and both are blind
To what is generous in the other's mind.

"I was the only boy, and father thought
I'd farm the Spital after he was dead,
And many a time he took me out and taught
About manures and seed-corn white and red,
And soils and hops, but I'd an empty head;
Harvest or seed, I would not do a turn—
I loathed the farm, I didn't want to learn.

"He did not mind at first, he thought it youth
Feeling the collar, and that I should change.
Then time gave him some inklings of the truth,
And that I loathed the farm, and wished to range.
Truth to a man of fifty's always strange;
It was most strange and terrible to him,
That I, his heir, should be the devil's limb.

"Yet still he hoped the Lord might change my mind.
I'd see him bridle in his wrath and hate,
And almost break my heart he was so kind,
Biting his lips sore with resolve to wait.
And then I'd try awhile; but it was Fate:
I didn't want to learn; the farm to me
Was mire and hopeless work and misery.

"Though there were things I loved about it, too—
The beasts, the apple-trees, and going haying.
And then I tried; but no, it wouldn't do,
The farm was prison, and my thoughts were straying
And there'd come father, with his grey head, praying,

'O, my dear son, don't let the Spital pass;
It 's my old home, boy, where your grandfer was.

" 'And now you won't learn farming; you don't care,
The old home's nought to you. I've tried to teach you;
I've begged Almighty God, boy, all I dare,
To use His hand if word of mine won't reach you.
Boy, for your grandfer's sake I do beseech you,
Don't let the Spital pass to strangers. Squire
Has said he'd give it you if we require.

" 'Your mother used to walk here, boy, with me,
It was her favourite walk down to the mill;
And there we'd talk how little death would be,
Knowing our work was going on here still.
You've got the brains, you only want the will—
Don't disappoint your mother and your father.
I'll give you time to travel, if you'd rather.'

"But, no, I'd wander up the brooks to read.
Then sister Jane would start with nagging tongue,
Saying my sin made father's heart to bleed,
And how she feared she'd live to see me hung.
And then she'd read me bits from Dr. Young.
And when we three would sit to supper, Jane
Would fillip dad till dad began again.

" 'I've been here all my life, boy. I was born
Up in the room above—looks on the mead.
I never thought you'd cockle my clean corn,
And leave the old home to a stranger's seed.
Father and I have made here 'thout a weed:
We've give our lives to make that. Eighty years.
And now I go down to the grave in tears.'

"And then I'd get ashamed and take off coat,
And work maybe a week, ploughing and sowing,
And then I'd creep away and sail my boat,
Or watch the water when the mill was going.
That's my delight—to be near water flowing,
Dabbling or sailing boats or jumping stanks,
Or finding moorhens' nests along the banks.

"And one day father found a ship I'd built;
He took the cart-whip to me over that,

113

And I, half mad with pain, and sick with guilt,
Went up and hid in what we called the flat,
A dusty hole given over to the cat.
She kittened there; the kittens had worn paths
Among the cobwebs, dust, and broken laths.

"And putting down my hand between the beams
I felt a leather thing, and pulled it clear:
A book with white cocoons stuck in the seams,
Where spiders had had nests for many a year.
It was my mother's sketch-book; hid, I fear,
Lest dad should ever see it. Mother's life
Was not her own while she was father's wife.

"There were her drawings, dated, pencilled faint.
March was the last one, eighteen eighty-three,
Unfinished that, for tears had smeared the paint.
The rest was landscape, not yet brought to be.
That was a holy afternoon to me;
That book a sacred book; the flat a place
Where I could meet my mother face to face.

"She had found peace of spirit, mother had,
Drawing the landscape from the attic there—
Heart-broken, often, after rows with dad,
Hid like a wild thing in a secret lair.
That rotting sketch-book showed me how and where
I, too, could get away; and then I knew
That drawing was the work I longed to do.

"Drawing became my life. I drew, I toiled,
And every penny I could get I spent
On paints and artist's matters, which I spoiled
Up in the attic to my heart's content,
Till one day father asked me what I meant;
The time had come, he said, to make an end.
Now it must finish: what did I intend?

"Either I took to farming, like his son,
In which case he would teach me, early and late
(Provided that my daubing mood was done),
Or I must go; it must be settled straight.
If I refused to farm, there was the gate.
I was to choose, his patience was all gone,
The present state of things could not go on.

114

"Sister was there; she eyed me while he spoke.
The kitchen clock ran down and struck the hour,
And something told me father's heart was broke,
For all he stood so set and looked so sour.
Jane took a duster, and began to scour
A pewter on the dresser; she was crying.
I stood stock still a long time, not replying.

"Dad waited, then he snorted and turned round.
'Well, think of it,' he said. He left the room,
His boots went clop along the stony ground
Out to the orchard and the apple-bloom.
A cloud came past the sun and made a gloom;
I swallowed with dry lips, then sister turned.
She was dead white but for her eyes that burned.

" 'You're breaking father's heart, Joe,' she began;
'It's not as if—' she checked, in too much pain.
'O, Joe, don't help to kill so fine a man;
You're giving him our mother over again.
It's wearing him to death, Joe, heart and brain;
You know what store he sets on leaving this
To (it's too cruel) to a son of his.

" 'Yet you go painting all the day. O Joe,
Couldn't you make an effort? Can't you see
What folly it is of yours? It's not as though
You are a genius, or could ever be.
O Joe, for father's sake, if not for me,
Give up this craze for painting, and be wise
And work with father, where you duty lies.'

" It goes too deep,' I said; 'I loathe the farm;
I couldn't help, even if I'd the mind.
Even if I helped, I'd only do him harm;
Father would see it, if he were not blind.
I was not built to farm, as he would find.
O Jane, it's bitter hard to stand alone
And spoil my father's life or spoil my own.'

"Spoil both,' she said, 'the way you're shaping now.
You're only a boy not knowing your own good.
Where will you go, suppose you leave here? How
Do you propose to earn your daily food?
Draw? Daub the pavements? There's a feckless brood

115

Goes to the devil daily, Joe, in cities
Only from thinking how divine their wit is.

" 'Clouds are they, without water, carried away.
And you'll be one of them, the way you're going,
Daubing at silly pictures all the day,
And praised by silly fools who're always blowing.
And you chose this when you might go a-sowing,
Casting the good corn into chosen mould
That shall in time bring forth a hundredfold.'

"So we went on, but in the end it ended.
I felt I'd done a murder; I felt sick.
There's much in human minds cannot be mended,
And that, not I, played dad a cruel trick.
There was one mercy: that it ended quick.
I went to join my mother's brother: he
Lived down the Severn. He was kind to me.

"And there I learned house-painting for a living.
I'd have been happy there, but that I knew
I'd sinned before my father past forgiving,
And that they sat at home, that silent two,
Wearing the fire out and the evening through,
Silent, defeated, broken, in despair,
My plate unset, my name gone, and my chair.

"I saw all that; and sister Jane came white—
White as a ghost, with fiery, weeping eyes.
I saw her all day long and half the night,
Bitter as gall, and passionate and wise.
'Joe, you have killed your father: there he lies.
You have done your work—you with our mother's ways.'
She said it plain, and then her eyes would blaze.

"And then one day I had a job to do
Down below bridge, by where the docks begin,
And there I saw a clipper towing through,
Up from the sea that morning, entering in.
Raked to the nines she was, lofty and thin,
Her ensign ruffling red, her bunts in pile,
Beauty and strength together, wonder, style.

"She docked close to the gates, and there she lay
Over the water from me, well in sight;

And as I worked I watched her all the day,
Finding her beauty ever fresh delight.
Her house-flag was bright green with strips of white;
High in the sunny air it rose to shake
Above the skysail poles most splendid rake.

"And when I felt unhappy I would look
Over the river at her, and her pride,
So calm, so quiet, came as a rebuke
To half the passionate pathways which I tried;
And though the autumn ran its term and died,
And winter fell and cold December came,
She was still splendid there, and still the same.

"Then on a day she sailed; but when she went
My mind was clear on what I had to try:
To see the sea and ships, and what they meant,
That was the thing I longed to do; so I
Drew and worked hard, and studied and put by,
And thought of nothing else but that one end,
But let all else go hang—love, money, friend.

"And now I've shipped as Dauber I've begun.
It was hard work to find a dauber's berth;
I hadn't any friends to find me one,
Only my skill, for what it may be worth;
But I'm at sea now, going about the earth,
And when the ship's paid off, when we return,
I'll join some Paris studio and learn."

He stopped, the air came moist, Si did not speak;
The Dauber turned his eyes to where he sat,
Pressing the sail-room hinges with his cheek,
His face half covered with a drooping hat.
Huge dewdrops from the staysails dropped and spat,
Si did not stir, the Dauber touched his sleeve,
A little birdlike noise came from a sheave.

Si was asleep, sleeping a calm deep sleep,
Still as a warden of the Egyptian dead
In some old haunted temple buried deep
Under the desert sand, sterile and red.
The Dauber shook his arm; Si jumped and said,
"Good yarn, I swear! I say, you have a brain—
Was that eight bells that went?" He slept again.

Then waking up, "I've had a nap," he cried.
"Was that one bell? What, Dauber, you still here? "
"Si there? " the Mate's voice called. "Sir," he replied.
The order made the lad's thick vision clear;
A something in the Mate's voice made him fear
"Si," said the Mate, "I hear you've made a friend—
Dauber, in short. That friendship's got to end.

"You're a young gentleman. Your place aboard
Is with the gentlemen abaft the mast.
You're learning to command; you can't afford
To yarn with any man. But there . . . it's past.
You've done it once; let this time be the last.
The Dauber's place is forward. Do it again,
I'll put you bunking forward with the men.

"Dismiss." Si went, but Sam, beside the Mate,
Timekeeper there, walked with him to the rail
And whispered him the menace of "You wait"—
Words which have turned full many a reefer pale.
The watch was changed; the watch on deck trimmed sail.
Sam, going below, called all the reefers down,
Sat in his bunk and eyed them with a frown.

"Si here," he said, "has soiled the half-deck's name
Talking to Dauber—Dauber, the ship's clout.
A reefer takes the Dauber for a flame,
The half-deck take the round-house walking out.
He's soiled the half-deck's honour; now, no doubt,
The Bosun and his mates will come here sneaking,
Asking for smokes, or blocking gangways speaking.

"I'm not a vain man, given to blow or boast;
I'm not a proud man, but I truly feel
That while I've bossed this mess and ruled this roast
I've kept this hooker's half-deck damned genteel.
Si must ask pardon, or be made to squeal.
Down on your knees, dog; them we love we chasten.
Jao, pasea, my son—in English, Hasten."

Si begged for pardon, meekly kneeling down
Before the reefer's mess assembled grim.
The lamp above them smoked the glass all brown;
Beyond the door the dripping sails were dim.
The Dauber passed the door; none spoke to him.

118

He sought his berth and slept, or, waking, heard
Rain on the deck-house—rain, no other word.

IV

Out of the air a time of quiet came.
Calm fell upon the heaven like a drowth;
The brass sky watched the brassy water flame,
Drowsed as a snail the clipper loitered south
Slowly, with no white bone across her mouth,
No rushing glory, like a queen made bold,
The Dauber strove to draw her as she rolled.

There the four leaning spires of canvas rose,
Royals and skysails lifting, gently lifting,
White like the brightness that a great fish blows
When billows are at peace and ships are drifting;
With mighty jerks that set the shadows shifting,
The courses tugged their tethers: a blue haze
Drifted like ghosts of flocks come down to graze.

There the great skyline made her perfect round,
Notched now and then by the sea's deeper blue;
A smoke-smutch marked a steamer homeward bound.
The haze wrought all things to intenser hue.
In tingling impotence the Dauber drew
As all men draw, keen to the shaken soul
To give a hint that might suggest the whole.

A naked seaman washing a red shirt
Sat at a tub whistling between his teeth;
Complaining blocks quavered like something hurt,
A sailor cut an old boot for a sheath,
The ship bowed to her shadow-ship beneath,
And little slaps of spray came at the roll
On to the deck-planks from the scupper-hole.

He watched it, painting patiently, as paints
With eyes that pierce behind the blue sky's veil,
The Benedictine in a Book of Saints
Watching the passing of the Holy Grail;
The green dish dripping blood, the trump, the hail,
The spears that pass, the memory, and the passion,
The beauty moving under this world's fashion.

But as he painted, slowly, man by man,
The seamen gathered near; the Bosun stood
Behind him, jeering; then the Sails began
Sniggering with comment that it was not good.
Chips flicked his sketch with little scraps of wood,
Saying, "That hit the top-knot," every time.
Cook mocked, "My lovely drawings; it's a crime."

Slowly the men came nearer, till a crowd
Stood at his elbow, muttering as he drew;
The Bosun, turning to them, spoke aloud,
"This is the ship that never got there. You
Look at her here, what Dauber's trying to do.
Look at her! lummy, like a Christmas-tree.
That thing's a ship; he calls this painting. See?"

Seeing the crowd, the Mate came forward; then
"Sir," said the Bosun, "Come and see the sight!
Here's Dauber makes a circus for the men.
He calls this thing a ship—this hell's delight!"
"Man," said the Mate, "you'll never get her right
Daubing like that. Look here!" He took a brush.
"Now, Dauber, watch; I'll put you to the blush.

"Look here. Look there. Now watch this ship of mine."
He drew her swiftly from a memory stored.
"God, sir," the Bosun said, "you do her fine!"
"Ay," said the Mate, "I do so, by the Lord!
I'll paint a ship with any man aboard."
They hung about his sketch like beasts at bait.
"There now, I taught him painting," said the Mate.

When he had gone, the gathered men dispersed;
Yet two or three still lingered to dispute
What errors made the Dauber's work the worst.
They probed his want of knowledge to the root.
"Bei Gott!" they swore, "der Dauber cannot do't;
He haf no knolich how to put der pense.
Der Mate's is goot. Der Dauber haf no sense."

"You hear?" the Bosun cried, "you cannot do it!"
"A gospel truth," the Cook said, "true as hell!
And wisdom, Dauber, if you only knew it;
A five year boy would do a ship as well."
"If that's the kind of thing you hope to sell,

God help you," echoed Chips. "I tell you true
The job's beyond you, Dauber; drop it, do.

"Drop it, in God's name drop it, and have done!
You see you cannot do it. Here's the Mate
Paints you to frazzles before everyone;
Paints you a dandy clipper while you wait.
While you, Lord love us, daub. I tell you straight,
We've had enough of daubing; drop it; quit.
You cannot paint, so make an end of it."

"That's sense," said all; "you cannot, why pretend? "
The Dauber rose and put his easel by.
"You've said enough," he said, "now let it end.
Who cares how bad my painting may be? I
Mean to go on, and, if I fail, to try.
However much I miss of my intent,
If I have done my best I'll be content.

"You cannot understand that. Let it be.
You cannot understand, nor know, nor share.
This is a matter touching only me;
My sketch may be a daub, for aught I care.
You may be right. But even if you were,
Your mocking should not stop this work of mine;
Rot though it be, its prompting is divine.

"You cannot understand that you, and you,
And you, you Bosun. You can stand and jeer,
This is the task your spirit fits you to,
That you can understand and hold most dear.
Grin, then, like collars, ear to donkey ear,
But let me daub. Try, you, to understand
Which task will bear the light best on God's hand."

V

The wester came as steady as the Trades;
Brightly it blew, and still the ship did shoulder
The brilliance of the water's white cockades
Into the milky green of smoky smoulder.
The sky grew bluer and the air grew colder.
Southward she thundered while the westers held,
Proud, with taut bridles, pawing, but compelled.

121

And still the Dauber strove, though all men mocked,
To draw the splendour of the passing thing,
And deep inside his heart a something locked.
Long pricking in him, now began to sting—
A fear of the disasters storm might bring;
His rank as painter would be ended then—
He would keep watch and watch like other men.

And go aloft with them to man the yard
When the great ship was rolling scuppers under,
Burying her snout all round the compass card,
While the green water struck at her and stunned her;
When the lee-rigging slacked, when one long thunder
Boomed from the black to windward, when the sail
Booted and spurred the devil in the gale.

For him to ride on men: that was the time
The Dauber dreaded; then the test would come,
When seas, half-frozen, slushed the decks with slime,
And all the air was blind with flying scum;
When the drenched sails were furled, when the fierce hum
In weather riggings died into the roar
Of God's eternal never tamed by shore.

Once in the passage he had worked aloft,
Shifting her suits one summer afternoon,
In the bright Trade wind, when the wind was soft,
Shaking the points, making the tackle croon.
But that was child's play to the future: soon
He would be ordered up when sails and spars
Were flying and going mad among the stars.

He had been scared that first time, daunted, thrilled,
Not by the height so much as by the size,
And then the danger to the man unskilled
In standing on a rope that runs through eyes.
"But in a storm," he thought, "the yards will rise
And roll together down, and snap their gear!"
The sweat came cold upon his palms for fear.

Sometimes in Gloucester he had felt a pang
Swinging below the house-eaves on a stage.
But stages carry rails; here he would hang
Upon a jerking rope in a storm's rage,
Ducked that the sheltering oilskin might assuage

122

The beating of the storm, clutching the jack,
Beating the sail, and being beaten back.

Drenched, frozen, gasping, blinded, beaten dumb,
High in the night, reeling great blinding arcs
As the ship rolled, his chappy fingers numb,
The deck below a narrow blur of marks,
The sea a welter of whiteness shot with sparks,
Now snapping up in bursts, now dying away,
Salting the horizontal snow with spray.

A hundred and fifty feet above the deck,
And there, while the ship rolls, boldly to sit
Upon a foot-rope moving, jerk and check,
While half a dozen seamen work on it;
Held by one hand, straining, by strength and wit
To toss a gasket's coil around the yard,
How could he compass that when blowing hard?

And if he failed in any least degree,
Or faltered for an instant, or showed slack,
He might go drown himself within the sea,
And add a bubble to the clipper's track.
He had signed his name, there was no turning back,
No pardon for default—this must be done.
One iron rule at sea binds everyone.

Till now he had been treated with contempt
As neither man nor thing, a creature borne
On the ship's articles, but left exempt
From all the seamen's life except their scorn.
But he would rank as seaman off the Horn,
Work as a seaman, and be kept or cast
By standards set for men before the mast.

Even now they shifted suits of sails; they bent
The storm-suit ready for the expected time;
The mighty wester that the Plate had lent
Had brought them far into the wintry clime.
At dawn, out of the shadow, there was rime,
The dim Magellan Clouds were frosty clear,
The wind had edge, the testing-time was near.

And then he wondered if the tales were lies
Told by old hands to terrify the new,

For, since the ship left England, only twice
Had there been need to start a sheet or clew,
Then only royals, for an hour or two,
And no seas broke aboard, nor was it cold.
What were these gales of which the stories told?

The thought went by. He had heard the Bosun tell
Too often, and too fiercely, not to know
That being off the Horn in June is hell:
Hell of continual toil in ice and snow,
Frost-bitten hell in which the westers blow
Shrieking for days on end, in which the seas
Gulf the starved seamen till their marrows freeze.

Such was the weather he might look to find,
Such was the work expected: there remained
Firmly to set his teeth, resolve his mind,
And be the first, however much it pained,
And bring his honour round the Horn unstained,
And win his mates' respect; and thence, untainted,
Be ranked as man however much he painted.

He drew deep breath; a gantline swayed aloft
A lower topsail, hard with rope and leather
Such as men's frozen fingers fight with oft
Below the Ramirez in Cape Horn weather.
The arms upon the yard hove all together,
Lighting the head along; a thought occurred
Within the painter's brain like a bright bird:

That this, and so much like it, of man's toil,
Compassed by naked manhood in strange places,
Was all heroic, but outside the coil
Within which modern art gleams or grimaces;
That if he drew that line of sailors' faces
Sweating the sail, their passionate play and change,
It would be new, and wonderful, and strange.

That that was what his work meant; it would be
A training in new vision—a revealing
Of passionate men in battle with the sea,
High on an unseen stage, shaking and reeling;
And men through him would understand their feeling,
Their might, their misery, their tragic power,
And all by suffering pain a little hour;

124

High on the yard with them, feeling their pain,
Battling with them; and it had not been done.
He was a door to new worlds in the brain,
A window opening letting in the sun,
A voice saying, "Thus is bread fetched and ports won
And life lived out at sea where men exist
Solely by man's strong brain and sturdy wrist."

So he decided, as he cleaned his brasses,
Hearing without, aloft, the curse, the shout
Where the taut gantline passes and repasses,
Heaving new topsails to be lighted out.
It was most proud, however self might doubt,
To share man's tragic toil and paint it true.
He took the offered Fate: this he would do.

That night the snow fell between six and seven.
A little feathery fall so light, so dry—
An aimless dust out of a confused heaven,
Upon an air no steadier than a sigh;
The powder dusted down and wandered by
So purposeless, so many, and so cold,
Then died, and the wind ceased and the ship rolled.

Rolled till she clanged—rolled till the brain was tired,
Marking the acme of the heaves, the pause
While the sea-beauty rested and respired,
Drinking great draughts of roller at her hawse.
Flutters of snow came aimless upon flaws.
"Lock up your paints." the Mate said, speaking light:
"This is the Horn; you'll join my watch to-night!"

All through the windless night the clipper rolled
In a great swell with oily gradual heaves
Which rolled her down until her time-bells tolled,
Clang, and the weltering water moaned like beeves.
The thundering rattle of slatting shook the sheaves,
Startles of water made the swing ports gush,
The sea was moaning and sighing and saying "Hush!"

It was all black and starless. Peering down
Into the water, trying to pierce the gloom,
One saw a dim, smooth, oily glitter of brown

Heaving and dying away and leaving room
For yet another. Like the march of doom
Came those great powers of marching silences;
Then fog came down, dead-cold, and hid the seas.

They set the Dauber to the foghorn. There
He stood upon the poop, making to sound
Out of the pump the sailors' nasal blare,
Listening lest ice should make the note resound.
She bayed there like a solitary hound
Lost in a covert; all the watch she bayed,
The fog, come closelier down, no answer made.

Denser it grew, until the ship was lost.
The elemental hid her; she was merged
In mufflings of dark death, like a man's ghost,
New to the change of death, yet thither urged.
Then from the hidden waters something surged—
Mournful, despairing, great, greater than speech,
A noise like one slow wave on a still beach.

Mournful, and then again mournful, and still
Out of the night that mighty voice arose;
The Dauber at his foghorn felt the thrill.
Who rode that desolate sea? What forms were those?
Mournful, from things defeated, in the throes
Of memory of some conquered hunting-ground,
Out of the night of death arose the sound.

"Whales!" said the mate. They stayed there all night long
Answering the horn. Out of the night they spoke,
Defeated creatures who had suffered wrong,
But were still noble underneath the stroke.
They filled the darkness when the Dauber woke;
The men came peering to the rail to hear,
And the sea sighed, and the fog rose up sheer.

A wall of nothing at the world's last edge,
Where no life came except defeated life.
The Dauber felt shut in within a hedge,
Behind which form was hidden and thought was rife;
And that a blinding flash, a thrust, a knife
Would sweep the hedge away and make all plain,
Brilliant beyond all words, blinding the brain.

So the night passed, but then no morning broke—
Only a something showed that night was dead.
A sea-bird, cackling like a devil, spoke,
And the fog drew away and hung like lead.
Like mighty cliffs it shaped, sullen and red;
Like glowering gods at watch it did appear,
And sometimes drew away, and then drew near.

Like islands, and like chasms, and like hell,
But always mighty and red, gloomy and ruddy,
Shutting the visible sea in like a well;
Slow heaving in vast ripples, blank and muddy,
Where the sun should have risen it streaked bloody.
The day was still-born; all the sea-fowl scattering
Splashed the still water, mewing, hovering, clattering.

Then Polar snow came down little and light,
Till all the sky was hidden by the small,
Most multitudinous drift of dirty white
Tumbling and wavering down and covering all—
Covering the sky, the sea, the clipper tall,
Furring the ropes with white, casing the mast,
Coming on no known air, but blowing past.

And all the air seemed full of gradual moan,
As though in those cloud-chasms the horns were blowing
The mort for gods cast out and overthrown,
Or for the eyeless sun plucked out and going.
Slow the low gradual moan came in the snowing;
The Dauber felt the prelude had begun.
The snowstorm fluttered by; he saw the sun

Snow and pass by, gleam from one towering prison
Into another, vaster and more grim,
Which in dull crags of darkness had arisen
To muffle-to a final door on him.
The gods upon the dull crags lowered dim,
The pigeons chattered, quarrelling in the track.
In the south-west the dimness dulled to black.

Then came the cry of "Call all hands on deck!"
The Dauber knew its meaning; it was come:
Cape Horn, that tramples beauty into wreck,
And crumples steel and smites the strong man dumb.

127

Down clattered flying kites and staysails: some
Sang out in quick, high calls; the fairleads skirled,
And from the south-west came the end of the world.

"Caught in her ball-dress," said the Bosun, hauling;
"Lee-ay, lee-ay!" quick, high, came the men's call;
It was all wallop of sails and startled calling.
"Let fly!" "Let go!" "Clew up!" and "Let go all!"
"Now up and make them fast!" "Here, give us a haul!"
"Now up and stow them! Quick! By God! we're done!"
The blackness crunched all memory of the sun.

"Up!" said the Mate. "Mizzen topgallants. Hurry!"
The Dauber ran, the others ran, the sails
Slatted and shook; out of the black a flurry
Whirled in fine lines, tattering the edge to trails.
Painting and art and England were old tales
Told in some other life to that pale man,
Who struggled with white fear and gulped and ran.

He struck a ringbolt in his haste and fell—
Rose, sick with pain, half-lamed in his left knee;
He reached the shrouds where clambering men pell-mell
Hustled each other up and cursed him; he
Hurried aloft with them: then from the sea
Came a cold, sudden breath that made the hair
Stiff on the neck, as though Death whispered there.

A man below him punched him in the side.
"Get up, you Dauber, or let me get past."
He saw the belly of the skysail skied,
Gulped, and clutched tight, and tried to go more fast.
Sometimes he missed his ratline and was grassed,
Scraped his shin raw against the rigid line.
The clamberers reached the futtock-shrouds' incline.

Cursing they came; one kicking out behind,
Kicked Dauber in the mouth, and one below
Punched at his calves; the futtock-shrouds inclined,
It was a perilous path for one to go.
"Up, Dauber, up!" A curse followed a blow.
He reached the top and gasped, then on, then on.
And one voice yelled "Let go!" and one "All gone!"

Fierce clamberers, some in oilskins, some in rags,
Hustling and hurrying up, up the steep stairs.
Before the windless sails were blown to flags,
And whirled like dirty birds athwart great airs,
Ten men in all, to get this mast of theirs
Snugged to the gale in time. "Up! Damn you, run,"
The mizzen topmast head was safely won.

"Lay out!" the Bosun yelled. The Dauber laid
Out on the yard, gripping the yard, and feeling
Sick at the mighty space of air displayed
Below his feet; where mewing birds were wheeling.
A giddy fear was on him; he was reeling.
He bit his lip half through, clutching the jack.
A cold sweat glued the shirt upon his back.

The yard was shaking, for a brace was loose.
He felt that he would fall; he clutched, he bent,
Clammy with natural terror to the shoes
While idiotic promptings came and went.
Snow fluttered on a wind-flaw and was spent;
He saw the water darken. Someone yelled,
"Frap it; don't stay to furl! Hold on!" He held.

Darkness came down—half darkness—in a whirl;
The sky went out, the waters disappeared.
He felt a shocking pressure of blowing hurl
The ship upon her side. The darkness speared
At her with wind; she staggered, she careered,
Then down she lay. The Dauber felt her go;
He saw his yard tilt downwards. Then the snow

Whirled all about—dense, multitudinous, cold—
Mixed with the wind's one devilish thrust and shriek.
Which whiffled out men's tears, deafened, took hold,
Flattening the flying drift against the cheek.
The yards buckled and bent, man could not speak.
The ship lay on her broadside; the wind's sound
Had devilish malice at having got her downed.

*　　　*　　　*　　　*

How long the gale had blown he could not tell,
Only the world had changed, his life had died.
A moment now was everlasting hell.

Nature an onslaught from the weather side,
A withering rush of death, a frost that cried,
Shrieked, till he withered at the heart; a hail
Plastered his oilskins with an icy mail.

"Cut!" yelled his mate. He looked—the sail was shred
Blown into rags in the first furious squall;
The tatters into tongues and stringers spread
A block upon the yard thumped like a mall.
The ship lay—the sea smote her, the wind's bawl!
Came, "loo, loo, loo!" The devil cried his hounds
On to the poor spent stag strayed in his bounds.

"Cut! Ease her!" yelled his mate; the Dauber heard.
His mate wormed up the tilted yard and slashed,
A rag of canvas skimmed like a darting bird.
The snow whirled, the ship bowed to it, the gear lashed,
The sea-tops were cut off and flung down smashed;
Tatters of shouts were flung, the rags of yells—
And clang, clang, clang, below beat the two bells.

"Oh God!" the Dauber moaned. A roaring rang,
Blasting the royals like a cannonade;
The backstays parted with a cracking clang,
The upper spars were snapped like twigs decayed—
Snapped at their heels, their jagged splinters splayed,
Like white and ghastly hair erect with fear.
The Mate yelled, "Gone, by God, and pitched them clear!"

"Up!" yelled the Bosun; "up and clear the wreck!"
The Dauber followed where he led: below
He caught one giddy glimpsing of the deck
Filled with white water, as though heaped with snow.
He saw the streamers of the rigging blow
Straight out like pennons from the splintered mast,
Then, all sense dimmed, all was an icy blast.

Roaring from nether hell and filled with ice,
Roaring and crashing on the jerking stage,
An utter bridle given to utter vice,
Limitless power mad with endless rage
Withering the soul; a minute seemed an age.
He clutched and hacked at ropes, at rags of sail,
Thinking that comfort was a fairy-tale

Told long ago—long, long ago—long since
Heard of in other lives—imagined, dreamed—
There where the basest beggar was a prince
To him in torment where the tempest screamed,
Comfort and warmth and ease no longer seemed
Things that a man could know: soul, body, brain,
Knew nothing but the wind, the cold, the pain.

"Leave that!" the Bosun shouted: "Crojick save!"
The splitting crojick, not yet gone to rags,
Thundered below, beating till something gave,
Bellying between its buntlines into bags.
Some birds were blown past, shrieking: dark, like shags,
Their backs seemed, looking down. "Leu, leu!" they cried.
The ship lay, the seas thumped her; she had died.

They reached the crojick yard, which buckled, buckled
Like a thin whalebone to the topsail's strain.
They laid upon the yard and heaved and knuckled,
Pounding the sail, which jangled and leapt again.
It was quite hard with ice, its rope like chain,
Its strength like seven devils; it shook the mast.
They cursed and toiled and froze: a long time passed

Two hours passed, then a dim lightening came.
Those frozen ones upon the yard could see
The mainsail and the foresail still the same,
Still battling with the hands and blowing free,
Rags tattered where the staysails used to be.
The lower topsails stood; the ship's lee deck
Seethed with four feet of water filled with wreck.

An hour more went by; the Dauber lost
All sense of hands and feet, all sense of all
But of a wind that cut him to the ghost,
And of a frozen fold he had to haul,
Of heavens that fell and never ceased to fall,
And ran in smoky snatches along the sea,
Leaping from crest to wave-crest, yelling. He

Lost sense of time; no bells went, but he felt
Ages go over him. At last, at last
They frapped the cringled crojick's icy pelt;
In frozen bulge and bunt they made it fast.

131

Then, scarcely live, they laid in to the mast.
The Captain's speaking-trumpet gave a blare,
"Make fast the topsail, Mister, while you're there."

Some seamen cursed, but up they had to go—
Up to the topsail yard to spend an hour
Stowing a topsail in a blinding snow,
Which made the strongest man among them cower.
More men came up, the fresh hands gave them power,
They stowed the sail; then with a rattle of chain
One half the crojick burst its bonds again.

*   *   *   *

They stowed the sail, frapping it round with rope,
Leaving no surface for the wind, no fold,
Then down the weather-shrouds, half dead, they grope;
That struggle with the sail had made them old.
They wondered if the crojick furl would hold.
"Lucky," said one, "It didn't spring the spar."
"Lucky," the Bosun said, "lucky! We are!

"She came within two shakes of turning top
Or stripping all her shroud-screws, that first quiff.
Now fish those wash-deck buckets out of the slop.
Here's Dauber says he doesn't like Cape Stiff.
This isn't wind, man, this is only a whiff.
Hold on, all hands, hold on!" a sea, half seen,
Paused, mounted, burst, and filled the main-deck green.

The Dauber felt a mountain of water fall.
It covered him deep, deep, he felt it fill,
Over his head, the deck, the fife-rails, all
Quieting the ship, she trembled and lay still.
Then with a rush and shatter and clanging shrill
Over she went; he saw the water cream
Over the bitts; he saw the half-deck stream.

Then in the rush he swirled, over she went;
Her lee-rail dipped, he struck, and something gave;
His legs went through a port as the roll spent;
She paused, then rolled, and back the water drave.
He drifted with it as a part of the wave,
Drowning, half-stunned, exhausted, partly frozen,
He struck the booby hatchway; then the Bosun

Leaped, seeing his chance, before the next sea burst,
And caught him as he drifted, seized him, held,
Up-ended him against the bitts, and cursed.
"This ain't the George's Swimming Baths," he yelled;
"Keep on your feet!" Another grey-back felled
The two together, and the Bose, half-blind,
Spat: "One's a joke," he cursed, "but two's unkind."

"Now, damn it, Dauber!" said the Mate. "Look out,
Or you'll be over the side!" The water freed;
Each clanging freeing-port became a spout.
The men cleared up the decks as there was need.
The Dauber's head was cut, he felt it bleed
Into his oilskins as he clutched and coiled.
Water and sky were devils' brews which boiled,

Boiled, shrieked, and glowered; but the ship was saved,
Snugged safely down, though fourteen sails were split.
Out of the dark a fiercer fury raved.
The grey-backs died and mounted, each crest lit
With a white toppling gleam that hissed from it
And slid, or leaped, or ran with whirls of cloud,
Mad with inhuman life that shrieked aloud.

The watch was called; Dauber might go below.
"Splice the main brace!" the Mate called. All laid aft
To get a gulp of momentary glow
As some reward for having saved the craft.
The steward ladled mugs, from which each quaffed
Whisky, with water, sugar, and lime-juice, hot,
A quarter of a pint each made the tot.

Beside the lamp-room door the steward stood
Ladling it out, and each man came in turn,
Tipped his sou' wester, drank it, grunted "Good!"
And shambled forward, letting it slowly burn.
When all were gone the Dauber lagged astern.
Torn by his frozen body's lust for heat,
The liquor's pleasant smell, so warm, so sweet,

And by a promise long since made at home
Never to taste strong liquor. Now he knew
The worth of liquor; now he wanted some.
His frozen body urged him to the brew;
Yet it seemed wrong, an evil thing to do

To break that promise. "Dauber," said the Mate,
"Drink, and turn in, man; why the hell d'ye wait?"

"Please, sir, I'm temperance." "Temperance are you, hey?
That's all the more for me! So you're for slops?
I thought you'd had enough slops for to-day.
Go to your bunk and ease her when she drops.
And—damme, steward! you brew with too much hops!
Stir up the sugar, man!—and tell your girl
How kind the Mate was teaching you to furl."

Then the Mate drank the remnants, six men's share,
And ramped into his cabin, where he stripped
And danced unclad, and was uproarious there.
In waltzes with the cabin cat he tripped,
Singing in tenor clear that he was pipped—
That "he who strove the tempest to disarm,
Must never first embrail the lee yard-arm,"

And that his name was Ginger. Dauber crept
Back to the round-house, gripping by the rail.
The wind howled by; the passionate water leapt;
The night was all one roaring with the gale.
Then at the door he stopped, uttering a wail;
His hands were perished numb and blue as veins.
He could not turn the knob for both the Spains.

A hand came shuffling aft, dodging the seas,
Singing "her nut-brown hair" between his teeth;
Taking the ocean's tumult at his ease
Even when the wash about his thighs did seethe.
His soul was happy in its happy sheath;
"What, Dauber, won't it open? Fingers cold?
You'll talk of this time, Dauber, when you're old."

He flung the door half open, and a sea
Washed them both in, over the splashboard, down
"You silly, salt miscarriage!" sputtered he.
"Dauber, pull out the plug before we drown!
That's spoiled my laces and my velvet gown.
Where is the plug? " Groping in pitch dark water,
He sang between his teeth "The Farmer's Daughter."

In was pitch dark within there; at each roll
The chests slid to the slant; the water rushed,

134

Making full many a clanging tin pan bowl
Into the black below-bunks as it gushed.
The dog-tired men slept through it; they were hushed.
The water drained, and then with matches damp
The man struck heads off till he lit the lamp.

"Thank you," the Dauber said; the seaman grinned.
"This is your first foul weather?" "Yes." "I thought
Up on the yard you hadn't seen much wind.
Them's rotten sea-boots, Dauber, that you brought.
Now I must cut on deck before I'm caught."
He went; the lamp-flame smoked; he slammed the door;
A film of water loitered across the floor.

The Dauber watched it come and watched it go;
He had had revelation of the lies
Cloaking the truth men never choose to know;
He could bear witness now and cleanse their eyes
He had beheld in suffering; he was wise;
This was the sea, this searcher of the soul—
This never-dying shriek fresh from the Pole.

He shook with cold; his hands could not undo
His oilskin buttons, so he shook and sat,
Watching his dirty fingers, dirty blue,
Hearing without the hammering tackle slat,
Within, the drops from dripping clothes went pat,
Running in little patters, gentle, sweet,
And "Ai, ai!" went the wind, and the seas beat.

His bunk was sopping wet; he clambered in.
None of his clothes were dry, his fear recurred.
Cramps bunched the muscles underneath his skin.
The great ship rolled until the lamp was blurred.
He took his Bible and tried to read a word;
Trembled at going aloft again, and then
Resolved to fight it out and show it to men.

Faces recurred, fierce memories of the yard,
The frozen sail, the savage eyes, the jests,
The oaths of one great seaman syphilis-scarred,
The tug of leeches jammed beneath their chests,
The buntlines bellying bunts out into breasts.
The deck so desolate-grey, the sky so wild,
He fell asleep, and slept like a young child.

135

But not for long; the cold awoke him soon,
The hot-ache and the skin-cracks and the cramp,
The seas thundering without, the gale's wild tune,
The sopping misery of the blankets damp.
A speaking-trumpet roared; a sea-boot's stamp
Clogged at the door. A man entered to shout:
"All hands on deck! Arouse here! Tumble out!"

The caller raised the lamp; his oilskins clicked
As the thin ice upon them cracked and fell.
"Rouse out!" he said. "This lamp is frozen wicked.
Rouse out!" His accent deepened to a yell.
"We're among ice; it's blowing up like hell.
We're going to hand both topsails. Time, I guess,
We're sheeted up. Rouse out! Don't stay to dress!"

"Is it cold on deck?" said Dauber. "Is it cold?
We're sheeted up, I tell you, inches thick!
The fo'c's'le 's like a wedding-cake, I'm told.
Now tumble out, my sons; on deck here, quick!
Rouse out, away and come and climb the stick.
I'm going to call the half-deck. Bosun! Hey!
Both topsails coming in. Heave out! Away!"

He went; the Dauber tumbled from his bunk,
Clutching the side. He heard the wind go past,
Making the great ship wallow as if drunk.
There was a shocking tumult up the mast.
"This is the end," he muttered, "come at last!
I've got to go aloft, facing this cold.
I can't. I can't. I'll never keep my hold.

"I cannot face the topsail yard again.
I never guessed what misery it would be."
The cramps and hot-ache made his sick with pain.
The ship stopped suddenly from a devilish sea,
Then, with a triumph of wash, a rush of glee,
The door burst in, and in the water rolled,
Filling the lower bunks, black, creaming, cold.

The lamp sucked out. "Wash!" went the water back,
Then in again, flooding; the Bosun swore.
"You useless thing! You Dauber! You lee slack!
Get out, you heekapoota! Shut the door!
You coo-ilyaira, what are you waiting for?

Out of my way, you thing—you useless thing!"
He slammed the door indignant, clanging the ring.

And then he lit the lamp, drowned to the waist;
"Here's a fine house! Get at the scupper-holes"—
He bent against it as the water raced—
"And pull them out to leeward when she rolls.
They say some kinds of landsmen don't have souls.
I well believe. A Port Mahon baboon
Would make more soul than you got with a spoon."

Down in the icy water Dauber groped
To find the plug; the racing water sluiced
Over his head and shoulders as she sloped.
Without, judged by the sound, all hell was loosed,
He felt cold Death about him tightly noosed.
That Death was better than the misery there
Iced on the quaking foothold high in air.

And then the thought came: "I'm a failure. All
My life has been a failure. They were right.
It will not matter if I go and fall;
I should be free then from this hell's delight.
I'll never paint. Best let it end to-night.
I'll slip over the side. I've tried and failed."
So in the ice-cold in the night he quailed.

Death would be better, death, than this long hell
Of mockery and surrender and dismay—
This long defeat of doing nothing well,
Playing the part too high for him to play.
"O Death! who hides the sorry thing away,
Take me; I've failed. I cannot play these cards."
There came a thundering from the topsail yards.

And then be bit his lips, clenching his mind,
And staggered out to muster, beating back
The coward frozen self of him that whined.
Come what cards might he meant to play the pack.
"Ai!" screamed the wind; the topsail sheets went clack.
Ice filled the air with spikes; the grey-backs burst.
"Here's Dauber," said the Mate, "on deck the first.

"Why, holy sailor, Dauber, you're a man!
I took you for a soldier. Up now, come!"

Up on the yards already they began
That battle with a gale which strikes men dumb
The leaping topsail thundered like a drum.
The frozen snow beat in the face like shots.
The wind spun whipping wave-crests into clots.

So up upon the topsail yard again,
In the great tempest's fiercest hour, began
Probation to the Dauber's soul, of pain
Which crowds a century's torment in a span.
For the next month the ocean taught this man,
And he, in that month's torment, while she wested,
Was never warm nor dry, nor full nor rested.

But still it blew, or, if it lulled, it rose
Within the hour and blew again; and still
The water as it burst aboard her froze.
The wind blew off an ice-field, raw and chill,
Daunting man's body, tampering with his will,
But after thirty days a ghostly sun
Gave sickly promise that the storms were done.

VII

A great grey sea was running up the sky,
Desolate birds flew past; their mewings came
As that lone water's spiritual cry,
Its forlorn voice, its essence, its soul's name.
The ship limped in the water as if lame.
Then in the forenoon watch to a great shout
More sail was made, the reefs were shaken out.

A slant came from the south; the singers stood
Clapped to the halliards, hauling to a tune,
Old as the sea, a fillip to the blood.
The upper topsail rose like a balloon.
"So long, Cape Stiff. In Valparaiso soon,"
Said one to other, as the ship lay over,
Making her course again—again a rover.

Slowly the sea went down as the wind fell.
Clear rang the songs, "Hurrah! Cape Horn is bet!"
The combless seas were lumping into swell;
The leaking fo'c's'les were no longer wet.
More sail was made; the watch on deck was set

To cleaning up the ruin broken bare
Below, aloft, about her, everywhere.

The Dauber, scrubbing out the round-house, found
Old pantiles pulped among the mouldy gear,
Washed underneath the bunks and long since drowned
During the agony of the Cape Horn year.
He sang in scrubbing, for he had done with fear—
Fronted the worst and looked it in the face;
He had got manhood at the testing-place.

Singing he scrubbed, passing his watch below,
Making the round-house fair; the Bosun watched,
Bringing his knitting slowly to the toe.
Sails stretched a mizzen skysail which he patched;
They thought the Dauber was a bad egg hatched.
"Daubs," said the Bosun cheerly, "can you knit?
I've made a Barney's Bull of this last bit."

Then, while the Dauber counted, Bosun took
Some marline from his pocket. "Here," he said,
"You want to know square sennit? So fash. Look!
Eight foxes take, and stop the ends with thread.
I've known an engineer would give his head
To know square sennit." As the Bose began,
The Dauber felt promoted into man.

It was his warrant that he had not failed—
That the most hard part in his difficult climb
Had not been past attainment; it was scaled:
Safe footing showed above the slippery clime.
He had emerged out of the iron time,
And knew that he could compass his life's scheme
He had the power sufficient to his dream.

Then dinner came, and now the sky was blue.
The ship was standing north, the Horn was rounded
She made a thundering as she weltered through.
The mighty grey-backs glittered as she bounded.
More sail was piled upon her; she was hounded
North, while the wind came; like a stag she ran
Over grey hills and hollows of seas wan.

She had a white bone in her mouth: she sped;
Those in the round-house watched her as they ate

Their meal of pork-fat fried with broken bread.
"Good old!" they cried. "She's off; she's gathering gait!"
Her track was whitening like a Lammas spate.
"Good old!" they cried. "Oh, give her cloth! Hurray!
For three weeks more to Valparaiso Bay!"

"She smells old Vallipo," the Bosun cried.
"We'll be inside the tier in three weeks more,
Lying at double-moorings where they ride
Off of the market, half a mile from shore,
And bumboat pan, my sons, and figs galore,
And girls in black mantillas fit to make a
Poor seaman frantic when they dance the cueca."

Eight bells were made, the watch was changed, and now
The Mate spoke to the Dauber: "This is better.
We'll soon be getting mudhooks over the bow.
She'll make her passage still if this'll let her.
Oh, run, you drogher! dip your fo'c's'le wetter.
Well, Dauber, this is better than Cape Horn.
Them topsails made you wish you'd not been born."

"Yes, sir," the Dauber said. "Now," said the Mate,
"We've got to smart her up. Them Cape Horn seas
Have made her paint-work like a rusty grate.
Oh, didn't them topsails make your fish-hooks freeze?
A topsail don't pay heed to 'Won't you, please?'
Well, you have seen Cape Horn, my son; you've learned.
You've dipped you hand and had your fingers burned.

"And now you'll stow that folly, trying to paint.
You've had your lesson; you're a sailor now.
You come on board a female ripe to faint.
All sorts of slush you'd learned, the Lord knows how.
Cape Horn has sent you wisdom over the bow
If you've got sense to take it. You're a sailor.
My God! before you were a woman's tailor.

"So throw your paints to blazes and have done.
Words can't describe the silly things you did
Sitting before your easel in the sun,
With all your colours on the paint-box lid.
I blushed for you . . . and then the daubs you hid.
My God! you'll have more sense now, eh? You've quit?"
"No, sir." "You've not?" "No, sir." "God give you wit.

140

"I thought you'd come to wisdom." Thus they talked,
While the great clipper took her bit and rushed
Like a skin-glistening stallion not yet baulked,
Till fire-bright water at her swing-ports gushed;
Poising and bowing down her fore-foot crushed
Bubble on glittering bubble; on she went.
The Dauber watched her, wondering what it meant.

To come, after long months, at rosy dawn,
Into the placid blue of some great bay.
Treading the quiet water like a fawn
Ere yet the morning haze was blown away.
A rose-flushed figure putting by the grey,
And anchoring there before the city smoke
Rose, or the church-bells rang, or men awoke.

And then, in the first light, to see grow clear
That long-expected haven filled with strangers—
Alive with men and women; see and hear
Its clattering market and its money-changers;
And hear the surf beat, and be free from dangers,
And watch the crinkled ocean blue with calm
Drowsing beneath the Trade, beneath the palm.

Hungry for that he worked; the hour went by,
And still the wind grew, still the clipper strode,
And now a darkness hid the western sky,
And sprays came flicking off at the wind's goad.
She stumbled now, feeling her sail a load.
The Mate gazed hard to windward, eyed his sail,
And said the Horn was going to flick her tail.

Boldly he kept it on her till she staggered,
But still the wind increased; it grew, it grew,
Darkening the sky, making the water haggard:
Full of small snow the mighty wester blew.
"More fun for little fish-hooks," sighed the crew.
They eyed the taut topgallants stiff like steel.
A second hand was ordered to the wheel.

The Captain eyed her aft, sucking his lip,
Feeling the sail too much, but yet refraining
From putting hobbles on the leaping ship,
The glad sea-shattering stallion, halter-straining,
Wind-musical, uproarious, and complaining;

But, in a gust, he cocked his finger, so:
"You'd better take them off, before they go."

All saw. They ran at once without the word
"Leeay! Leeay!" Loud rang the clew-line cries;
Sam in his bunk within the half-deck heard,
Stirred in his sleep, and rubbed his drowsy eyes.
"There go the lower to 'gallants." Against the skies
Rose the thin bellying strips of leaping sail.
The Dauber was the first man over the rail.

Three to a mast they ran; it was a race.
"God!" said the Mate; "that Dauber, he can go."
He watched the runners with an upturned face
Over the futtocks, struggling heel to toe,
Up to the topmast cross-trees into the blow
Where the three sails were leaping. "Dauber wins!"
The yards were reached, and now the race begins.

Which three will furl their sail first and come down?
Out to the yard-arm for the leech goes one,
His hair blown flagwise from a hatless crown,
His hands at work like fever to be done.
Out of the gale a fiercer fury spun.
The three sails leaped together, yanking high,
Like talons darting up to clutch the sky.

The Dauber on the fore-topgallant yard
Out at the weather yard-arm was the first
To lay his hand upon the buntline-barred
Topgallant yanking to the wester's burst;
He craned to catch the leech; his comrades cursed;
One at the buntlines, one with oaths observed,
"The eye of the outer jib-stay isn't served."

"No," said the Dauber. "No," the man replied.
They heaved, stowing the sail, not looking round,
Panting, but full of life and eager-eyed;
The gale roared at them with its iron sound.
"That's you," the Dauber said. His gasket wound
Swift round the yard, binding the sail in bands;
There came a gust, the sail leaped from his hands,

So that he saw it high above him grey,
And there his mate was falling; quick he clutched

142

An arm in oilskins swiftly snatched away.
A voice said "Christ!" a quick shape stooped and touched,
Chain struck his hands, ropes shot, the sky was smutched
With vast black fires that ran, that fell, that furled,
And then he saw the mast, the small snow hurled.

The fore-topgallant yard far, far aloft,
And blankness settling on him and great pain;
And snow beneath his fingers wet and soft
And topsail-sheet-blocks shaking at the chain.
He knew it was he who had fallen; then his brain
Swirled in a circle while he watched the sky.
Infinite multitudes of snow blew by.

"I thought it was Tom who fell," his brain's voice said
"Down on the bloody deck!" the Captain screamed.
The multitudinous little snow-flakes sped,
His pain was real enough, but all else seemed.
Si with a bucket ran, the water gleamed
Tilting upon him, others came, the Mate . . .
They knelt with eager eyes like things that wait

For other things to come. He saw them there.
"It will go on," he murmured, watching Si.
Colours and sounds seemed mixing in the air,
The pain was stunning him, and the wind went by.
"More water," said the Mate. "Here, Bosun, try.
Ask if he's got a message. Hell, he's gone!
Here, Dauber, paints." He said, "It will go on."

Not knowing his meaning rightly, but he spoke
With the intenseness of a fading soul
Whose share of Nature's fire turns to smoke,
Whose hand on Nature's wheel loses control.
The eager faces glowered red like coal.
They glowed, the great storm glowed, the sails, the mast.
"It will go on," he cried aloud, and passed.

Those from the yard came down to tell the tale.
"He almost had me off," said Tom. "He slipped.
There came one hell of a jump-like from the sail. . . .
He clutched at me and almost had me pipped.
He caught my 'ris'band, but the oilskin ripped. . . .
It tore clean off. Look here. I was near gone.
I made a grab to catch him; so did John.

"I caught his arm. My God! I was near done.
He almost had me over; it was near.
He hit the ropes and grabbed at every one."
"Well," said the Mate, "we cannot leave him here.
Run, Si, and get the half-deck table clear.
We'll lay him there. Catch hold there, you, and you.
He's dead, poor son; there's nothing more to do."

Night fell, and all night long the Dauber lay
Covered upon the table; all night long
The pitiless storm exulted at her prey,
Huddling the waters with her icy thong.
But to the covered shape she did no wrong.
He lay beneath the sailcloth. Bell by bell
The night wore through; the stars rose, the stars fell.

Blowing most pitiless cold out of clear sky
The wind roared all night long; and all night through
The green seas on the deck went washing by,
Flooding the half-deck; bitter hard it blew.
But little of it all the Dauber knew—
The sopping bunks, the floating chests, the wet
The darkness, and the misery, and the sweat.

He was off duty. So it blew all night,
And when the watches changed the men would come
Dripping within the door to strike a light
And stare upon the Dauber lying dumb,
And say, "He come a cruel thump, poor chum."
Or, "He'd a-been a fine big man"; or "He . . .
A smart young seaman he was getting to be."

Or, "Damn it all, it's what we've all to face! . . .
I knew another fellow one time . . ." then
Came a strange tale of death in a strange place
Out on the sea, in ships, with wandering men.
In many ways Death puts us into pen.
The reefers came down tired and looked and slept.
Below the skylight little dribbles crept

Along the painted woodwork, glistening, slow,
Following the roll and dripping, never fast,
But dripping on the quiet form below,

Like passing time talking to time long past.
And all night long "Ai, ai!" when the wind's blast,
And creaming water swished below the pale,
Unheeding body stretched beneath the sail.

At dawn they sewed him up, and at eight bells
They bore him to the gangway, wading deep,
Through the green-clutching, white-toothed water-hells
That flung his carriers over in their sweep.
They laid an old red ensign on the heap,
And all hands stood bare-headed, stooping, swaying,
Washed by the sea while the old man was praying

Out of a borrowed prayer-book. At a sign
They twitched the ensign back and tipped the grating.
A creamier bubbling broke the bubbling brine.
The muffled figure tilted to the weighting;
It dwindled slowly down, slowly gyrating.
Some craned to see; it dimmed, it disappeared;
The last green milky bubble blinked and cleared.

"Mister, shake out your reefs." the Captain called.
"Out topsail reefs!" the Mate cried; then all hands
Hurried, the great sails shook, and all hands hauled,
Singing that desolate song of lonely lands,
Of how a lover came in dripping bands,
Green with the wet and cold, to tell his lover
That Death was in the sea, and all was over.

Fair came the falling wind; a seaman said
The Dauber was a Jonah; once again
The clipper held her course, showing red lead,
Shattering the sea-tops into golden rain.
The waves bowed down before her like blown grain;
Onwards she thundered, on; her voyage was short,
Before the tier's bells rang her into port.

Cheerly they rang her in, those beating bells,
The new-come beauty stately from the sea,
Whitening the blue heave of the drowsy swells,
Treading the bubbles down. With three times three
They cheered her moving beauty in, and she
Came to her berth so noble, so superb;
Swayed like a queen, and answered to the curb.

Then in the sunset's flush they went aloft,
And unbent sails in that most lovely hour
When the light gentles and the wind is soft,
And beauty in the heart breaks like a flower.
Working aloft they saw the mountain tower,
Snow to the peak; they heard the launchmen shout;
And bright along the bay the lights came out.

And then the night fell dark, and all night long
The pointed mountain pointed at the stars,
Frozen, alert, austere; the eagle's song
Screamed from her desolate screes and splintered scars.
On her intense crags where the air is sparse
The stars looked down; their many golden eyes
Watched her and burned, burned out, and came to rise.

Silent the finger of the summit stood,
Icy in pure, thin air, glittering with snows.
Then the sun's coming turned the peak to blood.
And in the rest-house the muleteers arose,
And all day long, where only the eagle goes,
Stones, loosened by the sun, fall; the stones falling
Fill empty gorge on gorge with echoes calling.

EXPLANATIONS OF SOME OF THE SEA
TERMS USED IN THE POEM

Backstays — Wire poles which support the masts against lateral and
after strains.

Barney's Bull — A figure in marine proverb. A jewel in marine repartee.

Bells — Two bells (one forward, one aft), which are struck every half-
hour in a certain manner to mark the passage of the watches.

Bitts — Strong wooden structures (built round each mast) upon which
running rigging is secured.

Block — A sheaved pulley.

Boatswain — A supernumerary or idler, generally attached to the mate's
watch, and holding considerable authority over the crew.

Bouilli Tin — Any tin that contains, or has contained, preserved meat.

Bows — The forward extremity of a ship.

Brace-Blocks —Pulleys through which the braces travel.

Braces — Ropes by which the yards are inclined forward or aft.

Bumboat Pan — Soft bread sold by the bumboat man, a kind of sea costermonger who trades with ships in port.

Bunt — Those cloths of a square sail which are nearest to the mast when the sail is set. The central portion of a furled square sail. The human abdomen (figuratively).

Buntlines — Ropes which help to confine square sails to the yards in the operation of furling.

Chocks — Wooden stands on which the boats rest.

Cleats — Iron or wooden contrivances to which ropes may be secured.

Clew-lines — Ropes by which the lower corners of square sails are lifted.

Clews — The lower corners of square sails.

Clipper — A title of honour given to ships of more than usual speed and beauty.

Coaming -- The raised rim of a hatchway; a barrier at a doorway to keep water from entering.

Courses — The large square sails set upon the lower yards of sailing ships. The mizzen course is called the "crojick".

Cringled — Fitted with iron rings or cringles, many of which are let into sails or sail-roping for various purposes.

Crojick or cross-jack — A square sail set upon the lower yard of the mizzen mast.

Dungarees — Thin blue or khaki-coloured overalls made from coconut fibre.

Fairleads — Rings of wood or iron by means of which running rigging is led in any direction.

Fife rails — Strong wooden shelves fitted with iron pins, to which ropes may be secured.

Fish-hooks — Fingers.

Foot-ropes — Ropes on which men stand when working aloft.

Fo'c's'le — The cabin or cabins in which the men are berthed. It is usually an iron deck-house divided through the middle into two compartments for the two watches, and fitted with wooden bunks. Sometimes it is even fitted with lockers and an iron water-tank.

Foxes — Strands, yarns, or arrangements of yarns of rope.

Frap — To wrap round with rope.

Freeing-ports — Iron doors in the ship's side which open outwards to free the decks of water.

Futtock-shrouds — Iron bars to which the topmast rigging is secured. As they project outward and upward from the masts they are difficult to clamber over.

Galley — The ship's kitchen.

Gantline (girtline) — A rope used for the sending of sails up and down from aloft.

Gaskets — Ropes by which the sails are secured in furling.

Half-deck — A cabin or apartment in which the apprentices are berthed. Its situation is usually the ship's waist; but it is sometimes further aft, and occasionally it is under the poop or even right forward under the top-gallant fo'c's'le.

Halliards — Ropes by which sails are hoisted.

Harness-room — An office or room from which the salt meat is issued, and in which it is sometimes stored.

Hawse — The bows or forward end of a ship.

Head — The forward part of a ship. That upper edge of a square sail which is attached to the yard.

House-flag — The special flag of the firm to which a ship belongs.

Idlers — The members of the round-house mess, generally consisting of the carpenter, cook, sailmaker, boatswain, painter, etc., are known as the idlers.

Jack or jackstay — An iron bar (fitted along all yards in sailing ships) to which the head of a square sail is secured when bent.

Kites — Light upper sails.

Leeches — The outer edges of square sails. In furling some square sails the leech is dragged inwards till it lies level with the head upon the surface of the yard. This is done by the first man who gets upon the yard, beginning at the weather side.

Logship — A contrivance by which a ship's speed is measured.

Lower topsail — The second sail from the deck on square-rigged masts. It is a very strong, important sail.

Marline — Tarry line or coarse string made of rope-yarns twisted together.

Mate — The First or Chief Mate is generally called the Mate.

Mizzen-topmast-head — The summit of the second of the three or four spars which make the complete mizzen-mast.

Mudhooks — Anchors.

Pins — Iron or wooden bars to which running rigging is secured.

Pointing — A kind of neat plait with which ropes are sometimes ended off or decorated.

Poop-break — The forward end of the after superstructure.

Ratlines — The rope steps placed across the shrouds to enable the seamen to go aloft.

Reefers — Apprentices.

Reef-points — Ropes by which the area of some sails may be reduced in the operation of reefing. Reef-points are securely fixed to the sails fitted with them, and when not in use their ends patter continually upon the canvas with a gentle drumming noise.

Reel — A part of the machinery used with a logship.

Round-house — A cabin (of all shapes except round) in which the idlers are berthed.

Royals — Light upper square sails; the fourth, fifth, or sixth sails from the deck according to the mast's rig.

Sail-room — A large room or compartment in which the ship's sails are stored.

"Sails" — The sailmaker is meant.

Scuttle-butt — A cask containing fresh water.

Shackles — Rope handles for a sea-chest.

Sheet-blocks — Iron blocks, by means of which sails are sheeted home. In any violent wind they beat upon the mast with great rapidity and force.

Sheets — Ropes or chains which extend the lower corners of square sails in the operation of sheeting home.

Shifting suits (of sails) — The operation of removing a ship's sails and replacing them with others.

Shrouds — Wire ropes of great strength, which support lateral strains on masts.

Shroud-screws — Iron contrivances by which shrouds are hove taut.

Sidelights — A sailing ship carries two of these between sunset and sunrise: one green, to starboard; one red, to port.

Sights — Observations to help in the finding of a ship's position.

Skid — A wooden contrivance on which ship's boats rest.

Skysails — The uppermost square sails; the fifth, sixth, or seventh sails from the deck according to the mast's rig.

Slatting — The noise made by sails flogging in the wind.

Slush — Grease, melted fat.

South-wester — A kind of oilskin hat. A gale from the south-west.

Spit brown — To chew tobacco.

Square sennit — A cunning plait which makes a four-square bar.

Staysails — Fore and aft sails set upon the stays between the masts.

Stow — To furl.

Strop (the putting on) — A strop is a grummet or rope ring. The two players kneel down facing each other, the strop is placed over their heads, and the men then try to pull each other over by the strength of their neck-muscles.

Swing ports — Iron doors in the ship's side which open outwards to free the decks from water.

Tackle (pronounced "taykel") — Blocks, ropes, pulleys, etc.
Take a caulk — To sleep upon the deck.
Topsails — The second and third sails from the deck on the masts of a modern square-rigged ship are known as the lower and upper topsails.
Trucks — The summits of the masts.

Upper topsail — The third square sail from the deck on the masts of square-rigged ships.

Yards — The steel or wooden spars (placed across masts) from which square sails are set.

THE *WANDERER*

All day they loitered by the resting ships,
Telling their beauties over, taking stock;
At night the verdict left my messmates' lips,
"The *Wanderer* is the finest ship in dock."

I had not seen her, but a friend, since drowned,
Drew her, with painted ports, low, lovely, lean,
Saying, "The *Wanderer*, clipper, outward bound,
The loveliest ship my eyes have ever seen—

"Perhaps to-morrow you will see her sail.
She sails at sunrise": but the morrow showed
No *Wanderer* setting forth for me to hail;
Far down the stream men pointed where she rode.

Rode the great trackway to the sea, dim, dim,
Already gone before the stars were gone.
I saw her at the sea-line's smoky rim
Grow swiftly vaguer as they towed her on.

Soon even her masts were hidden in the haze
Beyond the city; she was on her course

To trample billows for a hundred days;
That afternoon the norther gathered force,

Blowing a small snow from a point of east.
"Oh, fair for her," we said, "to take her south."
And in our spirits, as the wind increased,
We saw her there, beyond the river mouth,

Setting her side-lights in the wildering dark,
To glint upon mad water, while the gale
Roared like a battle, snapping like a shark,
And drunken seamen struggled with the sail.

While with sick hearts her mates put out of mind
Their little children left astern, ashore,
And the gale's gathering made the darkness blind.
Water and air one intermingled roar.

Then we forgot her, for the fiddlers played,
Dancing and singing held our merry crew;
The old ship moaned a little as she swayed.
It blew all night, oh, bitter hard it blew!

So that at midnight I was called on deck
To keep an anchor-watch: I heard the sea
Roar past in white procession filled with wreck:
Intense bright frosty stars burned over me,

And the Greek brig beside us dipped and dipped,
White to the muzzle like a half-tide rock,
Drowned to the mainmast with the seas she shipped;
Her cable-swivels clanged at every shock.

And like a never-dying force, the wind
Roared till we shouted with it, roared until
Its vast vitality of wrath was thinned,
Had beat its fury breathless and was still.

By dawn the gale had dwindled into flaw,
A glorious morning followed: with my friend
I climbed the fo'c's'le-head to see; we saw
The waters hurrying shorewards without end.

Haze blotted out the river's lowest reach;
Out of the gloom the steamers, passing by,

Called with their sirens, hooting their sea-speech;
Out of the dimness others made reply.

And as we watched, there came a rush of feet
Charging the fo'c's'le till the hatchway shook.
Men all about us thrust their way, or beat,
Crying, "The *Wanderer!* Down the river! Look!"

I looked with them towards the dimness; there
Gleamed like a spirit striding out of night,
A full-rigged ship unutterably fair,
Her masts like trees in winter, frosty-bright.

Foam trembled at her bows like wisps of wool;
She trembled as she towed. I had not dreamed
That work of man could be so beautiful,
In its own presence and in what it seemed.

"So, she is putting back again," I said.
"How white with frost her yards are on the fore!"
One of the men about me answer made,
"That is not frost, but all her sails are tore,

"Torn into tatters, youngster, in the gale;
Her best foul-weather suit gone." It was true,
Her masts were white with rags of tattered sail
Many as gannets when the fish are due.

Beauty in desolation was her pride,
Her crowned array a glory that had been;
She faltered tow'rds us like a swan that died,
But although ruined she was still a queen.

"Put back with all her sails gone," went the word;
Then, from her signals flying, rumour ran,
"The sea that stove her boats in killed her third;
She has been gutted and has lost a man."

So, as though stepping to a funeral march,
She passed defeated homewards whence she came
Ragged with tattered canvas white as starch,
A wild bird that misfortune had made tame.

She was refitted soon: another took
The dead man's office; then the singers hove

Her capstan till the snapping hawsers shook;
Out, with a bubble at her bows, she drove.

Again they towed her seawards, and again
We, watching, praised her beauty, praised her trim,
Saw her fair house-flag flutter at the main,
And slowly saunter seawards, dwindling dim;

And wished her well, and wondered, as she died,
How, when her canvas had been sheeted home,
Her quivering length would sweep into her stride,
Making the greenness milky with her foam.

But when we rose next morning, we discerned
Her beauty once again a shattered thing;
Towing to dock the *Wanderer* returned,
A wounded sea-bird with a broken wing.

A spar was gone, her rigging's disarray
Told of a worse diaster than the last;
Like draggled hair dishevelled hung the stay,
Drooping and beating on the broken mast.

Half-mast upon her flagstaff hung her flag;
Word went among us how the broken spar
Had gored her captain like an angry stag,
And killed her mate a half-day from the bar.

She passed to dock upon the top of flood.
An old man near me shook his head and swore:
"Like a bad woman, she has tasted blood—
There'll be no trusting in her any more."

We thought it truth, and when we saw her there
Lying in dock, beyond, across the stream,
We would forget that we had called her fair,
We thought her murderess and the past a dream.

And when she sailed again, we watched in awe,
Wondering what bloody act her beauty planned,
What evil lurked behind the thing we saw,
What strength was there that thus annulled man's hand.

How next its triumph would compel man's will
Into compliance with external Fate,

How next the powers would use her to work ill
On suffering men; we had not long to wait.

For soon the outcry of derision rose,
"Here comes the *Wanderer!*" the expected cry.
Guessing the cause, our mockings joined with those
Yelled from the shipping as they towed her by.

She passed us close, her seamen paid no heed
To what was called: they stood, a sullen group,
Smoking and spitting, careless of her need,
Mocking the orders given from the poop.

Her mates and boys were working her; we stared.
What was the reason of this strange return,
This third annulling of the thing prepared?
No outward evil could our eyes discern.

Only like one who having formed a plan
Beyond the pitch of common minds, she sailed,
Mocked and deserted by the common man,
Made half divine to me for having failed.

We learned the reason soon; below the town
A stay had parted like a snapping reed,
"Warning," the men thought, "not to take her down."
They took the omen, they would not proceed.

Days passed before another crew would sign.
The *Wanderer* lay in dock alone, unmanned,
Feared as a thing possessed by powers malign,
Bound under curses not to leave the land.

But under passing Time fear passes too;
That terror passed, the sailors' hearts grew bold.
We learned in time that she had found a crew
And was bound out and southwards as of old.

And in contempt we thought, "A little while
Will bring her back again, dismantled, spoiled.
It is herself; she cannot change her style;
She has the habit now of being foiled."

So when a ship appeared among the haze,
We thought, "The *Wanderer* back again"; but no,

No *Wanderer* showed for many, many days,
Her passing lights made other waters glow.

But we would often think and talk of her,
Tell newer hands her story, wondering, then,
Upon what ocean she was *Wanderer*,
Bound to the cities built by foreign men.

And one by one our little conclave thinned,
Passed into ships and sailed and so away,
To drown in some great roaring of the wind,
Wanderers themselves, unhappy fortune's prey.

And Time went by me making memory dim,
Yet still I wondered if the *Wanderer* fared
Still pointing to the unreached ocean's rim,
Brightening the water where her breast was bared.

And much in ports abroad I eyed the ships,
Hoping to see her well-remembered form
Come with a curl of bubbles at her lips
Bright to her berth, the sovereign of the storm.

I never did and many years went by,
Then, near a Southern port, one Christmas Eve,
I watched a gale go roaring through the sky,
Making the caldrons of the clouds upheave.

Then the wrack tattered and the stars appeared,
Millions of stars that seemed to speak in fire;
A byre cock cried aloud that morning neared,
The swinging wind-vane flashed upon the spire.

And soon men looked upon a glittering earth,
Intensely sparkling like a world new-born;
Only to look was spiritual birth,
So bright the raindrops ran along the thorn.

So bright they were, that one could almost pass
Beyond their twinkling to the source, and know
The glory pushing in the blade of grass,
That hidden soul which makes the flowers grow.

That soul was there apparent, not revealed,
Unearthly meanings covered every tree

That wet grass grew in an immortal field,
Those waters fed some never-wrinkled sea.

The scarlet berries in the hedge stood out
Like revelations but the tongue unknown;
Even in the brooks a joy was quick: the trout
Rushed in a dumbness dumb to me alone.

All of the valley was aloud with brooks;
I walked the morning, breasting up the fells,
Taking again lost childhood from the rooks,
Whose cawing came above the Christmas bells.

I had not walked that glittering world before,
But up the hill a prompting came to me,
"This line of upland runs along the shore:
Beyond the hedgerow I shall see the sea."

And on the instant from beyond away
That long familiar sound, a ship's bell broke
The hush below me in the unseen bay.
Old memories came: that inner prompting spoke.

And bright above the hedge a seagull's wings
Flashed and were steady upon empty air.
"A Power unseen," I cried, "prepares these things,
Those are her bells, the *Wanderer* is there."

So, hurrying to the hedge and looking down
I saw a mighty bay's wind-crinkled blue
Ruffling the image of a tranquil town,
With lapsing waters glittering as they grew.

And near me in the road the shipping swung,
So stately and so still in such great peace
That like to drooping crests their colours hung,
Only their shadows trembled without cease.

I did but glance upon those anchored ships.
Even as my thought had told, I saw her plain;
Tense, like a supple athlete with lean hips,
Swiftness at pause, the *Wanderer* come again—

Come as of old a queen, untouched by Time,
Resting the beauty that no seas could tire,

Sparkling, as though the midnight's rain were rime,
Like a man's thought transfigured into fire.

And as I look, one of her men began
To sing some simple tune of Christmas day;
Among her crew the song spread, man to man,
Until the singing rang across the bay;

And soon in other anchored ships the men
Joined in the singing with clear throats, until
The farm-boy heard it up the windy glen,
Above the noise of sheep-bells on the hill.

Over the water came the lifted song—
Blind pieces in a mighty game we swing;
Life's battle is a conquest for the strong;
The meaning shows in the defeated thing.

AUGUST, 1914

How still this quiet cornfield is tonight!
By an intenser glow the evening falls,
Bringing, not darkness, but a deeper light;
Among the stooks a partridge covey calls.

The windows glitter on the distant hill;
Beyond the hedge the sheep-bells in the fold
Stumble on sudden music and are still;
The forlorn pinewoods droop above the wold.

An endless quiet valley reaches out
Past the blue hills into the evening sky;
Over the stubble, cawing, goes a rout
Of rooks from harvest, flagging as they fly.

So beautiful it is, I never saw
So great a beauty on these English fields,
Touched by the twilight's coming into awe,
Ripe to the soul and rich with summer's yields.

      *   *   *   *

These homes, this valley spread below me here,
The rooks, the tilted stacks, the beasts in pen,

Have been the heartfelt things, past-speaking dear
To unknown generations of dead men,

Who, century after century, held these farms,
And, looking out to watch the changing sky,
Heard, as we hear, the rumours and alarms
Of war at hand and danger pressing nigh.

And knew, as we know, that the message meant
The breaking off of ties, the loss of friends,
Death, like a miser getting in his rent,
And no new stones laid where the trackway ends.

The harvest not yet won, the empty bin,
The friendly horses taken from the stalls,
The fallow on the hill not yet brought in,
The cracks unplastered in the leaking walls.

Yet heard the news, and went discouraged home,
And brooded by the fire with heavy mind,
With such dumb loving of the Berkshire loam
As breaks the dumb hearts of the English kind,

Then sadly rose and left the well-loved Downs,
And so by ship to sea, and knew no more
The fields of home, the byres, the market towns,
Nor the dear outline of the English shore,

But knew the misery of the soaking trench,
The freezing in the rigging, the despair
In the revolting second of the wrench
When the blind soul is flung upon the air,

And died (uncouthly, most) in foreign lands
For some idea but dimly understood
Of an English city never built by hands
Which love of England prompted and made good.

*   *   *   *

If there be any life beyond the grave,
It must be near the men and things we love,
Some power of quick suggestion how to save,
Touching the living soul as from above.

158

An influence from the Earth from those dead hearts
So passionate once, so deep, so truly kind,
That in the living child the spirit starts,
Feeling companioned still, not left behind.

Surely above these fields a spirit broods
A sense of many watchers muttering near
Of the lone Downland with the forlorn woods
Loved to the death, inestimably dear.

A muttering from beyond the veils of Death
From long-dead men, to whom this quiet scene
Came among blinding tears with the last breath,
The dying soldier's vision of his queen.

All the unspoken worship of those lives
Spent in forgotten wars at other calls
Glimmers upon these fields where evening drives
Beauty like breath, so gently darkness falls.

Darkness that makes the meadows holier still,
The elm-trees sadden in the hedge, a sigh
Moves in the beech-clump on the haunted hill,
The rising planets deepen in the sky,

And silence broods like spirit on the brae,
A glimmering moon begins, the moonlight runs
Over the grasses of the ancient way
Rutted this morning by the passing guns.

from BIOGRAPHY

By many waters and on many ways
I have known golden instants and bright days;
The day on which, beneath an arching sail,
I saw the Cordilleras and gave hail;
The summer day on which in heart's delight
I saw the Swansea Mumbles bursting white;
The glittering day when all the waves wore flags,
And the ship *Wanderer* came with sails in rags;
That curlew-calling time in Irish dusk,
When life became more splendid than its husk,
When the rent chapel on the brae at Slains
Shone with a doorway opening beyond brains;
The dawn when, with a brace-block's creaking cry,

Out of the mist a little barque slipped by,
Spilling the mist with changing gleams of red,
Then gone, with one raised hand and one turned head
The howling evening when the spindrift's mists
Broke to display the Four Evangelists,
Snow-capped, divinely granite, lashed by breakers,
Wind-beaten bones of long since buried acres;

The night alone near water when I heard
All the sea's spirit spoken by a bird;
The English dusk when I beheld once more
(With eyes so changed) the ship, the citied shore,
The lines of masts, the streets so cheerly trod
(In happier seasons), and gave thanks to God.
All had their beauty, their bright moments' gift,
Their something caught from Time, the ever-swift.

All of those gleams were golden; but life's hands
Have given more constant gifts in changing lands,
And when I count those gifts, I think them such
As no man's bounty could have bettered much:
The gift of country life, near hills and woods,
Where happy waters sing in solitudes;
The gift of being near ships, of seeing each day
A city of ships with great ships under weigh;
The great street paved with water, filled with shipping
And all the world's flags flying and seagulls dipping.

SONG

One sunny time in May
When lambs were sporting,
The sap ran in the spray
And I went courting,
And all the apple-boughs
Were bright with blossom,
I picked an early rose
For my love's bosom.

And then I met her friend,
Down by the water,
Who cried, "She's met her end,
That grey-eyed daughter,
That voice of hers is stilled.
Her beauty broken."

Oh, me! my love is killed,
My love unspoken.

She was too sweet, too dear,
To die so cruel.
O Death, why leave me here
And take my jewel?
Her voice went to the bone,
So true, so ringing,
And now I go alone
Winter or springing.

SHIPS

I cannot tell their wonder nor make known
Magic that once thrilled through me to the bone,
But all men praise some beauty, tell some tale,
Vent a high mood which makes the rest seem pale.
Pour their heart's blood to flourish one green leaf,
Follow some Helen for her gift of grief,
And fail in what they mean, whate'er they do:
You should have seen, man cannot tell to you
The beauty of the ships of that my city.

That beauty now is spoiled by the sea's pity:
For one may haunt the pier a score of times
Hearing St. Nicholas' bells ring out the chimes,
Yet never see those proud ones swaying home,
With mainyards backed and bows a cream of foam,
Those bows so lovely-curving, cut so fine
Those coulters of the many-bubbled brine,
As once, long since, when all the docks were filled
With that sea beauty man has ceased to build.

Yet though their splendour may have ceased to be,
Each played her sovereign part in making me;
Now I return my thanks with heart and lips
For the great queenliness of all those ships.

And first the first bright memory, still so clear,
An autumn evening in a golden year,
When in the last lit moments before dark
The *Chepica*, a steel-gray lovely barque,

Her trucks aloft in sun-glow red as blood,
Came to an anchor near us on the flood.
Then come so many ships that I could fill
Three docks with their fair hulls remembered still,
Each with her special memory's special grace,
Riding the sea, making the waves give place
To delicate high beauty; man's best strength,
Noble in every line in all their length.
Ailsa, Genista, ships, with long jib-booms,
The *Wanderer* with great beauty and strange dooms,
Liverpool (mightiest then) superb, sublime,
The *California* huge, as slow as Time.
The *Cutty Sark,* the perfect *J.T. North,*
The loveliest barque my city has sent forth.
Dainty *Redgauntlet,* well remembered yet,
The splendid *Argus* with her skysail set,
Stalwart *Drumcliff,* white-blocked majestic *Sierras,*
Divine bright ships, the water's standard bearers.
Melpomene, Euphrosyne, and their sweet
Sea-troubling sisters of the Fernie Fleet.
Corunna (in whom my friend died) and the old
Long since loved *Esmeralda* long since sold.

Centurion passed in Rio, *Glaucus* spoken,
Aladdin burnt, the *Bidston* water broken,
Yola in whom my friend sailed, *Dawpool* trim,
Fierce-bowed *Egeria* plunging to the swim,
Stanmore wide-sterned, sweet *Cupica,* tall *Bard,*
Queen in all harbours with her moonsail yard.

Though I tell many there must still be others,
M'Vickar Marshall's ships and Fernie Brothers'
Lochs, Counties, Shires, Drums, the countless lines
Whose house-flags all were once familiar signs
At high main trucks on Mersey's windy ways
When sun made all the wind-white water blaze.
Their names bring back old mornings when the docks
Shone with their house-flags and their painted blocks,
Their raking masts below the Custom House
And all the marvellous beauty of their bows.

Familiar steamers, too, majestic steamers,
Shearing Atlantic roller-tops to streamers,
Umbria, Etruria, noble, still at sea,
The grandest, then, that man had brought to be.

Majestic, City of Paris, City of Rome,
Forever jealous racers, out and home.
The Alfred Holt's blue smokestacks down the stream,
The fair *Arabian* with her bows a-cream.
Booth liners, Anchor liners, Red Star liners,
The marks and styles of countless ship designers.
The *Magdalena, Puno, Potosi,*
Lost *Cotopaxi*, all well known to me.

These splendid ships, each with her grace, her glory,
Her memory of old song or comrade's story,
Still in my mind the image of life's need,
Beauty in hardest action, beauty indeed.
"They built great ships and sailed them" sounds most brave,
Whatever arts we have or fail to have;
I touch my country's mind, I come to grips
With half her purpose thinking of these ships.

That art untouched by softness, all that line
Drawn ringing hard to stand the test of brine;
That nobleness and grandeur, all that beauty
Born of a manly life and bitter duty;
That splendour of fine bows which yet could stand
The shock of rollers never checked by land.
That art of masts, sail-crowded, fit to break,
Yet stayed to strength, and back-stayed into rake,
The life demanded by that art, the keen
Eye-puckered, hard-case seamen, silent, lean,
They are grander things than all the art of towns,
Their tests are tempests and the sea that drowns.
They are my country's line, her great art done
By strong brains labouring on the thought unwon,
They mark our passage as a race of men,
Earth will not see such ships as those agen.

THE RIVER

All other waters have their time of peace,
Calm, or the turn of tide or summer drought;
But on these bars the tumults never cease,
In violent death this river passes out.

Brimming she goes, a bloody-coloured rush,
Hurrying her heaped disorder, rank on rank,

Bubbleless speed so still that in the hush
One hears the mined earth dropping from the bank,

Slipping in little falls whose tingeings drown,
Sunk by the waves for ever pressing on,
Till with a stripping crash the tree goes down,
Its washing branches flounder and are gone.

Then, roaring out aloud, her water spreads,
Making a desolation where her waves
Shriek and give battle, tossing up their heads.
Tearing the shifting sandbanks into graves,

Changing the raddled ruin of her course
So swiftly, that the pilgrim on the shore
Hears the loud whirlpool laughing like a horse
Where the scurfed sand was parched an hour before.

And always underneath that heaving tide
The changing bottom runs, or piles, or quakes,
Flinging immense heaps up to wallow wide,
Sucking the surface into whirls like snakes.

If anything should touch that shifting sand,
All the blind bottom sucks it till it sinks;
It takes the clipper ere she comes to land,
It takes the thirsting tiger as he drinks.

And on the river pours—it never tires;
Blind, hungry, screaming, day and night the same
Purposeless hurry of a million ires,
Mad as the wind, as merciless as flame.

*   *   *   *

There was a full-rigged ship, the *Travancore*,
Towing to port against that river's rage—
A glittering ship made sparkling for the shore,
Taut to the pins in all her equipage.

Clanging, she topped the tide; her sails were furled
Her men came loitering downwards from the yards;
They who had brought her half across the world,
Trampling so many billows into shards,

164

Now looking up, beheld their duty done,
The ship approaching port, the great masts bare.
Gaunt as three giants striding in the sun,
Proud, with the colours tailing out like hair.

So, having coiled their gear, they left the deck;
Within the fo'c's'le's gloom of banded steel,
Mottled like wood with many a painted speck,
They brought their plates and sat about a meal.

Then pushing back the tins, they lit their pipes,
Or slept, or played at cards, or gently spoke,
Light from the portholes shot in dusty stripes
Tranquilly moving, sometimes blue with smoke.

These sunbeams sidled with the vessel rolled,
Their lazy yellow dust-strips crossed the floor,
Lighting a man-hole leading to the hold,
A man-hole leaded down the day before.

Like gold the solder on the man-hole shone;
A few flies threading in a drowsy dance
Slept in their pattern, darted, and were gone.
The river roared against the ship's advance.

And quietly sleep came upon the crew,
Man by man drooped upon his arms and slept;
Without, the tugboat dragged the vessel through,
The rigging whined, the yelling water leapt,

Till blindly a careering wave's collapse
Rose from beneath her bows and spouted high,
Spirting the fo'c's'le floor with noisy slaps;
A sleeper at the table heaved a sigh,

And lurched, half-drunk with sleep, across the floor,
Muttering and blinking like a man insane,
Cursed at the river's tumult, shut the door,
Blinked, and lurched back and fell asleep again.

Then there was greater silence in the room,
Ship's creakings ran along the beams and died,
The lazy sunbeams loitered up the gloom,
Stretching and touching till they reached the side.

*　　　*　　　*　　　*

165

Yet something jerking in the vessel's course
Told that the tug was getting her in hand
As, at a fence, one steadies down a horse,
To rush the whirlpool on Magellan Sand;

And in the uneasy water just below
Her Mate inquired "if the men should stir
And come on deck?" Her Captain answered "No,
Let them alone, the tug can manage her."

Then, as she settled down and gathered speed,
Her Mate inquired again "if they should come
Just to be ready there in case of need,
Since, on such godless bars, there might be some."

But "No," the Captain said, "the men have been
Boxing about since midnight, let them be.
The pilot's able and the ship's a queen,
The hands can rest until we come to quay."

They ceased, they took their stations; right ahead
The whirlpool heaped and sucked; in tenor tone
The steady leadsman chanted at the lead,
The ship crept forward trembling to the bone.

And just above the worst a passing wave
Brought to the line such unexpected stress
That as she tossed her bows her towrope gave,
Snapped at the collar like a stalk of cress.

Then, for a ghastly moment, she was loose,
Blind in a whirlpool, groping for a guide,
Swinging adrift without a moment's truce,
She struck the sand and fell upon her side.

And instantly the sand beneath her gave
So that she righted and again was flung,
Grinding the quicksand open for a grave,
Straining her masts until the steel was sprung.

The foremast broke; its mighty bulk of steel
Fell on the fo'c's'le door and jammed it tight;
The sand-rush heaped her to an even keel,
She settled down, resigned, she made no fight,

But, like an overladen beast, she lay
Dumb in the mud with billows at her lips,
Broken, where she had fallen in the way,
Grinding her grave among the bones of ships.

*   *   *   *

At the first crashing of the mast, the men
Sprang from their sleep to hurry to the deck;
They found that Fate had caught them in a pen,
The door that opened out was jammed with wreck.

Then, as with shoulders down, their gathered strength
Hove on the door, but could not make it stir,
They felt the vessel tremble through her length;
The tug, made fast again, was plucking her.

Plucking, and causing motion, till it seemed
That she would get her off; they heard her screw
Mumble the bubbled rip-rap as she steamed;
"Please God, the tug will shift her!" said the crew.

"She's off!" the seamen said; they felt her glide,
Scraping the bottom with her bilge, until
Something collapsing clanged along her side;
The scraping stopped, the tugboat's screw was still.

"She's holed!" a voice without cried; "holed and jammed—
Holed on the old *Magellan*, sunk last June.
I lose my ticket and the men are damned;
They'll drown like rats unless we free them soon.

"My God, they shall not!" and the speaker beat
Blows with a crow upon the foremast's wreck;
Minute steel splinters fell about his feet,
No tremor stirred the ruin on the deck.

And as their natures bade, the seamen learned
That they were doomed within that buried door;
Some cursed, some raved, but one among them turned
Straight to the manhole leaded in the floor,

And sitting down astride it, drew his knife,
And staidly dug to pick away the lead,

167

While at the ports his fellows cried for life:
"Burst in the door, or we shall all be dead!"

For like a brook the leak below them clucked.
They felt the vessel settling; they could feel
How the blind bog beneath her gripped and sucked.
Their fingers beat their prison walls of steel.

And then the gurgling stopped—the ship was still.
She stayed; she sank no deeper—an arrest
Fothered the pouring leak; she ceased to fill,
She trod the mud, drowned only to the breast.

And probing at the well, the captain found
The leak no longer rising, so he cried:
"She is not sinking—you will not be drowned;
The shifting sand has silted up her side.

"Now there is time. The tug shall put ashore
And fetch explosives to us from the town;
I'll burst the house or blow away the door
(It will not kill you if you all lie down).

"Be easy in your minds, for you 'll be free
As soon as we've the blast." the seamen heard
The tug go townwards, butting at the sea;
Some lit their pipes, the youngest of them cheered.

But still the digger bent above the lid,
Gouging the solder from it as at first,
Pecking the lead, intent on what he did;
The other seamen mocked at him or cursed.

And some among them nudged him as he picked.
He cursed them, grinning, but resumed his game;
His knife-point sometimes struck the lid and clicked.
The solder-pellets shone like silver flame.

And still his knife-blade clicked like ticking time
Counting the hour till the tug's return,
And still the ship stood steady on the slime,
While Fate above her fingered with her urn.

*   *   *   *

168

Then from the tug beside them came the hail:
"They have none at the stores, nor at the dock,
Nor at the quarry, so I tried the gaol.
They thought they had, but it was out of stock.

"So then I telephoned to town; they say
They've sent an engine with some to the pier;
I did not leave till it was on its way,
A tug is waiting there to bring it here:

"It can't be here, though, for an hour or more;
I've lost an hour in trying, as it is.
For want of thought commend me to the shore.
You'd think they'd know their river's ways by this."

"So there is nothing for it but to wait,"
The Captain answered, fuming. "Until then,
We'd better go to dinner, Mr. Mate."
The cook brought dinner forward to the men.

          *   *   *   *

Another hour of prison loitered by;
The strips of sunlight stiffened at the port,
But still the digger made the pellets fly,
Paying no heed to his companions' sport,

While they, about him spooning at their tins,
Asked if he dug because he found it cold,
Or whether it was penance for his sins,
Or hope of treasure in the forward hold.

He grinned and cursed, but did not cease to pick,
His sweat dropped from him when he bent his head.
His knife-blade quarried down, till with a click
Its grinded thinness snapped against the lead.

Then, dully rising, brushing back his sweat,
He asked his fellows for another knife.
"Never," they said; "man, what d'ye hope to get?"
"Nothing," he said, "except a chance for life."

169

"Havers," they said, and one among them growled,
"You'll get no knife from any here to break.
You've dug the manhole since the door was fouled,
And now your knife's broke, quit, for Jesus' sake."

But one, who smelt a bargain, changed his tone,
Offering a sheath-knife for the task in hand
At twenty times its value, as a loan
To be repaid him when they reached the land.

And there was jesting at the lender's greed
And mockery at the digger's want of sense,
Closing with such a bargain without need,
Since in an hour the tug would take them thence.

But "Right," the digger said. The deal was made,
He took the borrowed knife, and sitting down
Gouged at the channelled solder with the blade,
Saying, "Let be, it's better dig than drown."

And nothing happened for a while; the heat
Grew in the stuffy room, the sunlight slid,
Flies buzzed about and jostled at the meat,
The knife-blade clicked upon the manhole lid:

And one man said, "She takes a hell of time
Bringing the blaster," and another snored;
One, between pipe-puffs, hummed a smutty rhyme,
One, who was weaving, thudded with his sword.

It was as though the ship were in a dream,
Caught in a magic ocean, calm like death,
Tranced, till a presence should arise and gleam,
Making the waters conscious with her breath.

It was so drowsy that the river's cries,
Roaring aloud their ever-changing tune,
Came to those sailors like the drone of flies,
Filling with sleep the summer afternoon.

So that they slept, or, if they spoke, it was
Only to worry lest the tug should come:
Such power upon the body labour has
That prison seemed a blessed rest to some,

Till one man leaning at the port-hole, stared,
Checking his yawning at the widest stretch,
Then blinked and swallowed, while he muttered, scared,
"That blasting-cotton takes an age to fetch."

Then swiftly passing from the port he went
Up and then down the fo'c's'le till he stayed,
Fixed at the port-hole with his eyes intent,
Round-eyed and white, as if he were afraid,

And muttered as he stared, "My God! she is.
She's deeper than she was, she's settling down.
That palm-tree top was steady against this,
And now I see the quay below the town.

"Look here at her. She's sinking in her tracks.
She's going down by inches as she stands;
The water's darker and it stinks like flax,
Her going down is churning up the sands."

And instantly a panic took the crew,
Even the digger blenched; his knife-blade's haste
Cutting the solder witnessed that he knew
Time on the brink with not a breath to waste.

While far away the tugboat at the quay
Under her drooping pennon waited still
For that explosive which would set them free,
Free, with the world a servant to their will.

Then from a boat beside them came a blare,
Urging that tugboat to be quick; and men
Shouted to stir her from her waiting there,
"Hurry the blast, and get us out of pen.

"She's going down. She's going down, man! Quick!"
The tugboat did not stir, no answer came;
They saw her tongue-like pennon idly lick
Clear for an instant, lettered with her name,

Then droop again. The engine had not come,
The blast had not arrived. The prisoned hands
Saw her still waiting though their time had come,
Their ship was going down among the sands,

Going so swiftly now, that they could see
The banks arising as she made her bed;
Full of sick sound she settled deathward, she
Gurgled and shook, the digger picked the lead.

And, as she paused to take a final plunge,
Prone like a half-tide rock, the men on deck
Jumped to their boats and left, ere like a sponge
The river's rotten heart absorbed the wreck;

And on the perilous instant ere Time struck
The digger's work was done, the lead was cleared,
He cast the manhole up; below it muck
Floated, the hold was full, the water leered.

All of his labour had but made a hole
By which to leap to death; he saw black dust
Float on the bubbles of that brimming bowl,
He drew a breath and took his life in trust,

And plunged head foremost into that black pit,
Where floating cargo bumped against the beams
He groped a choking passage blind with grit,
The roaring in his ears was shot with screams.

So, with a bursting heart and roaring ears
He floundered in that sunk ship's inky womb.
Drowned in deep water for what seemed like years,
Buried alive and groping through the tomb,

Till suddenly the beams against his back
Gave, and the water on his eyes was bright;
He shot up through a hatchway foul with wrack
Into clean air and life and dazzling light,

And striking out, he saw the fo'c's'le gone,
Vanished, below the water, and the mast
Standing columnar from the sea; it shone
Proud, with its colours flying to the last.

And all about, a many-wrinkled tide
Smoothed and erased its eddies, wandering chilled,
Like glutted purpose, trying to decide
If its achievement had been what it willed.

And men in boats were there; they helped him in.
He gulped for breath and watched that patch of smooth,
Shaped like the vessel, wrinkle into grin,
Furrow to waves and bare a yellow tooth.

Then the masts leaned until the shroud-screws gave.
All disappeared—her masts, her colours, all.
He saw the yardarms tilting to the grave;
He heard the siren of a tugboat call,

And saw her speeding, foaming at the bow,
Bringing the blast charge that had come too late.
He heard one shout, "It isn't wanted now."
Time's minute-hand had been the hand of Fate.

Then the boats turned; they brought him to the shore.
Men crowded round him, touched him, and were kind;
The Mate walked with him, silent, to the store.
He said, "We've left the best of us behind."

Then, as he wrung his sodden clothes, the Mate
Gave him a drink of rum, and talked awhile
Of men and ships and unexpected Fate;
And darkness came and cloaked the river's guile,

So that its huddled hurry was not seen,
Only made louder, till the full moon climbed
Over the forest, floated, and was queen.
Within the town a temple belfry chimed.

Then, upon silent pads, a tiger crept
Down to the river-brink, and crouching there
Watched it intently, till you thought he slept
But for his ghastly eye and stiffened hair.

Then, trembling at a lust more fell than his,
He roared and bounded back to coverts lone,
Where, among moonlit beauty, slaughter is,
Filling the marvellous night with myriad groan.

LOLLINGDON DOWNS

I could not sleep for thinking of the sky,
The unending sky, with all its million suns
Which turn their planets everlastingly
In nothing, where the fire-haired comet runs.
If I could sail that nothing, I should cross
Silence and emptiness with dark stars passing;
Then, in the darkness, see a point of gloss
Burn to a glow, and glare, and keep amassing,
And rage into a sun with wandering planets,
And drop behind; and then, as I proceed,
See his last light upon his last moon's granites
Die to a dark that would be night indeed:
Night where my soul might sail a million years
In nothing, not even Death, not even tears.

How did the nothing come, how did these fires,
These million-leagues of fires, first toss their hair,
Licking the moons from heaven in their ires,
Flinging them forth for them to wander there?
What was the Mind? Was it a mind which thought?
Or chance? or law? or conscious law? or power?
Or a vast balance by vast clashes wrought?
Or Time at trial with Matter for an hour?
Or is it all a body where the cells
Are living things supporting something strange,
Whose mighty heart the singing planet swells
As it shoulders nothing in unending change?
Is this green earth of many-peopled pain
Part of a life, a cell within a brain?

"NIGHT IS ON THE DOWNLAND"

Night is on the downland, on the lonely moorland,
On the hills where the wind goes over sheep-bitten turf,
Where the bent grass beats upon the unploughed poorland
And the pine-woods roar like the surf.

Here the Roman lived on the wind-barren lonely,
Dark now and haunted by the moorland fowl;
None comes here now but the peewit only,
And moth-like death in the owl.

Beauty was here, on this beetle-droning downland;
The thought of a Cæsar in the purple came
From the palace by the Tiber in the Roman townland
To this wind-swept hill with no name.

Lonely Beauty came here and was here in sadness,
Brave as a thought on the frontier of the mind,
In the camp of the wild upon the march of madness,
The bright-eyed Queen of the Blind.

Now where Beauty was are the wind-withered gorses,
Moaning like old men in the hill-wind's blast;
The flying sky is dark with running horses,
And the night is full of the past.

"A HUNDRED YEARS AGO . . . ."

A hundred years ago they quarried for the stone here;
The carts came through the wood by the track still plain;
The drills show in the rock where the blasts were blown here
They show up dark after rain.

Then the last cart of stone went away through the wood,
To build the great house for some April of a woman,
Till her beauty stood in stone; as her man's thought made it good,
And the dumb rock was made human.

The house still stands, but the April of its glory
Is gone, long since, with the beauty that has gone;
She wandered away west, it is an old sad story:
It is best not talked upon.

And the man has gone, too, but the quarry that he made,
Whenever April comes as it came in old time,
Is a dear delight to the man who loves a maid.
For the primrose comes from the lime. . . .

And the blackbird builds below the catkin shaking,
And the sweet white violets are beauty in the blood,
And daffodils are there, and the blackthorn blossom breaking
Is a wild white beauty in bud.

SONNETS
XXX

There, on the darkened deathbed, dies the brain
That flared three several times in seventy years.
It cannot lift the silly hand again,
Nor speak, nor sing, it neither sees nor hears;
And muffled mourners put it in the ground
And then go home, and in the earth it lies
Too dark for vision and too deep for sound,
The million cells that made a good man wise.
Yet for a few short years an influence stirs,
A sense or wraith or essence of him dead,
Which makes insensate things its ministers
To those beloved, his spirit's daily bread;
Then that, too, fades; in book or deed a spark
Lingers, then that, too, fades; then all is dark.

LXII

There was an evil in the nodding wood
Above the quarry long since overgrown,
Something which stamped it as a place of blood
Where tortured spirit cried from murdered bone.
Then, after years, I saw a rusty knife
Stuck in a woman's skull, just as 'twas found,
Blackt with a centuried crust of clotted life,
In the red clay of that unholy ground.
So that I knew the unhappy thing had spoken,
That tongueless thing for whom the quarry spoke,
The evil seals of murder had been broken
By the red earth, the grass, the rooted oak,
The inarticulate dead had forced the spade,
The hand, the mind, till murder was displayed.

REYNARD THE FOX
PART II

On old Cold Crendon's windy tops
Grows wintrily Blown Hilcote Copse,
Wind-bitten beech with badger barrows,
Where brocks eat wasp-grubs with their marrows
And foxes lie on short-grassed turf,
Nose between paws, to hear the surf
Of wind in the beeches drowsily.
There was our fox bred lustily
Three years before, and there he berthed,

Under the beech-roots snugly earthed,
With a roof of flint and a floor of chalk
And ten bitten hens' heads each on its stalk,
Some rabbits' paws, some fur from scuts,
A badger's corpse and a smell of guts.
And there on the night before my tale
He trotted out for a point in the vale.

He saw, from the cover edge, the valley
Go trooping down with its droops of sally
To the brimming river's lipping bend,
And a light in the inn at Water's End.
He heard the owl go hunting by
And the shriek of the mouse the owl made die,
And the purr of the owl as he tore the red
Strings from between his claws and fed;
The smack of joy of the horny lips
Marbled green with the blobby strips.
He saw the farms where the dogs were barking,
Cold Crendon Court and Copsecote Larking;
The fault with the spring as bright as gleed,
Green-slash-laced with water-weed.
A glare in the sky still marked the town,
Though all folk slept and the blinds were down,
The street lamps watched the empty square,
The night-cat sang his evil there.

The fox's nose tipped up and round,
Since smell is a part of sight and sound.
Delicate smells were drifting by,
The sharp nose flaired them heedfully;
Partridges in the clover stubble,
Crouched in a ring for the stoat to nubble.
Rabbit bucks beginning to box;
A scratching place for the pheasant cocks,
A hare in the dead grass near the drain,
And another smell like the spring again.

A faint rank taint like April coming,
It cocked his ears and his blood went drumming,
For somewhere out by Ghost Heath Stubs
Was a roving vixen wanting cubs.
Over the valley, floating faint
On a warmth of windflaw, came the taint;

He cocked his ears, he upped his brush,
And he went upwind like an April thrush.

By the Roman Road to Braiches Ridge,
Where the fallen willow makes a bridge,
Over the brook by White Hart's Thorn
To the acres thin with pricking corn,
Over the sparse green hair of the wheat,
By the Clench Brook Mill at Clench Brook Leat,
Through Cowfoot Pastures to Nonely Stevens,
And away to Poltrewood St. Jevons.
Past Tott Hill Down all snaked with meuses,
Past Clench St. Michael and Naunton Crucis,
Past Howle's Oak Farm where the raving brain
Of a dog who heard him foamed his chain;
Then off, as the farmer's window opened,
Past Stonepits Farm to Upton Hope End,
Over short sweet grass and worn flint arrows
And the three dumb hows of Tencombe Barrows.
And away and away with a rolling scramble,
Through the sally and up the bramble,
With a nose for the smells the night wind carried,
And his red fell clean for being married;
For clicketting time and Ghost Heath Wood
Had put the violet in his blood.

At Tencombe Rings near the Manor Linney
His foot made the great black stallion whinny,
And the stallion's whinny aroused the stable
And the bloodhound bitches stretched their cable,
And the clink of the bloodhounds' chain aroused
The sweet-breathed kye as they chewed and drowsed,
And the stir of the cattle changed the dream
Of the cat in the loft to tense green gleam.
The red-wattled black cock hot from Spain
Crowed from his perch for dawn again,
His breast-pufft hens, one-legged on perch,
Gurgled, beak-down, like men in church,
They crooned in the dark, lifing one red eye
In the raftered roost as the fox went by.

By Tencombe Regis and Slaughters Court,
Through the great grass square of Roman Fort,
By Nun's Wood Yews and the Hungry Hill,
And the Corpse Way Stones all standing still.

178

By Seven Springs Mead to Deerlip Brook,
And a lolloping leap to Water Hook.
Then with eyes like sparks and his blood awoken,
Over the grass to Water's Oaken,
And over the hedge and into ride
In Ghost Heath Wood for his roving bride.

Before the dawn he had loved and fed
And found a kennel, and gone to bed
On a shelf of grass in a thick of gorse
That would bleed a hound and blind a horse.
There he slept in the mild west weather
With his nose and brush well tucked together,
He slept like a child, who sleeps yet hears
With the self who needs neither eyes nor ears.

He slept while the pheasant cock untucked
His head from his wing flew down and kukked,
While the drove of the starlings whirred and wheeled
Out of the ash-trees into field,
While with great black flags that flogged and paddled
The rooks went out to the plough and straddled,
Straddled wide on the moist red cheese
Of the furrows driven at Uppat's Leas.

Down in the village men awoke,
The chimneys breathed with a faint blue smoke.
The fox slept on, though tweaks and twitches,
Due to his dreams, ran down his flitches.

The cows were milked and the yards were sluiced,
And the cocks and hens let out of roost,
Windows were opened, mats were beaten,
All men's breakfasts were cooked and eaten;
But out in the gorse on the grassy shelf
The sleeping fox looked after himself.

Deep in his dream he heard the life
Of the woodland seek for food or wife,
The hop of a stoat, a buck that thumped,
The squeal of a rat as a weasel jumped,
The blackbird's chackering scattering crying,
The rustling bents from the rabbits flying,
Cows in a byre, and distant men,
And Condicote church-clock striking ten.

At eleven o'clock a boy went past,
With a rough-haired terrier following fast.
The boy's sweet whistle and dog's quick yap
Woke the fox from out of his nap.

He rose and stretched till the claws in his pads
Stuck hornily out like long black gads.
He listened a while, and his nose went round
To catch the smell of the distant sound.

The windward smells came free from taint—
They were rabbit, strongly, with lime-kiln, faint,
A wild-duck, likely, at Sars Holt Pond,
And sheep on the Sars Holt Down beyond.

The leeward smells were much less certain,
For the Ghost Heath Hill was like a curtain,
Yet vague, from the leeward, now and then,
Came muffled sounds like the sound of men.

He moved to his right to a clearer space,
And all his soul came into his face,
Into his eyes and into his nose,
As over the hill a murmur rose.
His ears were cocked and his keen nose flaired,
He sneered with his lips till his teeth were bared,
He trotted right and lifted a pad
Trying to test what foes he had.

On Ghost Heath turf was a steady drumming
Which sounded like horses quickly coming,
It died as the hunt went down the dip,
Then Malapert yelped at Myngs's whip.
A bright iron horseshoe clinked on stone,
Then a man's voice spoke, not one alone,
Then a burst of laughter, swiftly still,
Muffled away by Ghost Heath Hill.
Then, indistinctly, the clop, clip, clep,
On Brady Ride, of a horse's step.
Then silence, then, in a burst, much clearer,
Voices and horses coming nearer,
And another noise, of a pit-pat beat
On the Ghost Hill grass, of foxhound feet.

He sat on his haunches listening hard,
While his mind went over the compass card.
Men were coming and rest was done,
But he still had time to get fit to run;
He could outlast horse and outrace hound,
But men were devils from Lobs's Pound.
Scent was burning, the going good,
The world one lust for a fox's blood,
The main earths stopped and the drains put to,
And fifteen miles to the land he knew.
But of all the ills, the ill least pleasant
Was to run in the light when men were present.
Men in the fields to shout and sign
For a lift of hounds to a fox's line.
Men at the earth, at the long point's end,
Men at each check and none his friend,
Guessing each shift that a fox contrives;
But still, needs must when the devil drives.

He readied himself, then a soft horn blew,
Then a clear voice carolled, "Ed-hoick! Eleu!"
Then the wood-end rang with the clear voice crying
And the cackle of scrub where hounds were trying.
Then the horn blew nearer, a hound's voice quivered,
Then another, then more, till his body shivered,
He left his kennel and trotted thence
With his ears flexed back and his nerves all tense.

He trotted down with his nose intent
For a fox's line to cross his scent,
It was only fair (he being a stranger)
That the native fox should have the danger.
Danger was coming, so swift, so swift,
That the pace of his trot began to lift
The blue-winged Judas, a jay began
Swearing, hounds whimpered, air stank of man.

He hurried his trotting, he now felt frighted,
It was his poor body made hounds excited.
He felt as he ringed the great wood through
That he ought to make for the land he knew.

Then the hound's excitement quivered and quickened,
Then a horn blew death till his marrow sickened,

Then the wood behind was a crash of cry
For the blood in his veins; it made him fly.

They were on his line; it was death to stay.
He must make for home by the shortest way,
But with all this yelling and all this wrath
And all these devils, how find a path?

He ran like a stag to the wood's north corner,
Where the hedge was thick and the ditch a yawner,
But the scarlet glimpse of Myngs on Turk,
Watching the woodside, made him shirk.

He ringed the wood and looked at the south.
What wind there was blew into his mouth.
But close to the woodland's blackthorn thicket
Was Dansey, still as a stone, on picket.
At Dansey's back were a twenty more
Watching the cover and pressing fore.

The fox drew in and flaired with his muzzle.
Death was there if he messed the puzzle.

There were men without and hounds within,
A crying that stiffened the hair on skin.
Teeth in cover and death without,
Both deaths coming, and no way out.

His nose ranged swiftly, his heart beat fast,
Then a crashing cry rose up in a blast,
Then horse-hooves trampled, then horses' flitches
Burst their way through the hazel switches.
Then the horn again made the hounds like mad,
And a man, quite near, said, "Found, by Gad!"
And a man, quite near, said, "Now he'll break.
Larks Leybourne Copse is the line he'll take."
And men moved up with their talk and stink
And the traplike noise of the horseshoe clink.
Men whose coming meant death from teeth
In a worrying wrench, with him beneath.

The fox sneaked down by the cover side
(With his ears flexed back) as a snake would glide;
He took the ditch at the cover-end,
He hugged the ditch as his only friend.

The blackbird cock with the golden beak
Got out of his way with a jabbering shriek,
And the shriek told Tom on the raking bay
That for eighteenpence he was gone away.

He ran in the hedge in the triple growth
Of bramble and hawthorn, glad of both,
Till a couple of fields were past, and then
Came the living death of the dread of men.

Then, as he listened, he heard a "Hoy!"
Tom Dansey's horn and "Awa-wa-woy!"
Then all hounds crying with all their forces,
Then a thundering down of seventy horses.
Robin Dawe's horn and halloes of "Hey
Hark Hollar, Hoik!" and "Gone away!"
"Hark Hollar Hoik!" and a smack of the whip,
A yelp as a tail hound caught the clip.

"Hark Hollar, Hark Hollar!" then Robin made
Pip go crash through the cut and laid.
Hounds were over and on his line
With a head like bees upon Tipple Tine.
The sound of the nearness sent a flood
Of terror of death through the fox's blood.
He upped his brush and he cocked his nose,
And he went upwind as a racer goes.

Bold Robin Dawe was over first,
Cheering his hounds on at the burst;
The field were spurring to be in it.
"Hold hard, sirs, give them half a minute,"
Came from Sir Peter on his white.
The hounds went romping with delight
Over the grass and got together,
The tail hounds galloped hell-for-leather
After the pack at Myngs's yell.
A cry like every kind of bell
Rang from these rompers as they raced.

The riders, thrusting to be placed,
Jammed down their hats and shook their horses;
The hounds romped past with all their forces,
They crashed into the blackthorn fence.
The scent was heavy on their sense,

So hot, it seemed the living thing,
It made the blood within them sing;
Gusts of it made their hackles rise,
Hot gulps of it were agonies
Of joy, and thirst for blood and passion.
"Forward!" cried Robin, "that's the fashion."
He raced beside his pack to cheer.

The field's noise died upon his ear,
A faint horn, far behind, blew thin
In cover, lest some hound were in.
Then instantly the great grass rise
Shut field and cover from his eyes,
He and his racers were alone.
"A dead fox or a broken bone,"
Said Robin, peering for his prey.

The rise, which shut the field away,
Showed him the vale's great map spread out,
The down's lean flank and thrusting snout,
Pale pastures, red-brown plough, dark wood,
Blue distance, still as solitude,
Glitter of water here and there,
The trees so delicately bare,
The dark green gorse and bright green holly.
"O glorious God," he said, "how jolly!"
And there downhill two fields ahead
The lolloping red dog-fox sped
Over Poor Pastures to the brook.
He grasped these things in one swift look,
Then dived into the bullfinch heart
Through thorns that ripped his sleeves apart
And skutched new blood upon his brow.
"His point's Lark's Leybourne Covers now,"
Said Robin, landing with a grunt.
"Forrard, my beautifuls!"

       The hunt
Followed downhill to race with him,
White Rabbit, with his swallow's skim,
Drew within hail. "Quick burst, Sir Peter."
"A traveller. Nothing could be neater.
Making for Godsdown Clumps, I take it?"
"Lark's Leybourne, sir, if he can make it.
Forrard!"

Bill Ridden thundered down,
His big mouth grinned beneath his frown,
The hounds were going away from horses.
He saw the glint of watercourses,
Yell Brook and Wittold's Dyke, ahead,
His horseshoes sliced the green turf red.
Young Cothill's chaser rushed and past him,
Nob Manor, running next, said "Blast him!

The poet chap who thinks he rides."
Hugh Colway's mare made straking strides
Across the grass, the Colonel next,
Then Squire, volleying oaths, and vext,
Fighting his hunter for refusing;
Bell Ridden, like a cutter cruising,
Sailing the grass; then Cob on Warder,
Then Minton Price upon Marauder;
Ock Gurney with his eyes intense,
Burning as with a different sense,
His big mouth muttering glad "By damns!"
Then Pete, crouched down from head to hams,
Rapt like a saint, bright focussed flame;
Bennett, with devils in his wame,
Chewing black cud and spitting slanting;
Copse scattering jests and Stukely ranting;
Sal Ridden taking line from Dansey;
Long Robert forcing Necromancy;
A dozen more with bad beginnings;
Myngs riding hard to snatch an innings.
A wild last hound with high shrill yelps
Smacked forrard with some whipthong skelps.
Then last of all, at top of rise,
The crowd on foot, all gasps and eyes;
The run up hill had winded them.

They saw the Yell Brook like a gem
Blue in the grass a short mile on;
They heard faint cries, but hounds were gone
A good eight fields and out of sight,
Except a rippled glimmer white
Going away with dying cheering,
And scarlet flappings disappearing,
And scattering horses going, going,
Going like mad, White Rabbit snowing
Far on ahead, a loose horse taking

185

Fence after fence with stirrups shaking,
And scarlet specks and dark specks dwindling.

Nearer, were twigs knocked into kindling,
A much bashed fence still dropping stick,
Flung clods still quivering from the kick;
Cut hoof-marks pale in cheesy clay,
The horse-smell blowing clean away;
Birds flitting back into the cover.
One last faint cry, then all was over.
The hunt had been, and found, and gone.

At Neaking's Farm three furlongs on,
Hounds raced across the Waysmore Road,
Where many of the riders slowed
To tittup down a grassy lane
Which led as hounds led in the main,
And gave no danger of a fall.
There as they tittupped one and all,
Big Twenty Stone came scattering by,
His great mare made the hoof-casts fly.
"By leave!" he cried. "Come on! Come up!
This fox is running like a tup;
Let's leave this lane and get to terms,
No sense in crawling here like worms.
Come, let me pass and let me start.
This fox is running like a hart,
And this is going to be a run.
Come on, I want to see the fun.
Thanky. By leave! Now, Maiden, do it."
He faced the fence and put her through it,
Shielding his eyes lest spikes should blind him;
The crashing blackthorn closed behind him.
Mud-scatters chased him as he scudded;
His mare's ears cocked, her neat feet thudded.

The kestrel cruising over meadow
Watched the hunt gallop on his shadow,
Wee figures, almost at a stand,
Crossing the multicoloured land,
Slow as a shadow on a dial.

Some horses, swerving at a trial,
Balked at a fence; at gates they bunched.
The mud about the gates was dunched

Like German cheese; men pushed for places
And kicked the mud into the faces
Of those who made them room to pass.
The half-mile's gallop on the grass
Had tailed them out and warmed their blood.
"His point's the Banner Barton Wood."
"That, or Goat's Gorse." "A stinger, this."
"You're right in that; by Jove, it is."
"An upwind travelling fox, by George!"
"They say Tom viewed him at the forge."
"Well, let me pass and let's be on."

They crossed the lane to Tolderton,
The hill-marl died to valley clay,
And there before them ran the grey
Yell Water, swirling as it ran,
The Yell Brook of the hunting man.
The hunters eyed it and were grim.

They saw the water snaking slim
Ahead, like silver; they could see
(Each man) his pollard willow-tree
Firming the bank; they felt their horses
Catch the gleam's hint and gather forces.
They heard the men behind draw near.
Each horse was trembling as a spear
Trembles in hand when tense to hurl.
They saw the brimmed brook's eddies curl;
The willow-roots like water-snakes;
The beaten holes the ratten makes.
They heard the water's rush; they heard
Hugh Colway's mare come like a bird;
A faint cry from the hounds ahead,
Then saddle-strain, the bright hooves' tread,
Quick words, the splash of mud, the launch,
The sick hope that the bank be staunch,
Then Souse, with Souse to left and right.
Maroon across, Sir Peter's white
Down but pulled up, Tom over, Hugh
Mud to the hat but over too,
Well splashed by Squire, who was in.

With draggled pink struck close to skin
The Squire leaned from bank and hauled
His mired horse's rein; he bawled

For help from each man racing by.
"What, help you pull him out? Not I.
What made you pull him in?" They said.
Nob Manor cleared and turned his head,
And cried, "Wade up. The ford's upstream."
Ock Gurney in a cloud of steam
Stood by his dripping cob and wrung
The taste of brook mud from his tongue,
And scraped his poor cob's pasterns clean.
"Lord, what a crowner we've a-been.
This jumping brook's a mucky job."
He muttered, grinning, "Lord, poor cob!
Now, sir, let me." He turned to Squire
And cleared his hunter from the mire
By skill and sense and strength of arm.

Meanwhile the fox passed Nonesuch Farm,
Keeping the spinney on his right.
Hounds raced him here with all their might
Along the short firm grass, like fire.
The cowman viewed him from the byre
Lolloping on, six fields ahead,
Then hounds, still carrying such a head
It made him stare, then Rob on Pip,
Sailing the great grass like a ship,
Then grand Maroon in all his glory,
Sweeping his strides, his great chest hoary
With foam fleck and the pale hill-marl.
They strode the Leet, they flew the Snarl,
They knocked the nuts at Nonesuch Mill,
Raced up the spur of Gallows Hill
And viewed him there. The line he took
Was Tineton and the Pantry Brook,
Going like fun and hounds like mad.
Tom glanced to see what friends he had
Still within sight, before he turned
The ridge's shoulder; he discerned,
One field away, young Cothill sailing
Easily up. Peter Gurney failing,
Hugh Colway quartering on Sir Peter,
Bill waiting on the mate to beat her,
Sal Ridden skirting to the right.
A horse, with stirrups flashing bright
Over his head at every stride,
Looked like the Major's; Tom espied

Far back a scarlet speck of man
Running, and straddling as he ran.
Charles Copse was up, Nob Manor followed,
Then Bennett's big-boned black that wallowed,
Clumsy, but with the strength of ten.
Then black and brown and scarlet men,
Brown horses, white and black and grey,
Scattered a dozen fields away.
The shoulder shut the scene away.

From the Gallows Hill to the Tineton Copse
There were ten ploughed fields, like ten full-stops,
All wet red clay, where a horse's foot
Would be swathed, feet thick, like an ash-tree root.
The fox raced on, on the headlands firm,
Where his swift feet scared the coupling worm;
The rooks rose raving to curse him raw,
He snarled a sneer at their swoop and caw.
Then on, then on, down a half-ploughed field
Where a ship-like plough drove glitter-keeled,
With a bay horse near and a white horse leading,
And a man saying "Zook," and the red earth bleeding.
He gasped as he saw the ploughman drop
The stilts and swear at the team to stop.
The ploughman ran in his red clay clogs,
Crying, "Zick un, Towzer; zick, good dogs!"
A couple of wire-haired lurchers lean
Arose from his wallet, nosing keen;
With a rushing swoop they were on his track,
Putting chest to stubble to bite his back.
He swerved from his line with the curs at heel,
The teeth as they missed him clicked like steel.
With a worrying snarl, they quartered on him,
While the ploughman shouted, "Zick; upon him."

The lurcher dogs soon shot their bolt,
And the fox raced on by the Hazel Holt,
Down the dead grass tilt to the sandstone gash
Of the Pantry Brook at Tineton Ash.
The loitering water, flooded full,
Had yeast on its lip like raddled wool,
It was wrinkled over with Arab script
Of eddies that twisted up and slipped
The stepping-stones had a rush about them,
So the fox plunged in and swam without them.

189

He crossed to the cattle's drinking shallow,
Firmed up with rush and the roots of mallow;
He wrung his coat from his draggled bones
And romped away for the Sarsen Stones.

A sneaking glance with his ears flexed back
Made sure that his scent had failed the pack,
For the red clay, good for corn and roses,
Was cold for scent and brought hounds to noses

He slackened pace by the Tineton Tree
(A vast hollow ash-tree grown in three),
He wriggled a shake and padded slow,
Not sure if the hounds were on or no.

A horn blew faint, then he heard the sounds
Of a cantering huntsman, lifing hounds;
The ploughman had raised his hat for sign,
And the hounds were lifted and on his line.
He heard the splash in the Pantry Brook,
And a man's voice: "Thiccy's the line he took."
And a clear "Yoi doit!" and a whimpering quaver,
Though the lurcher dogs had dulled the savour.

The fox went off while the hounds made halt,
And the horses breathed and the field found fault,
But the whimpering rose to a crying crash
By the hollow ruin of Tineton Ash.

Then again the kettledrum horsehooves beat,
And the green blades bent to the fox's feet,
And the cry rose keen not far behind
Of the "Blood, blood, blood," in the foxhounds' mind.

The fox was strong, he was full of running,
He could run for an hour and then be cunning,
But the cry behind him made him chill,
They were nearer now and they meant to kill.
They meant to run him until his blood
Clogged on his heart as his brush with mud,
Till his back bent up and his tongue hung flagging,
And his belly and brush were filthed from dragging.
Till he crouched stone-still, dead-beat and dirty,
With nothing but teeth against the thirty.
And all the way to that blinding end

He would meet with men and have none his friend:
Men to holloa and men to run him,
With stones to stagger and yells to stun him;
Men to head him, with whips to beat him,
Teeth to mangle and mouths to eat him.
And all the way, that wild high crying.
To cold his blood with the thought of dying,
The horn and the cheer, and the drum-like thunder
Of the horsehooves stamping the meadows under.
He upped his brush and went with a will
For the Sarsen Stones on Wan Dyke Hill.

As he ran the meadow by Tineton Church
A christening party left the porch;
They stook stock still as he pounded by,
They wished him luck but they thought he'd die.
The toothless babe in his long white coat
Looked delicate meat, the fox took note;
But the sight of them grinning there, pointing finger,
Made him put on steam till he went a stinger.

Past Tineton Church, over Tineton Waste,
With the lolloping ease of a fox's haste,
The fur on his chest blown dry with the air,
His brush still up and his cheek-teeth bare.

Over the Waste, where the ganders grazed,
The long swift lilt of his loping lazed,
His ears cocked up as his blood ran higher,
He saw his point, and his eyes took fire.
The Wan Dyke Hill with its fir-tree barren,
Its dark of gorse and its rabbit-warren,
The Dyke on its heave like a tightened girth,
And holes in the Dyke where a fox might earth.
He had rabbited there long months before,
The earths were deep and his need was sore;
The way was new, but he took a bearing,
And rushed like a blown ship billow-sharing.

Off Tineton Common to Tineton Dean,
Where the wind-hid elders pushed with green;
Through the Dean's thin cover across the lane,
And up Midwinter to King of Spain.
Old Joe, at digging his garden grounds,
Said: 'A fox, being hunted; where be hounds?

191

O lord, my back, to be young again,
'Stead a zellin' zider in King of Spain!
O hark! I hear 'em, O sweet, O sweet.
Why there be redcoat in Gearge's wheat.
And there be redcoat, and there they gallop.
Thur go a browncoat down a wallop.
Quick, Ellen, quick! Come, Susan fly!
Here'm hounds. I zeed the fox go by,
Go by like thunder, go by like blasting,
With his girt white teeth all looking ghasting.
Look, there come hounds! Hark, hear 'em crying?
Lord, belly to stubble, ain't they flying!
There's huntsman, there. The fox come past
(As I was digging) as fast as fast.
He's only been gone a minute by;
A girt dark dog as pert as pye."

Ellen and Susan came out scattering
Brooms and dustpans till all was clattering;
They saw the pack come head-to-foot
Running like racers, nearly mute;
Robin and Dansey quartering near
All going gallop like startled deer.

A half-dozen flitting scarlets showing
In the thin green Dean where the pines were growing.
Black coats and brown coats thrusting and spurring,
Sending the partridge coveys whirring.
Then a rattle uphill and a clop up lane,
It emptied the bar of the King of Spain.

Tom left his cider, Dick left his bitter,
Granfer James left his pipe and spitter;
Out they came from the sawdust floor.
They said, "They'm going." They said, "O Lor'!"

The fox raced on, up the Barton Balks,
With a crackle of kex in the nettle stalks,
Over Hammond's grass to the dark green line
Of the larch-wood smelling of turpentine.
Scratch Steven Larches, black to the sky,
A sadness breathing with one long sigh,
Grey ghosts of trees under funeral plumes,
A mist of twig over soft brown glooms.
As he entered the wood he heard the smacks,

Chip-jar, of the fir-pole feller's axe.
He swerved to the left to a broad green ride,
Where a boy made him rush for the farther side.
He swerved to the left, to the Barton Road,
But there were the timberers come to load—
Two timber-carts and a couple of carters
With straps round their knees instead of garters.
He swerved to the right, straight down the wood,
The carters watched him, the boy hallooed.
He leaped from the larch-wood into tillage,
The cobbler's garden of Barton village.

The cobbler bent at his wooden foot,
Beating sprigs in a broken boot;
He wore old glasses with thick horn rim,
He scowled at his work, for his sight was dim.
His face was dingy, his lips were grey,
From primming sparrowbills day by day.
As he turned his boot he heard a noise
At his garden-end, and he thought, "It's boys."

He saw his cat nip up on the shed,
Where her back arched up till it touched her head;
He saw his rabbit race round and round
Its little black box three feet from ground.
His six hens cluckered and flocked to perch,
"That's boys," said cobbler, "so I'll go search."
He reached his stick and blinked in his wrath,
When he saw a fox in his garden path.

The fox swerved left and scrambled out,
Knocking crinked green shells from the brussels-sprout
He scrambled out through the cobbler's paling,
And up Pill's orchard to Purton's Tailing,
Across the plough at the top of bent,
Through the heaped manure to kill his scent,
Over to Aldam's, up to Cappell's,
Past Nursery Lot with its whitewashed apples,
Past Colston's Broom, past Gaunt's, past Shere's,
Past Foxwhelps' Oasts with their hooded ears,
Past Monk's Ash Clerewell, past Beggars' Oak,
Past the great elms blue with the Hinton smoke.
Along Long Hinton to Hinton Green,
Where the wind-washed steeple stood serene.
With its golden bird still sailing air.
Past Banner Barton, past Chipping Bare,

Past Maddings Hollow, down Dundry Dip,
And up Goose Grass to the Sailing Ship.

The three black firs of the Ship stood still
On the bare chalk heave of the Dundry Hill.
The fox looked back as he slackened past
The scaled red-hole of the mizzen-mast.

There they were coming, mute but swift—
A scarlet smear in the blackthorn rift,
A white horse rising, a dark horse flying,
And the hungry hounds too tense for crying.
Stormcock leading, his stern spear straight,
Racing as though for a piece of plate,
Little speck horsemen field on field;
Then Dansey viewed him and Robin squealed.

At the "View Halloo!" the hounds went frantic,
Back went Stormcock and up went Antic,
Up went Skylark as Antic sped,
It was zest to blood how they carried head.
Skylark drooped as Maroon drew by,
Their hackles lifted, they scorned to cry.

The fox knew well that, before they tore him,
They should try their speed on the downs before him.
There were three more miles to the Wan Dyke Hill,
But his heart was high that he beat them still.
The wind of the downland charmed his bones,
So off he went for the Sarsen Stones.

The moan of the three great firs in the wind
And the "Ai" of the foxhounds died behind;
Wind-dapples followed the hill-wind's breath
On the Kill Down Gorge where the Danes found death.
Larks scattered up; the peewits feeding
Rose in a flock from the Kill Down Steeding.
The hare leaped up from her form and swerved
Swift left for the Starveall, harebell-turved.
On the wind-bare thorn some longtails prinking
Cried sweet as though wind-blown glass were chinking.
Behind came thudding and loud halloo,
Or a cry from hounds as they came to view.

The pure clean air came sweet to his lungs,
Till he thought foul scorn of those crying tongues.
In a three mile more he would reach the haven
In the Wan Dyke croaked on by the raven.
In a three mile more he would make his berth
On the hard cool floor of a Wan Dyke earth,
Too deep for spade, too curved for terrier,
With the pride of the race to make rest the merrier.
In a three mile more he would reach his dream,
So his game heart gulped and he put on steam.

Like a rocket shot to a ship ashore
The lean red bolt of his body tore,
Like a ripple of wind running swift on grass:
Like a shadow on wheat when a cloud blows past,
Like a turn at the buoy in a cutter sailing
When the bright green gleam lips white at the railing.
Like the April snake whipping back to sheath,
Like the gannets' hurtle on fish beneath,
Like a kestrel chasing, like a sickle reaping,
Like all things swooping, like all things sweeping,
Like a hound for stay, like a stag for swift,
With his shadow beside like spinning drift.

Past the gibbet-stock all stuck with nails,
Where they hanged in chains what had hung at jails,
Past Ashmundshowe where Ashmund sleeps,
And none but the tumbling peewit weeps,
Past Curlew Calling, the gaunt grey corner
Where the curlew comes as a summer mourner,
Past Blowbury Beacon, shaking his fleece,
Where all winds hurry and none brings peace;
Then down on the mile-long green decline,
Where the turf's like spring and the air's like wine,
Where the sweeping spurs of the downland spill
Into Wan Brook Valley and Wan Dyke Hill.

On he went with a galloping rally
Past Maesbury Clump for Wan Brook Valley.
The blood in his veins went romping high,
"Get on, on, on, to the earth or die."
The air of the downs went purely past
Till he felt the glory of going fast,
Till the terror of death, though there indeed,

Was lulled for a while by his pride of speed.
He was romping away from hounds and hunt,
He had Wan Dyke Hill and his earth in front,
In a one mile more when his point was made
He would rest in safety from dog or spade;
Nose between paws he would hear the shout
Of the "Gone to earth!" to the hounds without,
The whine of the hounds, and their cat-feet gadding,
Scratching the earth, and their breath pad-padding:
He would hear the horn call hounds away,
And rest in peace till another day.

In one mile more he would lie at rest,
So for one mile more he would go his best.
He reached the dip at the long droop's end
And he took what speed he had still to spend.

So down past Maesbury beech-clump grey
That would not be green till the end of May,
Past Arthur's Table, the white chalk boulder,
Where pasque flowers purple the down's grey shoulder,
Past Quichelm's Keeping, past Harry's Thorn,
To Thirty Acre all thin with corn.

As he raced the corn towards Wan Dyke Brook
The pack had view of the way he took;
Robin hallooed from the downland's crest,
He capped them on till they did their best.
The quarter-mile to the Wan Brook's brink
Was raced as quick as a man can think.

And here, as he ran to the huntsman's yelling,
The fox first felt that the pace was telling;
His body and lungs seemed all grown old,
His legs less certain, his heart less bold,
The hound-noise nearer, the hill-slope steeper,
The thud in the blood of his body deeper.
His pride in his speed, his joy in the race,
Were withered away, for what use was pace?
He had run his best, and the hounds ran better,
Then the going worsened, the earth was wetter.
Then his brush drooped down till it sometimes dragged,
And his fur felt sick and his chest was tagged
With taggles of mud, and his pads seemed lead,
It was well for him he'd an earth ahead.

Down he went to the brook and over,
Out of the corn and into the clover,
Over the slope that the Wan Brook drains,
Past Battle Tump where they earthed the Danes,
Then up the hill that the Wan Dyke rings
Where the Sarsen Stones stand grand like kings.

Seven Sarsens of granite grim,
As he ran them by they looked at him;
As he leaped the lip of their earthen paling
The hounds were gaining and he was failing.

He passed the Sarsens, he left the spur,
He pressed uphill to the blasted fir,
He slipped as he leaped the hedge; he slithered.
"He's mine," thought Robin. "He's done; he's dithered."

At the second attempt he cleared the fence,
He turned half-right where the gorse was dense,
He was leading hounds by a furlong clear.
He was past his best, but his earth was near.
He ran up gorse to the spring of the ramp,
The steep green wall of the dead men's camp,
He sidled up it and scampered down
To the deep green ditch of the Dead Men's Town.

Within, as he reached that soft green turf,
The wind, blowing lonely, moaned like surf,
Desolate ramparts rose up steep
On either side, for the ghosts to keep.
He raced the trench, past the rabbit warren,
Close-grown with moss which the wind made barren;
He passed the spring where the rushes spread,
And there in the stones was his earth ahead.
One last short burst upon failing feet—
There life lay waiting, so sweet, so sweet,
Rest in a darkness, balm for aches.

The earth was stopped. It was barred with stakes.

With the hounds at head so close behind
He had to run as he changed his mind.
This earth, as he saw, was stopped, but still
There was one earth more on the Wan Dyke Hill—
A rabbit burrow a furlong on,

He could kennel there till the hounds were gone.
Though his death seemed near he did not blench,
He upped his brush and he ran the trench.

He ran the trench while the wind moaned treble,
Earth trickled down, there were falls of pebble.
Down in the valley of that dark gash
The wind-withered grasses looked like ash.
Trickles of stones and earth fell down
In that dark alley of Dead Men's Town.
A hawk arose from a fluff of feathers,
From a distant fold came a bleat of wethers.
He heard no noise from the hounds behind
But the hill-wind moaning like something blind.

He turned the bend in the hill, and there
Was his rabbit-hole with its mouth worn bare;
But there, with a gun tucked under his arm,
Was young Sid Kissop of Purlpit's Farm,
With a white hob ferret to drive the rabbit
Into a net which was set to nab it.
And young Jack Cole peered over the wall,
And loosed a pup with a "Z'bite en, Saul!"
The terrier pup attacked with a will,
So the fox swerved right and away downhill.

Down from the ramp of the Dyke he ran
To the brackeny patch where the gorse began,
Into the gorse, where the hill's heave hid
The line he took from the eyes of Sid;
He swerved downwind and ran like a hare
For the wind-blown spinney below him there.

He slipped from the gorse to the spinney dark
(There were curled grey growths on the oak-tree bark);
He saw no more of the terrier pup,
But he heard men speak and the hounds come up.

He crossed the spinney with ears intent
For the cry of hounds on the way he went;
His heart was thumping, the hounds were near now,
He could make no sprint at a cry and cheer now,
He was past his perfect, his strength was failing,
His brush sag-sagged and his legs were ailing.

He felt, as he skirted Dead Men's Town,
That in one mile more they would have him down.

Through the withered oak's wind-crouching tops
He saw men's scarlet above the copse,
He heard men's oaths, yet he felt hounds slacken,
In the frondless stalks of the brittle bracken.
He felt that the unseen link which bound
His spine to the nose of the leading hound
Was snapped, that the hounds no longer knew
Which way to follow nor what to do;
That the threat of the hounds' teeth left his neck,
They had ceased to run, they had come to check.
They were quartering wide on the Wan Hill's bent.

The terrier's chase had killed his scent.

He heard bits chink as the horses shifted,
He heard hounds cast, then he heard hounds lifted,
But there came no cry from a new attack;
His heart grew steady, his breath came back.

He left the spinney and ran its edge
By the deep dry ditch of the blackthorn hedge;
Then out of the ditch and down the meadow,
Trotting at ease in the blackthorn shadow,
Over the track called Godsdown Road,
To the great grass heave of the gods' abode.
He was moving now upon land he knew:
Up Clench Royal and Morton Tew,
The Pol Brook, Cheddesdon, and East Stoke Church,
High Clench St. Lawrence and Tinker's Birch.
Land he had roved on night by night,
For hot blood suckage or furry bite.
The threat of the hounds behind was gone;
He breathed deep pleasure and trotted on.

While young Sid Kissop thrashed the pup
Robin on Pip came heaving up,
And found his pack spread out at check.
"I'd like to wring your terrier's neck,"
He said, "you see? He's spoiled our sport.
He's killed the scent." He broke off short,
And stared at hounds and at the valley.

No jay or magpie gave a rally
Down in the copse, no circling rooks
Rose over fields; old Joyful's looks
Were doubtful in the gorse, the pack
Quested both up and down and back.
He watched each hound for each small sign.
They tried, but could not hit the line,
The scent was gone. The field took place
Out of the way of hounds. The pace
Had tailed them out; though four remained;
Sir Peter, on White Rabbit, stained
Red from the brooks, Bill Ridden cheery,
Hugh Colway with his mare dead weary,
The Colonel with Marauder beat.
They turned towards a thud of feet;
Dansey, and then young Cothill came
(His chestnut mare was galloped tame).
"There's Copse a field behind," he said.
"Those last miles put them all to bed.
They're strung along the downs like flies."
Copse and Nob Manor topped the rise.
"Thank God! A check," they said, "at last."

"They cannot own it; you must cast."
Sir Peter said. The soft horn blew,
Tom turned the hounds upwind. They drew
Upwind, downhill, by spinney-side.
They tried the brambled ditch; they tried
The swamp, all choked with bright green grass
And clumps of rush, and pools like glass,
Long since the dead men's drinking pond.
They tried the white-leaved oak beyond,
But no hound spoke to it or feathered.
The horse-heads drooped like horses tethered,
The men mopped brows. "An hour's hard run.
Ten miles," they said, "we must have done.
It 's all of six from Colston's Gorses."
The lucky got their second horses.

The time ticked by. "He's lost," they muttered.
A pheasant rose. A rabbit scuttered.
Men mopped their scarlet cheeks and drank.
They drew downwind along the bank
(The Wan Way) on the hill's south spur,
Grown with dwarf oak and juniper,

Like dwarves alive, but no hound spoke.
The seepings made the ground one soak.
They turned the spur; the hounds were beat.
Then Robin shifted in his seat
Watching for signs, but no signs showed.
"I'll lift across the Godsdown Road
Beyond the spinney," Robin said.
Tom turned them; Robin went ahead.

Beyond the copse a great grass fallow
Stretched towards Stoke and Cheddesdon Mallow,
A rolling grass where hounds grew keen.
"Yoi doit, then! This is where he's been."
Said Robin, eager at their joy.
"Yooi, Joyful, lad! Yooi, Cornerboy!
They're on to him."
                        At his reminders
The keen hounds hurried to the finders.
The finding hounds began to hurry,
Men jammed their hats, prepared to scurry.
The "Ai, Ai," of the cry began,
Its spirit passed to horse amd man;
The skirting hounds romped to the cry.
Hound after hound cried "Ai, Ai, Ai,"
Till all were crying, running, closing,
Their heads well up and no heads nosing.
Joyful ahead with spear-straight stern
They raced the great slope to the burn.
Robin beside them. Tom behind
Pointing past Robin down the wind.

For there, two furlongs on, he viewed
On Holy Hill or Cheddesdon Rood,
Just where the ploughland joined the grass,
A speck down the first furrow pass,
A speck the colour of the plough.
"Yonder he goes. We'll have him now,"
He cried. The speck passed slowly on,
It reached the ditch, paused, and was gone.

Then down the slope and up the Rood
Went the hunt's gallop. Godsdown Wood
Dropped its last oak-leaves at the rally.
Over the Rood to High Clench Valley
The gallop led: the redcoats scattered,

The fragments of the hunt were tattered
Over five fields, ev'n since the check.
"A dead fox or a broken neck,"
Said Robin Dawe. "Come up, the Dane."
The hunter lent against the rein,
Cocking his ears; he loved to see
The hounds at cry. The hounds and he
The chiefs in all that feast of pace.

The speck in front began to race.

The fox heard hounds get on to his line,
And again the terror went down his spine;
Again the back of his neck felt cold,
From the sense of the hounds' teeth taking hold.
But his legs were rested, his heart was good,
He had breath to gallop to Mourne End Wood;
It was four miles more, but an earth at end,
So he put on pace down the Rood Hill Bend.

Down the great grass slope which the oak-trees dot,
With a swerve to the right from the keeper's cot,
Over High Clench Brook in its channnel deep
To the grass beyond, where he ran to sheep.

The sheep formed line like a troop of horse,
They swerved, as he passed, to front his course.
From behind, as he ran, a cry arose:
"See the sheep there. Watch them. There he goes!"

He ran the sheep that their smell might check
The hounds from his scent and save his neck,
But in two fields more he was made aware
That the hounds still ran; Tom had viewed him there.

Tom had held them on through the taint of sheep;
They had kept his line, as they meant to keep.
They were running hard with a burning scent,
And Robin could see which way he went.
The pace that he went brought strain to breath,
He knew as he ran that the grass was death.

He ran the slope towards Morton Tew
That the heave of the hill might stop the view,
Then he doubled down to the Blood Brook red,

And swerved upstream in the brook's deep bed.
He splashed the shallows, he swam the deeps,
He crept by banks as a moorhen creeps;
He heard the hounds shoot over his line,
And go on, on, on, towards Cheddesdon Zine.

In the minute's peace he could slacken speed,
The ease from the strain was sweet indeed.
Cool to the pads the water flowed.
He reached the bridge on the Cheddesdon Road.

As he came to light from the culvert dim
Two boys on the bridge looked down on him;
They were young Bill Ripple and Harry Meun;
"Look, there be squirrel, a-swimmin', see 'un?"

"Noa, ben't a squirrel, be fox, be fox.
Now, Hal, get pebble, we'll give 'en socks."
"Get pebble, Billy, dub 'un a plaster;
There's for thy belly, I'll learn 'ee master."

The stones splashed spray in the fox's eyes,
He raced from brook in a burst of shies,
He ran for the reeds in the withy car,
Where the dead flags shake and wild-duck are.

He pushed through the reeds, which cracked at his passing,
To the High Clench Water, a grey pool glassing;
He heard Bill Ripple, in Cheddesdon Road,
Shout, "This way, huntsmen, it 's here he goed."

Then "Leu, Leu, Leu," went the soft horn's laughter,
The hounds (they had checked) came romping after;
The clop of the hooves on the road was plain,
Then the crackle of reeds, then cries again.

A whimpering first, then Robin's cheer,
Then the "Ai, Ai, Ai"; they were all too near,
His swerve had brought but a minute's rest;
Now he ran again, and he ran his best.

With a crackle of dead dry stalks of reed
The hounds came romping at topmost speed;
The redcoats ducked as the great hooves skittered
The Blood Brook's shallows to sheets that glittered;

With a cracking whip and a "Hoik, Hoik, Hoik,
Forrard!" Tom galloped. Bob shouted "Yoick!"
Like a running fire the dead reeds crackled;
The hounds' heads lifted, their necks were hackled.
Tom cried to Bob, as they thundered through,
"He is running short, we shall kill at Tew."
Bob cried to Tom as they rode in team,
"I was sure, that time, that he turned upstream.
As the hounds went over the brook in stride
I saw old Daffodil fling to side,
So I guessed at once, when they checked beyond."

The ducks flew up from the Morton Pond;
The fox looked up at their tailing strings,
He wished (perhaps) that a fox had wings.
Wings with his friends in a great V straining
The autumn sky when the moon is gaining;
For better the grey sky's solitude
Than to be two miles from the Mourne End Wood
With the hounds behind, clean-trained to run,
And your strength half spent and your breath half done.
Better the reeds and the sky and water
Than that hopeless pad from a certain slaughter.
At the Morton Pond the fields began—
Long Tew's green meadows; he ran, he ran.

First the six green fields that make a mile,
With the lip-ful Clench at the side the while,
With rooks above, slow-circling, showing
The world of men where a fox was going;
The fields all empty, dead grass, bare hedges,
And the brook's bright gleam in the dark of sedges.
To all things else he was dumb and blind;
He ran with the hounds a field behind.

At the sixth green field came the long slow climb
To the Mourne End Wood, as old as time;
Yew woods dark, where they cut for bows,
Oak woods green with the mistletoes,
Dark woods evil, but burrowed deep
With a brock's earth strong, where a fox might sleep.
He saw his point on the heaving hill,
He had failing flesh and a reeling will;
He felt the heave of the hill grow stiff,
He saw black woods, which would shelter—if

Nothing else, but the steepening slope
And a black line nodding, a line of hope—
The line of the yews on the long slope's brow,
A mile, three-quarters, a half-mile now.

A quarter-mile, but the hounds had viewed;
They yelled to have him this side the wood.
Robin capped them. Tom Dansey steered them;
With a "Yooi! Yooi! Yooi!" Bill Ridden cheered them.
Then up went hackles as Shatterer led.
"Mob him!" cried Ridden, "the wood's ahead.
Turn him, dam it! Yooi! beauties, beat him,
O God, let them get him; let them eat him!
O God!" said Ridden, "I'll eat him stewed,
If you'll let us get him this side the wood."

But the pace, uphill, made a horse like stone;
The pack went wild up the hill alone.

Three hundred yards and the worst was past,
The slope was gentler and shorter-grassed;
The fox saw the bulk of the woods grow tall
On the brae ahead, like a barrier-wall.
He saw the skeleton trees show sky
And the yew-trees darken to see him die,
And the line of the woods go reeling black:
There was hope in the woods—and behind, the pack.

Two hundred yards and the trees grew taller,
Blacker, blinder, as hope grew smaller;
Cry seemed nearer, the teeth seemed gripping,
Pulling him back; his pads seemed slipping.
He was all one ache, one gasp, one thirsting,
Heart on his chest-bones, beating, bursting;
The hounds were gaining like spotted pards,
And the wood hedge still was a hundred yards.

The wood hedge black was a two-year, quick
Cut-and-laid that had sprouted thick
Thorns all over and strongly plied.
With a clean red ditch on the take-off side.

He saw it now as a redness, topped
With a wattle of thorn-work spiky cropped,
Spiky to leap on, stiff to force,

No safe jump for a failing horse;
But beyond it darkness of yews together,
Dark green plumes over soft brown feather.

Darkness of woods where scents were blowing—
Strange scents, hot scents, of wild things going,
Scents that might draw these hounds away.
So he ran, ran, ran to that clean red clay.

Still, as he ran, his pads slipped back,
All his strength seemed to draw the pack,
The trees drew over him dark like Norns,
He was over the ditch and at the thorns.

He thrust at the thorns, which would not yield;
He leaped, but fell, in sight of the field.
The hounds went wild as they saw him fall,
The fence stood stiff like a Bucks flint wall.

He gathered himself for a new attempt;
His life before was an old dream dreamt,
All that he was was a blown fox quaking,
Jumping at thorns too stiff for breaking,
While over the grass in crowd, in cry,
Came the grip teeth grinning to make him die,
The eyes intense, dull, smouldering red,
The fell like a ruff round each keen head,
The pace like fire, and scarlet men
Galloping, yelling, "Yooi, eat him, then!"

He gathered himself, he leaped, he reached
The top of the hedge like a fish-boat beached.
He steadied a second and then leaped down
To the dark of the wood where bright things drown.

He swerved, sharp right, under young green firs.
Robin called on the Dane with spurs.
He cried, "Come, Dansey; if God's not good,
We shall change our fox in this Mourne End Wood."
Tom cried back as he charged like spate,
"Mine can't jump that, I must ride to gate."
Robin answered, "I'm going at him.
I'll kill that fox, if it kills me, drat him!
We'll kill in covert. Gerr on, now, Dane."
He gripped him tight and he made it plain,

He slowed him down till he almost stood,
While his hounds went crash into Mourne End Wood.

Like a dainty dancer, with footing nice
The Dane turned side for a leap in twice.
He cleared the ditch to the red clay bank,
He rose at the fence as his quarters sank,
He barged the fence as the bank gave way,
And down he came in a fall of clay.

Robin jumped off him and gasped for breath.
He said, "That's lost him as sure as death.
They've overrun him. Come up, the Dane.
We'll kill him yet, if we ride to Spain."

He scrambled up to his horse's back,
He thrust through cover, he called his pack;
He cheered them on till they made it good,
Where the fox had swerved inside the wood.

The fox knew well as he ran the dark,
That the headlong hounds were past their mark;
They had missed his swerve and had overrun,
But their devilish play was not yet done.

For a minute he ran and heard no sound,
Then a whimper came from a questing hound,
Then a "This way, beauties," and then "Leu, Leu,"
The floating laugh of the horn that blew.
Then the cry again, and the crash and rattle
Of the shrubs burst back as they ran to battle,
Till the wood behind seemed risen from root,
Crying and crashing, to give pursuit,
Till the trees seemed hounds and the air seemed cry,
And the earth so far that he needs must die,
Die where he reeled in the woodland dim,
With a hound's white grips in the spine of him.
For one more burst he could spurt, and then
Wait for the teeth, and the wrench, and men.

He made his spurt for the Mourne End rocks
The air blew rank with the taint of fox.
The yews gave way to a greener space
Of great stone strewn in a grassy place.
And there was his earth at the great grey shoulder

Sunk in the ground, of a granite boulder.
A dry, deep burrow with rocky roof,
Proof against crowbars, terrier-proof,
Life to the dying, rest for bones.

The earth was stopped; it was filled with stones.

Then, for a moment, his courage failed,
His eyes looked up as his body quailed,
Then the coming of death, which all things dread,
Made him run for the wood ahead.

The taint of fox was rank on the air,
He knew, as he ran, there were foxes there.
His strength was broken, his heart was bursting,
His bones were rotten, his throat was thirsting;
His feet were reeling, his brush was thick
From dragging the mud, and his brain was sick.

He thought as he ran of his old delight
In the wood in the moon in an April night,
His happy hunting, his winter loving,
The smells of things in the midnight roving,
The look of his dainty-nosing, red,
Clean-felled dam with her footpad's tread;
Of his sire, so swift, so game, so cunning,
With craft in his brain and power of running;
Their fights of old when his teeth drew blood,
Now he was sick, with his coat all mud.

He crossed the covert, he crawled the bank,
To a meuse in the thorns, and there he sank,
With his ears flexed back and his teeth shown white,
In a rat's resolve for a dying bite.

And there, as he lay, he saw the vale,
That a struggling sunlight silvered pale:
The Deerlip Brook like a strip of steel,
The Nun's Wood Yews where the rabbits squeal,
The great grass square of the Roman Fort,
And the smoke in the elms at Crendon Court.

And above the smoke in the elm-tree tops
Was the beech-clump's blur, Blown Hilcote Copse,

Where he and his mates had long made merry
In the bloody joys of the rabbit-herry.

And there as he lay and looked, the cry
Of the hounds at head came rousing by;
He bent his bones in the blackthorn dim.

But the cry of the hounds was not for him.
Over the fence with a crash they went,
Belly to grass, with a burning scent;
Then came Dansey, yelling to Bob:
"They've changed! Oh, damn it! now here's a job."
And Bob yelled back: "Well, we cannot turn 'em,
It's Jumper and Antic, Tom, we'll learn 'em!
We must just go on, and I hope we kill."
They followed hounds down the Mourne End hill.

The fox lay still in the rabbit meuse,
On the dry brown dust of the plumes of yews.
In the bottom below a brook went by,
Blue, in a patch, like a streak of sky.
There one by one, with a clink of stone,
Came a red or dark coat on a horse half-blown.
And man to man with a gasp for breath
Said: "Lord, what a run! I'm fagged to death."

After an hour no riders came,
The day drew by like an ending game;
The robin sang from a puft red breast,
The fox lay quiet and took his rest.
A wren on a tree-stump carolled clear,
Then the starlings wheeled in a sudden sheer,
The rooks came home to the twiggy hive
In the elm tree tops which the winds do drive.
Then the noise of the rooks fell slowly still,
And the lights came out in the Clench Brook Mill;
Then a pheasant cocked, then an owl began,
With the cry that curdles the blood of man.

The stars grew bright as the yews grew black,
The fox rose stiffly and stretched his back.
He flaired the air, then he padded out
To the valley below him, dark as doubt,
Winter-thin with the young green crops,
For old Cold Crendon and Hilcote Copse.

As he crossed the meadows at Naunton Larking
The dogs in the town all started barking,
For with feet all bloody and flanks all foam,
The hounds and the hunt were limping home;
Limping home in the dark dead-beaten,
The hounds all rank from a fox they'd eaten.
Dansey saying to Robin Dawe:
"The fastest and longest I ever saw."
And Robin answered: "Oh, Tom, 'twas good!
I thought they'd changed in the Mourne End Wood,
But now I feel that they did not change.
We've had a run that was great and strange;
And to kill in the end, at dusk, on grass!
We'll turn to the Cock and take a glass,
For the hounds, poor souls! are past their forces;
And a gallon of ale for our poor horses,
And some bits of bread for the hounds, poor things!
After all they've done (for they've done like kings)
Would keep them going till we get in.
We had it alone from Nun's Wood Whin."
Then Tom replied: "If they changed or not,
There've been few runs longer and none more hot,
We shall talk of to-day until we die."

The stars grew bright in the winter sky,
The wind came keen with a tang of frost,
The brook was troubled for new things lost,
The copse was happy for old things found,
The fox came home and he went to ground.

And the hunt came home and the hounds were fed,
They climbed to their bench and went to bed;
The horses in stable loved their straw.
"Good-night, my beauties," said Robin Dawe.

Then the moon came quiet and flooded full
Light and beauty on clouds like wool,
On a feasted fox at rest from hunting,
In the beech-wood grey where the brocks were grunting.

The beech-wood grey rose dim in the night
With moonlight fallen in pools of light,
The long dead leaves on the ground were rimed;
A clock struck twelve and the church-bells chimed.

THE LEMMINGS

Once in a hundred years the Lemmings come
Westward, in search of food, over the snow;
Westward until the salt sea drowns them dumb;
Westward, till all are drowned, those Lemmings go.

Once, it is thought, there was a westward land
(Now drowned) where there was food for those starved things,
And memory of the place has burnt its brand
In the little brains of all the Lemming kings.

Perhaps, long since, there was a land beyond
Westward from death, some city, some calm place
Where one could taste God's quiet and be fond
With the little beauty of a human face;

But now the land is drownèd. Yet still we press
Westward, in search, to death, to nothingness.

ON GROWING OLD

Be with me, Beauty, for the fire is dying;
My dog and I are old, too old for roving.
Man, whose young passion sets the spindrift flying,
Is soon too lame to march, too cold for loving.
I take the book and gather to the fire,
Turning old yellow leaves; minute by minute
The clock ticks to my heart. A withered wire,
Moves a thin ghost of music in the spinet.
I cannot sail your seas, I cannot wander
Your cornland, nor your hill-land, nor your valleys
Ever again, nor share the battle yonder
Where the young knight the broken squadron rallies.
Only stay quiet while my mind remembers
The beauty of fire from the beauty of embers.

Beauty, have pity! for the strong have power,
The rich their wealth, the beautiful their grace,
Summer of man its sunlight and its flower,
Spring-time of man all April in a face.
Only, as in the jostling in the Strand,
Where the mob thrusts or loiters or is loud,
The beggar with the saucer in his hand

Asks only a penny from the passing crowd,
So, from this glittering world with all its fashion,
Its fire, and play of men, its stir, its march,
Let me have wisdom, Beauty, wisdom and passion,
Bread to the soul, rain where the summers parch.
Give me but these, and, though the darkness close
Even the night will blossom as the rose.

KING COLE

King Cole was King before the troubles came,
The land was happy while he held the helm.
The valley-land from Condicote to Thame,
Watered by Thames and green with many an elm.
For many a year he governed well his realm,
So well-beloved, that, when at last he died,
It was bereavement to the countryside.

So good, so well-beloved, had he been
In life, that when he reached the judging-place
(There where the scales are even, the sword keen),
The Acquitting Judges granted him a grace,
Aught he might choose, red, black, from king to ace,
Beneath the bright arch of the heaven's span;
He chose, to wander earth, the friend of man.

So, since that time, he wanders shore and shire
An old, poor, wandering man, with glittering eyes,
Helping distressful folk to their desire
By power of spirit that within him lies.
Gentle he is, and quiet, and most wise,
He wears a ragged grey, he sings sweet words,
And where he walks there flutter little birds.

And when the planets glow as dusk begins
He pipes a wooden flute to music old.
Men hear him on the downs, in lonely inns,
In valley woods, or up the Chiltern wold;
His piping feeds the starved and warms the cold,
It gives the beaten courage; to the lost
It brings back faith, that lodestar of the ghost.

And most he haunts the beech-tree-pasturing chalk,
The Downs and Chilterns with the Thames between.

There still the Berkshire shepherds see him walk,
Searching the unhelped woe with instinct keen,
His old hat stuck with never-withering green,
His flute in poke, and little singings sweet
Coming from birds that flutter at his feet.

Not long ago a circus wandered there,
Where good King Cole most haunts the public way,
Coming from Reading for St. Giles's Fair
Through rain unceasing since Augustine's Day;
The horses spent, the waggons splashed with clay,
The men with heads bowed to the wester roaring,
Heaving the van-wheels up the hill at Goring.

Wearily plodding up the hill they went,
Broken by bitter weather and the luck,
Six vans, and one long waggon with the tent,
And piebald horses following in the muck,
Dragging their tired hooves out with a suck,
And heaving on, like some defeated tribe
Bound for Despair with Death upon their kibe.

All through the morn the circus floundered thus,
The nooning found them at the Crossing Roads,
Stopped by an axle splitting in its truss.
The horses drooped and stared before their loads,
Dark with the wet they were, and cold as toads,
The men were busy with the foundered van,
The showman stood apart, a beaten man.

He did not heed the dripping of the rain,
Nor the wood's roaring, nor the blotted hill,
He stood apart and bit upon his pain,
Biting the bitter meal with bitter will.
Focussed upon himself, he stood, stock still,
Staring unseeing, while his mind repeated,
"This is the end; I'm ruined; I'm defeated."

From time to time a haggard woman's face
Peered at him from a van, and then withdrew;
Seeds from the hayrack blew about the place,
The smoke out of the waggon chimneys blew,
From wicker creel the skinny cockerel crew.
The men who set the foundered axle straight
Glanced at their chief, and each man nudged his mate.

213

And one, the second clown, a snub-nosed youth,
Fair-haired, with broken teeth, discoloured black,
Muttered, "He looks a treat, and that's the truth.
I've had enough: I've given him the sack."
He took his wrench, arose, and stretched his back,
Swore at a piebald pony trying to bite,
And rolled a cigarette and begged a light.

Within, the second's wife, who leaped the hoops,
Nursed sour twins, her son and jealousy,
Thinking of love, in luckier, happier troupes
Known on the roads in summers now gone by
Before her husband had a roving eye,
Before the rat-eyed baggage with red hair
Came to do tight rope and make trouble there.

Beside the vans, the clown, old Circus John,
Growled to the juggler as he sucked his briar,
"How all the marrow of a show was gone
Since women came, to sing and walk the wire,
Killing the clown his act for half his hire,
Killing the circus trade: because," said he,
"Horses and us are what men want to see."

The juggler was a young man shaven-clean,
Even in the mud his dainty way he had,
Red-cheeked, with eyes like boxer's, quick and keen,
A jockey-looking youth with legs besprad,
Humming in baritone a ditty sad,
And tapping on his teeth his finger-nails,
The while the clown sucked pipe and spat his tales.

Molly, the singer, watched him wearily
With big black eyes that love had brimmed with tears,
Her mop of short cut hair was blown awry,
Her firm mouth showed her wiser than her years.
She stroked a piebald horse and pulled his ears,
And kissed his muzzle, while her eyes betrayed
This, that she loved the juggler, not the jade.

And growling in a group the music stood
Sucking short pipes, their backs against the rain,
Plotting rebellion in a bitter mood,

"A shilling more, or never play again."
Their old great coats were foul with many a stain,
Weather and living rough had stamped their faces,
They were cast clerks, old sailors, old hard cases.

Within the cowboy's van the rat-eyed wife,
Her reddish hair in papers twisted close,
Turned wet potatoes round against the knife,
And in a bucket dropped the peelèd Oes.
Her little girl was howling from her blows,
The cowboy smoked, and with a spanner whacked
The metal target of his shooting act.

And in another van more children cried
From being beaten or for being chid
By fathers cross or mothers haggard-eyed,
Made savage by the fortunes that betid.
The rain dripped from the waggons: the drops glid
Along the pony's flanks; the thick boots stamped
The running much for warmth, and hope was damped.

Yet all of that small troupe in misery stuck,
Were there by virtue of their nature's choosing
To be themselves and take the season's luck,
Counting the being artists worth the bruising.
To be themselves, as artists, even if losing
Wealth, comfort, health, in doing as they chose,
Alone of all life's ways brought peace to those.

So there below the forlorn woods, they grumbled,
Stamping for warmth and shaking off the rain.
Under the foundered van the tinkers fumbled,
Fishing the splitted truss with wedge and chain.
Soon, all was done, the van could go again,
Men cracked their whips, the horses' shoulders forged
Up to the collar while the mud disgorged.

So with a jangling of their chains they went,
Lean horses, swaying vans and creaking wheels,
Bright raindrops tilting off the van roof pent
And reedy cockerels crying in the creels,
Smoke driving down, men's shouts and children's squeals,
Whips cracking, and the hayrack sheddings blowing;
The showman stood aside to watch them going.

215

What with the rain misery making mad,
The showman never saw a stranger come
Till there he stood, a stranger roughly clad
In ragged grey of woollen spun at home.
Green sprigs were in his hat, and other some
Stuck in his coat; he bore a wooden flute,
And redbreasts hopped and carolled at his foot.

It was King Cole, who smiled and spoke to him.

King Cole. The van will hold until you reach a wright.
Where do you play?
The Showman. In Wallingford to-night.
King Cole. There are great doings there.
The Showman. I know of none.
King Cole. The Prince will lay the Hall's foundation stone
This afternoon: he and the Queen are there.
The Showman. Lord, keep this showman patient, lest he swear.
King Cole. Why should you swear? Be glad; your town is filled.
The Showman. What use are crowds to me with business killed?
King Cole. I see no cause for business to be crossed.
The Showman. Counter-attractions man at public cost.
Fireworks, dancing, bonfires, soldiers, speeches.
In all my tour along the river's reaches
I've had ill-luck: I've clashed with public feasts.
At Wycombe fair, we met performing beasts,
At Henley, waxworks, and at Maidenhead
The Psyche woman talking with the dead.
At Bray, we met the rain, at Reading, flood,
At Pangbourne, politics, at Goring, mud,
Now here, at Wallingford, the Royal Pair.
Counter-attraction killing everywhere,
Killing a circus dead: God give me peace;
If this be living, death will be release.
By God, it brims the cup; it fills the can.
What trade are you?
King Cole.   I am a wandering man.
The Showman. You mean, a tramp who flutes for bread and
   pence?
King Cole. I come, and flute, and then I wander thence.
The Showman. Quicksilver Tom who couldn't keep his place.
King Cole. My race being run, I love to watch the race.
The Showman. You ought to seek your rest.
King Cole.   My rest is this,
The world of men, wherever trouble is.

The Showman. If trouble rest you, God! your life is rest.
King Cole. Even the sun keeps moving, east to west.
The Showman. Little he gets by moving; less than I.
King Cole. He sees the great green world go floating by.
The Showman. A sorry sight to see, when all is said.
Why don't you set to work?
King Cole.   I have no trade.
The Showman. Where is your home?
King Cole.   All gone, a long time past.
The Showman. Your children, then?
King Cole.   All dead, sir, even the last.
I am a lonely man; no kith nor kin.
The Showman. There is no joy in life when deaths begin,
I know it, I. How long is't since you ate?
King Cole. It was so long ago that I forget.

The Showman. The proverb says a man can always find
One sorrier than himself in state and mind.
'Fore George, it's true. Well, come, then, to the van.
Jane, can you find a meal for this poor man?

"Yes," said his wife. "Thank God, we still are able
To help a friend; come in, and sit to table."
"Come," said her man, "I'll help you up aboard,
I'll save your legs as far as Wallingford."

They climbed aboard and sat; the woman spread
Food for King Cole, and watched him as he fed.
Tears trickled down her cheeks and much she sighed.
"My son," she said, "like you, is wandering wide,
I know not where; a beggar on the street
(For all I know), without a crust to eat,
He never could abide the circus life."

The Showman. It was my fault, I always tell my wife
I put too great constraint upon his will;
Things would be changed if he were with us still.
I ought not to have forced him to the trade.
King Cole. "A forced thing finds a vent," my father said;
And yet a quickening tells me that you son
Is not far from you now; for I am one
Who feels these things, like comfort in the heart.

The couple watched King Cole and shrank apart,
For brightness covered him with glittering.

217

"Tell me your present troubles," said the King,
"For you are worn. What sorrow makes you sad?"

The Showman. Why, nothing, sir, except that times are bad,
Rain all the season through, and empty tents,
And nothing earned for stock or winter rents.
My wife there, ill, poor soul, from very grief,
And now no hope nor prospect of relief;
The season's done, and we're as we began.

Now one can bear one's troubles, being a man,
But what I cannot bear is loss of friends.
This troupe will scatter when the season ends:
My clown is going, and the Tricksey Three,
Who juggle and do turns, have split with me;
And now, to-day, my wife's too ill to dance,
And all my music ask for an advance.
There must be poison in a man's distress
That makes him mad and people like him less.

Well, men are men. But what I cannot bear
Is my poor Bet, my piebald Talking Mare,
Gone curby in her hocks from standing up.
That's the last drop that overfills the cup.
My Bet's been like a Christian friend for years.

King Cole. Now courage, friend, no good can come from tears.
I know a treatment for a curby hock
Good both for inward sprain or outward knock.
Here's the receipt; it's sure as flowers in spring;
A certain cure, the Ointment of the King.

That cures your mare; your troubles Time will right;
A man's ill-fortune passes like the night.
Times are already mending at their worst;
Think of Spent Simmy when his roof-beam burst.
His ruined roof fell on him in a rain
Of hidden gold that built it up again.
So, courage, and believe God's providence.
Lo, here, the city shining like new pence,
To welcome you; the Prince is lodging there.
Lo, you, the banners flying like a fair.
Your circus will be crowded twenty deep.
This city is a field for you to reap,
For thousands must have come to see the Prince,

218

And all are here, all wanting fun. And since
The grass was green, all men have loved a show.
Success is here, so let your trouble go.
The Showman. Well, blessings on your heart for speaking so;
It may be that the tide will turn at last.
But royal tours have crossed me in the past
And killed my show, and maybe will again.
One hopes for little after months of rain,
And the little that one hopes one does not get.
The Wife. Look, Will, the city gates with sentries set.
The Showman. It looks to me as if the road were barred.
King Cole. They are some soldiers of the bodyguard.
I hope, the heralds of your fortune's change.

"Now take this frowsy circus off the range,"
The soldiers at the city entrance cried;
"Keep clear the town, you cannot pass inside,
The Prince is here, with other things to do
Than stare at gangs of strollers such as you."

The Showman. But I am billed to play here; and must play.
The Soldiers. No must at all. You cannot play to-day,
Nor pitch your tents within the city bound.
The Showman. Where can I, then?
The Soldiers.   Go, find some other ground.
A Policeman. Pass through the city. You can pitch and play
One mile beyond it, after five to-day.
The Showman. One mile beyond, what use is that to me?
A Policeman. Those are the rules, here printed, you can see.
The Showman. But let me see the Mayor, to make sure.
The Soldiers. These are his printed orders, all secure.
Pass through or back, you must not linger here,
Blocking the road with all this circus gear.
Which will you do, then; back or pass along?
The Showman. Pass.
The Soldiers. Then away, and save your breath for song.
We cannot bother with your right and wrong.
George, guide these waggons through the western gate.
Now, march d'ye hear? and do not stop to bait
This side a mile; for that's the order. March!

The Showman toppled like a broken arch.
The line squall roared upon them with loud lips.

A green-lit strangeness followed, like eclipse

219

They passed within, but, when within, King Cole
Slipped from the van to head the leading team.
He breathed into his flute his very soul,
A noise like waters in a pebbly stream,
And straight the spirits that inhabit dream
Came round him, and the rain-squall roared its last,
And bright the wind-vane shifted as it passed.

And in the rush of sun and glittering cloud
That followed on the storm, he led the way,
Fluting the sodden circus through the crowd
That trod the city streets in holiday.
And lo, a marvellous thing, the gouted clay
Splashed on the waggons and the horses, glowed,
They shone like embers as they trod the road.

And round the tired horses came the Powers
That stir men's spirits, waking or asleep,
To thoughts like planets and to acts like flowers,
Out of the inner wisdom's beauty deep:
These led the horses, and, as marshalled sheep
Fronting a dog, in line, the people stared
At those bright waggons led by the bright-haired.

And, as they marched, the spirits sang, and all
The horses crested to the tune and stepped
Like centaurs to a passionate festival
With shining throats that mantling criniers swept
And all the hearts of all the watchers leapt
To see those horses passing and to hear
That song that came like blessing to the ear.

And, to the crowd the circus artists seemed
Splendid, because the while that singing quired
Each artist was the part that he had dreamed
And glittered with the Power he desired,
Women and men, no longer wet or tired
From long despair, now shone like queens and kings,
There they were crowned with their imaginings.

And with them, walking by the vans, there came
The wild things from the woodland and the mead,
The red stag, with his tender-stepping dame,
Branched, and high-tongued and ever taking heed.
Nose-wrinkling rabbits nibbling at the weed,

220

The hares that box by moonlight on the hill,
The bright trout's death, the otter from the mill.

There, with his mask made virtuous, came the fox,
Talking of landscape while he thought of meat;
Blood-loving weasels, honey-harrying brocks,
Stoats, and the mice that build among the wheat.
Dormice, and moles with little hands for feet,
The water-rat that gnaws the yellow flag,
Toads from the stone and merrows from the quag.

And over them flew birds of every kind,
Whose way, or song, or speed, or beauty brings
Delight and understanding to the mind;
The bright-eyed, feathery, thready-leggèd things.
There they, too, sang amid a rush of wings,
With sweet clear cries and gleams from wing and crest
Blue, scarlet, white, gold plume and speckled breast.

And all the vans seemed grown with living leaves
And living flowers, the best September knows,
Moist poppies scarlet from the Hilcote sheaves,
Green-fingered bine that runs the barley-rows,
Pale candylips, and those intense blue blows
That trail the porches in the autumn dusk,
Tempting the noiseless moth to tongue their musk.

So, tired thus, so tended, and so sung,
They crossed the city through the marvelling crowd.
Maids with wide eyes from upper windows hung,
The children waved their toys and sang aloud.
But in his van the beaten showman bowed
His head upon his hands, and wept, not knowing
Aught of what passed except that wind was blowing.

All through the town the fluting led them on,
But near the western gate King Cole retired;
And, as he ceased, the vans no longer shone,
The bright procession dimmed like lamps expired;
Again with muddy vans and horses tired,
And artists cross and women out of luck,
The sodden circus plodded through the muck.

The crowd of following children loitered home;
Maids shut the windows lest more rain should come:

The circus left the streets of flowers and flags,
King Cole walked with it, huddling in his rags.
They reached the western gate and sought to pass.

"Take back this frowsy show to where it was,"
The sergeant of the gateway-sentry cried;
"You know quite well you cannot pass outside."

The Showman. But we were told to pass here, by the guard.
The Sergeant. Here are the printed orders on the card.
No traffic, you can read. Clear out.
The Showman.   But where?
The Sergeant. Where you're not kicked from, or there's room
    to spare.
Go back and out of town the way you came.
The Showman. I've just been sent from there. Is this a game?
The Sergeant. You'll find it none, my son, if that's your tone.
The Showman. You redcoats; ev'n your boots are not your own.
The Sergeant. No, they're the Queen's; I represent the Queen.
The Showman. Pipeclay your week's account, you red marine.
The Sergeant. Thank you, I will. Now vanish. Right about,
The Showman. Right, kick the circus in or kick it out.
But kick us, kick us hard, we've got no friends,
We've no Queen's boots or busbies on our ends;
We're poor, we like it, no one cares; besides,
These dirty artists ought to have thick hides.
The dust, like us, is fit for boots to stamp,
None but Queen's redcoats are allowed to camp
In this free country.
A Policeman.   What's the trouble here?
The Showman. A redcoat, sadly needing a thick ear.
The Policeman. The show turned back? No, sergeant, let them
    through.
They can't turn back, because the Prince is due.
Best let them pass.
The Sergeant.   Then pass; and read the rules
Another time.
The Showman. You fat, red-coated fools.
The Policeman. Pass right along.

                    They passed. Beyond the town
A farmer gave them leave to settle down
In a green field beside the Oxford road.
There the spent horses ceased to drag the load;
The tent was pitched beneath a dropping sky,

The green-striped tent with all its gear awry.
The men drew close to grumble: in the van
The showman parted from the wandering man.

The Showman. You see; denied a chance; denied bare bread.
King Cole. I know the stony road that artists tread.
The Showman. You take it very mildly, if you do.
How would you act if this were done to you?
King Cole. Go to the mayor.
The Showman.   I am not that kind.
I'll kneel to no Court prop with painted rind.
You and your snivelling to them may go hang.
I say: "God curse the Prince and all his gang."
The Wife. Ah, no, my dear, for Life hurts every one,
Without our cursing. Let the poor Prince be;
We artist folk are happier folk than he,
Hard as it is.
The Showman. I say: God let him see.
And taste and know this misery that he makes.
He strains a poor man's spirit till it breaks,
And then he hangs him, while a poor man's gift
He leaves unhelped, to wither or to drift.
Sergeants at city gates are all his care.
We are but outcast artists in despair.
They dress in scarlet and he gives them gold.
King Cole. Trust still to Life, the day is not yet old.
The Showman. By God! our lives are all we have to trust.
King Cole. Life changes every day and ever must.
The Showman. It has not changed with us, this season, yet.
King Cole. Life is as just as Death; Life pays its debt.
The Showman. What justice is there in our suffering so?
King Cole. This: that not knowing, we should try to know.
The Showman. Try. A sweet doctrine for a broken heart.
King Cole. The best (men say) in every manly part.
The Showman. Is it, by Heaven? I have tried it, I.
I tell you, friend, your justice is a lie;
Your comfort is a lie, your peace a fraud;
Your trust a folly and your cheer a gaud.
I know what men are, having gone these roads.
Poor bankrupt devils, sweating under loads
While others suck their blood and smile and smile.
You be an artist on the roads awhile,
You'll know what justice comes with suffering then.
King Cole. Friend, I am one grown old with sorrowing men.
The Showman. The old are tamed, they have not blood to feel.

223

King Cole. They've blood to hurt, if not enough to heal.
I have seen sorrow close and suffering close.
I know their ways with men, if any knows.
I know the harshness of the way they have
To loose the base and prison up the brave.
I know that some have found the depth they trod
In deepest sorrow, is the heart of God.
Up on the bitter iron there is peace.
In the dark night of prison comes release,
In the black midnight still the cock will crow.
There is a help that the abandoned know
Deep in the heart, that conquerors cannot feel.
Abide in hope the turning of the wheel,
The luck will alter and the star will rise.

His presence seemed to change before their eyes.
The old, bent, ragged, glittering, wandering fellow,
With thready blood-streaks in the rided yellow
Of cheek and eye, seemed changed to one who held
Earth and the spirit like a king of old.
He spoke again: "You have been kind," said he.
"In your own trouble you have thought of me.
God will repay. To him who gives is given,
Corn, water, wine, th world, the starry heaven."

Then, like a poor old man, he took his way
Back to the city, while the showman gazed
After his figure like a man amazed.

The Wife. I think that traveller was an angel sent.
The Showman. A most strange man, I wonder what he meant.
The Wife. Comfort was what he meant, in our distress.
The Showman. No words of his can make our trouble less.
The Wife. O, Will, he made me feel the luck would change.
Look at him, husband; there is something strange
About him there; a robin redbreast comes
Hopping about his feet as though for crumbs,
And little long-tailed tits and wrens that sing
Perching upon him.
The Showman.   What a wondrous thing!
I've read of such, but never seen it.
The Wife.   Look,
These were the dishes and the food he took.
The Showman. Yes; those were they. What of it?
The Wife.   Did he eat?

224

The Showman. Yes; bread and cheese; he would not touch the
meat.
The Wife. But see, the cheese is whole, the loaf unbroken,
And both are fresh. And see, another token:—
Those hard green apples that the farmer gave
Have grown to these gold globes, like Blenheims brave;
And look, how came these plums of Pershore here?
The Showman. We have been sitting with a saint, my dear.
The Wife. Look at the butterflies!

                       Like floating flowers
Came butterflies, the souls of summer hours,
Fluttering about the van; Red Admirals rich,
Scarlet and pale on breathing speeds of pitch,
Brimstones, like yellow poppy petals blown,
Brown ox-eyed Peacocks in their purpled roan,
Blue, silvered things that haunt the grassy chalk,
Green Hairstreaks bright as green shoots on a stalk,
And that dark prince, the oakwood haunting thing
Dyed with blue burnish like the mallard's wing.

"He was a saint of God," the showman cried.

Meanwhile, within the town, from man to man
The talk about the wondrous circus ran.
All were agreed, that nothing ever known
Had thrilled so tense the marrow in their bone.

All were agreed, that sights so beautiful
Made the Queen's Court with all its soldiers dull,
Made all the red-wrapped masts and papered strings
Seem fruit of death, no lovely living things.
And some said loudly that though time were short,
Men still might hire the circus for the Court.
And some, agreeing, sought the Mayor's hall,
To press petition for the show's recall.

But as they neared the hall, behold, there came
A stranger to them dressed as though in flame;
An old, thin, grinning glitterer, decked with green,
With thready blood-streaks on his visage lean,
And at his wrinkled eyes a look of mirth
Not common among men who walk the earth;
Yet from his pocket poked a flute of wood,
And little birds were following him for food.

"Sirs," said King Cole (for it was he), "I know
You seek the Mayor, but you need not so;
I have this moment spoken with his grace.
He grants the circus warrant to take place
Within the city, should the Prince see fit
To watch such pastime; here is his permit.
I go this instant to the Prince to learn
His wish herein: wait here till I return."

They waited while the old man passed the sentry
Beside the door, and vanished through the entry.
They thought, "This old man shining like New Spain,
Must be the Prince's lordly chamberlain.
His cloth of gold so shone, it seemed to burn;
Wait till he comes." They stayed for his return.

Meanwhile, above, the Prince stood still to bide
The nightly mercy of the eventide,
Brought nearer by each hour that chimed and ceased.
His head was weary with the city feast
But newly risen from. He stood alone
As heavy as the day's foundation stone.

The room he stood in was an ancient hall.
Portraits of long dead men were on the wall.
From the dull crimson of their robes there stared
Passionless eyes, long dead, that judged and glared.
Above them were the oaken corbels set,
Of angels reaching hands that never met,
Where in the spring the swallows came to build.

It was the meeting chamber of the Guild.

From where he stood, the Prince could see a yard
Paved with old slabs and cobbles cracked and scarred
Where weeds had pushed, and tiles and broken glass
Had fallen and been trodden in the grass.
A gutter dripped upon it from the rain.

"It puts a crown of lead upon my brain
To live this life of princes," thought the Prince.
"To be a king is to be like a quince,
Bitter himself, yet flavour to the rest.
To be a cat among the hay were best;

There in the upper darkness of the loft,
With green eyes bright, soft-lying, purring soft,
Hearing the rain without; not forced, as I,
To lay foundation stones until I die,
Or sign State-papers till my hand is sick.
The man who plaits straw crowns upon a rick
Is happier in his crown that I the King;
And yet, this day, a very marvellous thing
Came by me as I walked the chamber here.
Once in my childhood, in my seventh year,
I saw them come, and now they have returned,
Those strangers, riding upon cars that burned,
Or seemed to burn, with gold, while music thrilled,
Then beauty following till my heart was filled,
And life seemed peopled from eternity.

They brought down Beauty and Wisdom from the sky
Into the streets, those strangers; I could see
Beauty and wisdom looking up at me
As then, in childhood, as they passed below.

Men would not let me know them long ago,
Those strangers bringing joy. They will not now.
I am a prince with gold about my brow;
Duty, not joy, is all a prince's share
And yet, those strangers from I know not where,
From glittering lands, from unknown cities far
Beyond the sea-plunge of the evening star,
Would give me life, which princedom cannot give.
They would be revelation: I should live.

I may not deal with Wisdom, being a king."

There came a noise of some one entering;
He turned his weary head to see who came.
It was King Cole, arrayed as though in flame,
Like a white opal glowing from within,
He entered there in snowy cramoisin.
The Prince mistook him for a city lord,
He turned to him and waited for his word.

"Sir," said King Cole, "I come to bring you news.
Sir, in the weary life that princes use
There is scant time for any prince or king

227

To taste delights that artists have and bring.
But here, to-night, no other duty calls,
And circus artists are without the walls.
Will you not see them, sir?"

The Prince. Who are these artists; do they paint or write?
King Cole. No, but they serve the arts and love delight.
The Prince. What can they do?
King Cole.   They know full many a rite
That holds the watcher spell-bound, and they know
Gay plays of ghosts and jokes of long ago;
And beauty of bright speed their horses bring,
Ridden bare-backed at gallop round the ring
By girls who stand upon the racing team.
Jugglers they have, of whom the children dream,
Who pluck live rabbits from between their lips
And balance marbles on their finger-tips.
Will you not see them, sir? And then, they dance.

"Ay," said the Prince, "and thankful for the chance.
So thankful, that these bags of gold shall buy
Leave for all comers to be glad as I.
And yet, I know not if the Court permits.
Kings' pleasures must be sifted throught the wits
Or want of wit of many a courtly brain.
I get the lees and chokings of the drain,
Not the bright rippling that I perish for."

King Cole. Sir, I will open the forbidden door,
Which, opened, they will enter all in haste.
The life of man is stronger than good taste.
The Prince. Custom is stronger than the life of man.
King Cole. Custom is but a way that life began.
The Prince. A withering way that makes the leafage fall.
Custom, like Winter, is the King of all.
King Cole. Winter makes water solid, yet the spring,
That is but flowers, is a stronger thing.
Custom, the ass man rides, will plod for years,
But laughter kills him and he dies at tears.
One word of love, one spark from beauty's fire,
And custom is a memory; listen, sire.

Then at a window looking on the street
He played his flute like leaves or snowflakes falling,
Till men and women, passing, thought: "How sweet;

These notes are in our hearts like flowers falling."
And then, they thought, "An unknown voice is calling
Like April calling to the seed in earth;
Madness is quickening deadness into birth."

And then, as in the spring when first men hear,
Beyond the black-twigged hedge, the lambling's cry
Coming across the snow, a note of cheer
Before the storm-cock tells that spring is nigh,
Before the first green bramble pushes shy,
And all the blood leaps at the lambling's notes,
The piping brought men's hearts into their throats.

Till all were stirred, however old and grand;
Generals bestarred, old statesmen, courtiers prim
(Whose lips kissed nothing but the monarch's hand),
Stirred in their courtly minds' recesses dim,
The sap of life stirred in the dreary limb.
The old eyes brightened o'er the pouncet-box,
Remembering loves, and brawls, and mains of cocks.

And through the town the liquid piping's gladness
Thrilled on its way, rejoicing all who heard,
To thrust aside their dulness or their sadness
And follow blithely as the fluting stirred.
They hurried to the guild like horses spurred.
There in the road they mustered to await,
They knew not what, a dream, a joy, a fate.

And man to man in exaltation cried:
"Something has come to make us young again:
Wisdom has come, and Beauty, Wisdom's bride,
And youth like flowering April after rain."
But still the fluting piped and men were fain
To sing and ring the bells, they knew not why
Save that their hearts were in an ecstasy.

Then to the balcony above them came
King Cole the shining in his robe of flame;
Behind him came the Prince, who smiled and bowed.
King Cole made silence: then addressed the crowd.

"Friends, fellow mortals, bearers of the ghost
That burns, and breaks its lamp, but is not lost,
This day, for one brief hour, a key is given

To all, however poor, to enter heaven.
The Bringers Down of Beauty from the stars
Have reached this city in their golden cars.
They ask, to bring you beauty, if you will.

You do not answer: rightly, you are still.
But you will come, to watch the image move
Of all you dreamed or had the strength to love.
Come to the Ring, the image of the path
That this our planet through the Heaven hath;
Behold man's skill, man's wisdom, man's delight,
And women's beauty, imaged to the height.

Come, for our rulers come; and Death, whose feet
Tread at the door, permits a minute's sweet:
To each man's soul vouchsafes a glimpse, a gleam,
A touch, a breath of his intensest dream.

Now, to that glimpse, that moment, come with me;
Our rulers come.
                    O brother, let there be
Such welcome to our Prince as never was.
Let there be flowers under foot, not grass,
Flowers and scented rushes and the sprays
Of purple bramble reddening into blaze.

Let there be bells rung backward till the tune
Be as the joy of all the bees in June.
Let float your flags, and let your lanterns rise
Like fruit upon the trees in Paradise,
In many-coloured lights as rich as Rome
O'er road and tent; and let the children come,
It is their world, these Beauty Dwellers bring."

Then, like the song of all the birds of spring
He played his flute, and all who heard it cried,
"Strew flowers before our rulers to the Ring."
The courtiers hurried for their coats of pride,
The upturned faces in that market wide
Glowed in the sunset to a beauty grave
Such as the faces of immortals have.

And work was laid aside on desk and bench,
The red-lined ledger summed no penny more,
From lamp-blacked fingers the mechanic's wrench

Dropped to the kinking wheel chains on the floor,
The farmer shut the hen roost: at the store
The boys put up the shutters and ran hooting
Wild with delight in freedom to the fluting.

And now the fluting let that gathered tide
Of men and women forward through the town,
And flowers seemed to fall from every side,
White starry blossoms such as brooks bow down,
White petals clinging in the hair and gown;
And those who marched there thought that starry flowers
Grew at their sides, as though the streets were bowers.

And all, in marching, thought, "We go to see
Life, not the daily coil, but as it is
Lived in its beauty in eternity,
Above base aim, beyond our miseries;
Life that is speed and colour and bright bliss,
And beauty seen and strained for, and possessed
Even as a star forever in the breast."

The fluting led them through the western gate,
From many a tossing torch their faces glowed,
Bright-eyed and ruddy-featured and elate;
They sang and scattered flowers upon the road.
Still in their hair the starry blossoms snowed;
They saw ahead the green-striped tent, their mark,
Lit now and busy in the gathering dark.

There at the vans and in the green-striped tent
The circus artists growled their discontent.
Close to the gate a lighted van there was;
The showman's wife thrust back its window glass
And leaned her head without to see who came
To buy a ticket for the evening's game.

A roll of tickets and a plate of pence
(For change) lay by her as she leaned from thence.
She heard the crowd afar, but in her thought
She said: "That's in the city; it is nought.
They glorify the Queen."

                              Though sick at heart
She wore her spangles for her evening's part.
To dance upon the barebacked horse and sing.

231

Green velvet was her dress, with tinselling.
Her sad, worn face had all the nobleness
That lovely spirits gather from distress.

"No one to-night," she thought, "no one to-night."

Within the tent, a flare gave blowing light.
There, in their scarlet cart, the bandsmen tuned
Bugles that whinnied, flageolets that crooned
And strings that whined and grunted.
                                    Near the band
Piebald and magpie horses stood at hand
Nosing at grass beneath the green-striped dome
While men caressed them with the curry-comb.

The clowns, with whited, raddled faces, heaped
Old horse cloths round them to the chins; they peeped
Above the rugs; their cigarette ends' light
Showing black eyes, and scarlet smears and white.

They watched the empty benches, and the wry
Green curtain door which no one entered by.
Two little children entered and sat still
With bright wide opened eyes that stared their fill,
And red lips round in wonder smeared with tints
From hands and handkerchiefs and peppermints.

A farm lad entered. That was all the house.

"Strike up the band to give the folk a rouse,"
The showman said. "They must be all outside."
He said it boldly, though he knew he lied.

Sad as a funeral march for pleasure gone
The band lamented out, "He's got them on."
Then paused, as usual, for the crowd to come.

Nobody came, though from without a hum
Of instruments and singing slowly rose.
"Free feast, with fireworks and public shows,"
The bandsmen growled. "An empty house again.
Two children and a ploughboy and the rain.
And then a night march through the mud," they said.

Now to the gate, King Cole his piping played.
The showman's wife from out her window peering
Saw, in the road, a crowd with lanterns nearing,
And, just below her perch, a man who shone
As though white flame were his caparison;
One upon whom the great-eyed hawk-moths tense
Settled with feathery feet and quivering sense,
Till the white, gleaming robe seemed stuck with eyes.

It was the grinning glitterer, white and wise,
King Cole, who said, "Madam, the Court is here,
The Court, the Prince, the Queen, all drawing near,
We here, the vanguard, set them on their way.
They come intent to see your circus play.
They ask that all who wish may enter free,
And in their princely hope that this may be
They send you these plump bags of minted gold."
He gave a sack that she could scarcely hold.

She dropped it trembling, muttering thanks, and then
She cried: "O master, I must tell the men."
She rushed out of her van: she reached the Ring;
Called to her husband, "Will, the Queen and King,
Here at the very gate to see the show!"

"Light some more flares," said Will, "to make a glow.
'God save the Queen,' there, bandsmen; lively, boys.
Come on, 'God save our gracious', make a noise.
Here, John, bring on the piebalds to the centre,
We'll have the horses kneeling as they enter."
All sang, and rushed. Without, the trumpets brayed.

Now children, carrying paper lanterns, made
A glowing alley to the circus door;
Then others scattered flowers to pave a floor,
Along the highway leading from the town.
Rust-spotted bracken green they scattered down,
Blue cornflowers and withering poppies red,
Gold charlock, thrift, the purple hardihead,
Harebells, the milfoil white, September clover,
And boughs that berry red when summer's over,
All autumn flowers, with yellow ears of wheat.

Then with bruised, burning gums that made all sweet,
Came censer-bearing pages, and then came

Bearers in white with cressets full of flame,
Whose red tongues made the shadows dance like devils.
Then the blithe flutes that pipe men to the revels
Thrilled to the marrow softly as men marched.
Then, tossing leopard-skins from crests that arched,
The horses of the kettle-drummers stepped.
Then with a glitter of bright steel there swept
The guard of knights, each pennon-bearer bold
Girt in a crimson cloak with spangs of gold.
Then came the Sword and Mace, and then the four
Long silver trumpets thrilling to the core
Of people's hearts their sound. Then two by two,
Proud in caparisons of kingly blue,
Bitted with bars of gold, in silver shod,
Treading like kings, cream-coloured stallions trod.
Dragging the carriage with the Prince and Queen.
The Corporation, walking, closed the scene.
Then came the crowd in-surging like the wave
That closes up the gash the clipper clave.

Swift in the path their majestics would tread
The showman flung green baize and turkey red.
Within the tent, with bunting, ropes and bags
They made a Royal Box festooned with flags.
Even as the Queen arrived, the work was done,
The seven piebald horses kneeled like one,
The bandsmen blew their best, while, red as beet,
The showman bowed his rulers to their seat.

Then, through the door, came courtiers wigged and starred;
The crimson glitterers of the bodyguard;
The ladies of the Court, broad-browed and noble
Lovely as evening stars o'er seas in trouble;
The aldermen, in furs, with golden chains,
Old cottagers in smocks from country lanes,
Shepherds half dumb from silence on the down,
And merchants with their households from the town,
And, in the front, two rows of eager-hearted
Children with shining eyes and red lips parted.

Even as the creeping waves that brim the pool
One following other filled the circus full.

The showman stood beside his trembling wife.
"Never," he said, "in all our travelling life

Has this old tent looked thus, the front seats full
With happy little children beautiful.
Then all this glorious Court, tier after tier!
O would our son, the wanderer, were here,
Then we'd die happy!"
                              "Would he were!" said she,
"It was my preaching forced him to be free,"
The showman said.
                              "Ah, no," his wife replied,
"The great world's glory and the young blood's pride,
Those forced him from us, never you, my dear."
"I would be different if we had him here
Again," the showman said; "but we must start.
But all this splendour takes away my heart,
I am not used to playing to the King."

"Look," said his wife, "the stranger, in the Ring."

There in the Ring indeed, the stranger stood,
King Cole, the shining, with his flute of wood,
Waiting until the chattering Court was stilled.

Then from his wooden flute his piping thrilled,
Till all was tense, and then the leaping fluting
Clamoured as flowering clamours for the fruiting.
And round the Ring came Dodo, the brown mare,
Pied like a tiger-moth; her bright shoes tare
The scattered petals, while the clown came after
Like life, a beauty chased by tragic laughter.
The showman entered in and cracked his whip.

Then followed fun and skill and horsemanship,
Marvellous all, for all were at their best.
Never had playing gone with such a zest
To those good jesters; never had the tent
So swiftly answered to their merriment
With cheers, the artist's help, the actor's life.
Then, at the end, the showman and his wife
Stood at the entrance listening to the cheers.
They were both happy to the brink of tears.

King Cole came close and whispered in their ears:
"There is a soldier here who says he knew
You, long ago, and asks to speak to you.
A sergeant in the guard, a handsome blade."

"Mother!" the sergeant said. "What, Jack!" she said,
"Our son come back! look, father, here's our son."

"Bad pennies do come home to everyone,"
The sergeant said. "And if you'll have me home,
And both forgive me, I'll be glad to come."

"Why, son," the showman said, "the fault was ours."

Now a bright herald trod across the flowers
To bid the artists to the Queen and King,
Who thanked them for the joyful evening,
And shook each artist's hand with words of praise.
"Our happiest hour," they said, "for many days.
You must perform at Court at Christmastide."

They left their box: men flung the curtains wide,
The horses kneeled like one as they withdrew.
They reached the curtained door and loitered through.
The audience, standing, sang, "God save the Queen."
The hour of the showman's life had been.

Now once again a herald crossed the green
To tell the showman that a feast was laid,
A supper for the artists who had played
By the Queen's order, in a tent without.

In the bright moonlight at the gate the rout
Of courtiers, formed procession to be gone,
Others were called, steel clinked, and jewels shone,
The watchers climbed the banks and took their stands.

The circus artists shook each other's hands,
Their quarrels were forgotten and forgiven,
Old friendships were restored and sinners shriven.
"We find we cannot part from Will," they said.

And while they talked, the juggler took the maid
Milly, the singer, to the hawthorn glade
Behind the green-striped tent, and told his love,
A wild delight, beyond her hope, enough
Beyond her dream to brim her eyes with tears.

Now came a ringing cry to march; and cheers
Rose from the crowd; the bright procession fared
Back to the city while the trumpets blared.

So the night ended, and the Court retired.
Back to the town the swaying torches reeked,
Within the green-striped tent the lights expired,
The dew dripped from the canvas where it leaked,
Dark, in the showman's van, a cricket creaked,
But, near the waggons, fire was glowing red
On happy faces where the feast was spread.

Gladly they supped, those artists of the show;
Then by the perfect moon, together timed,
They struck the green-striped tent and laid it low,
Even as the quarter before midnight chimed.
Then putting-to the piebald nags, they climbed
Into their vans and slowly stole way,
Along Blown Hilcote on the Icknield Way.

And as the rumbling of the waggons died
By Aston Tirrold and the Moretons twain,
With axle-clatter in the countryside,
Lit by the moon and fragrant from the rain,
King Cole moved softly in the Ring again,
Where now the owls and he were left alone:
The night was loud with water upon stone.

He watched the night; then taking up his flute,
He breathed a piping of this life of ours,
The half-seen prize, the difficult pursuit,
The passionate lusts that shut us in their towers,
The love that helps us on, the fear that lowers,
The pride that makes us and the pride that mars,
The beauty and the truth that are our stars.

And man, the marvellous thing, that in the dark
Works with his little strength to make a light,
His wit that strikes, his hope that tends, a spark,
His sorrow of soul in toil, that brings delight,
His friends, who make salt sweet and blackness bright,
His birth and growth and change; and death the wise,
His peace, that puts a hand upon his eyes.

All these his pipings breathed of, until twelve
Struck on the belfry tower with tremblings numb
(Such as will shudder in the axe's helve
When the head strikes) to tell his hour was come.
Out of the living world of Christendom

He dimmed like mist till one could scarcely note
The robins nestling to his old grey coat.

Dimmer he grew, yet still a glimmering stayed
Like light on cobwebs, but it dimmed and died.
Then there was naught but moonlight in the glade,
Moonlight and water and an owl that cried.
Far overhead a rush of birds' wings sighed,
From migrants going south until the spring.
The night seemed fanned by an immortal wing.

But where the juggler trudged beside his love
Each felt a touching from beyond our ken,
From that bright kingdom where the souls who strove,
Live now for ever, helping living men.
And as they kissed each other; even then
Their brows seemed blessed, as though a hand unseen
Had crowned their loves with never-withering green.

THE RIDER AT THE GATE

A windy night was blowing on Rome,
The cressets guttered on Cæsar's home,
The fish-boats, moored at the bridge, were breaking
The rush of the river to yellow foam.

The hinges whined to the shutters shaking,
When clip-clop-clep came a horse-hoof raking
The stones of the road at Cæsar's gate;
The spear-butts jarred at the guard's awaking.

"Who goes there?" said the guard at the gate.
"What is the news, that you ride so late?"
"News most pressing, that must be spoken
To Cæsar alone, and that cannot wait."

"The Cæsar sleeps; you must show a token
That the news suffice that he be awoken.
What is the news, and whence do you come?
For no light cause may his sleep be broken."

"Out of the dark of the sands I come,
From the dark of death, with news for Rome.

238

A word so fell that it must be uttered
Though it strike the soul of the Cæsar dumb."

Cæsar turned in his bed and muttered,
With a struggle for breath the lamp-flame guttered;
Calpurnia heard her husband moan:
                    "The house is falling,
The beaten men come into their own."

"Speak your word," said the guard at the gate;
"Yes, but bear it to Cæsar straight,
Say, 'Your murderers' knives are honing,
Your killers' gang is lying in wait.'

"Out of the wind that is blowing and moaning,
Through the city palace and the country loaning,
I cry, 'For the world's sake, Cæsar, beware,
And take this warning as my atoning.

" 'Beware of the Court, of the palace stair,
Of the downcast friend who speaks so fair,
Keep from the Senate, for Death is going
On many men's feet to meet you there.'

"I, who am dead, have ways of knowing
Of the crop of death that the quick are sowing.
I, who was Pompey, cry it aloud
From the dark of death, from the wind blowing.

"I, who was Pompey, once was proud,
Now I lie in the sand without a shroud;
I cry to Cæsar out of my pain,
'Cæsar, beware, your death is vowed.' "

The light grew grey on the window-pane,
The windcocks swung in a burst of rain,
The window of Cæsar flung unshuttered,
The horse-hoofs died into wind again.

Cæsar turned in his bed and muttered,
With a struggle for breath the lamp-flame guttered:
Calpurnia heard her husband moan:
                    "The house is falling,
The beaten men come into their own."

239

THE RACER

I saw the racer coming to the jump,
   Staring with fiery eyeballs as he rushed,
I heard the blood within his body thump,
   I saw him launch, I heard the toppings crushed.

And as he landed I beheld his soul
   Kindle, because, in front, he saw the Straight
With all its thousands roaring at the goal,
   He laughed, he took the moment for his mate.

Would that the passionate moods on which we ride
   Might kindle thus to oneness with the will;
Would we might see the end to which we stride,
   And feel, not strain, in struggle, only thrill.

And laugh like him and know in all our nerves
Beauty, the spirit, scattering dust and turves.

THE PATHFINDER

She lies at grace, at anchor, head to tide,
   The wind blows by in vain: she lets it be.
Gurgles of water run along her side,
   She does not heed them: they are not the sea.
She is at peace from all her wandering now,
   Quiet is in the very bones of her:
The glad thrust of the leaning of her bow
   Blows bubbles from the ebb but does not stir.

Rust stains her side, her sails are furled, the smoke
Streams from her galley funnel and is gone;
A gull is settled on her skysail truck.
Some dingy seamen, by her deckhouse, joke;
The river loiters by her with its muck,
And takes her image as a benison.

How shall a man describe this resting ship,
   Her heavenly power of lying down at grace,
This quiet bird by whom the bubbles slip,
   This iron home where prisoned seamen pace?
Three slenderest pinnacles, three sloping spires,
   Climbing the sky, supported but by strings

240

Which whine in the sea wind from all their wires,
  Yet stand the strain however hard it dings.
Then, underneath, the long lean fiery sweep
  Of a proud hull exulting in her sheer,
That rushes like a diver to the leap,
  And is all beauty without spot or peer.
Built on the Clyde, by men, of strips of steel
That once was ore trod by the asses' heel.

A Clyde-built ship of fifteen hundred tons,
  Black-sided, with a tier of painted ports,
Red lead just showing where the water runs,
  Her bow a leaping race where beauty sports.
Keen as a hawk above the water line
  Though full below it: an elliptic stern:
Her attitude a racer's, stripped and fine,
  Tense to be rushing under spires that yearn.

She crosses a main skysail: her jibboom
Is one steel spike: her mainsail has a spread
Of eighty-seven feet, earring to earring.
Her wind is a fresh gale, her joy careering
Some two points free before it, nought ahead
But sea, and the gale roaring, and blown spume.

SOUTH AND EAST

When good King Arthur ruled these western hursts,
That farmhouse held a farmer with three sons,
Gai, Kai and Kradoc, so the story runs.
All of the hollow where the water bursts
  They reckoned holy land,
  For there, they said, the gods came, hand in hand,
At midnight, in full moon, to quench their thirsts.

So by the hollow's western edge they fenced
With unhewn stone and hawthorn and wild rose.
A little meadow as a holy close
Not be trodden in by foot uncleansed . . .
  And from the harvests rare
  Which filled their granaries, they were aware
That the great gods this service recompensed.

Gai was a hunter through the country-side;
Kai was a braggart little prone to truth;
Kradoc was reckoned but a simple youth,
Though kind and good and all his mother's pride.
He loved his mother well;
He loved his mare and dog; but it befell
That sorrow smote him young, for all three died.

Now it befell in grass-time, late in May,
That Gai, the hunter, going out at dawn,
Found the grass trampled in that sacred lawn,
All trodden as by feet the flowers lay.
He thought, "Some godless men
Have done this evil; lest they come agen
I'll watch to-night beside the holy hay."

Yet in his watch he slept, and when the east
Grew bright with primrose-coloured morning, lo,
The grass again was laid past power to mow;
By godless men, it seemed, not any beast.
So, when the next night fell,
Kai came to watch, but slept, not waking well,
At dawn the trodden portion had increased.

Then, on the third night, Kradoc said, "Let me
Be guard to-night"; so, when the dusk was dim,
He took his hunting-spear and stationed him
Beside the close beneath a hawthorn-tree.
The thin moon westered out,
The midnight covered all things with her doubt,
The summer made the world one mystery.

Then, when the hunting owls had ceast to cry,
There came a sound like birds upon the wing,
And shapes within the close were glimmering,
Hushing, and putting glittering raiment by . . .
Then the shapes moved: they seemed
Three women, dancing, but their moving gleamed:
Or were they birds? because they seemed to fly.

"They are the goddesses," he thought, "at game . . .
Soon they will blast me"; but he watched intent . . .
Starlight and dawn a little colour lent;
They were three women, each like moving flame

In some old dance of glee,
All lovely, but the leader of the three
Beauty so great as hers can have no name.

For hours he stared, not moving, while they danced;
Then in the brightening dusk a blackbird cried;
The dancing stopped, the women slipped aside,
There to the grey wall where their plumage glanced.
They donned it and were gone
Up, upon wings; across the sky they shone,
Gleams on the darkness where the dawn advanced.

And being vanished, all his heart was sore
With love of that fair Queen. "Alas, I kept
Ill watch," he said, "and all the grass is stepped
As though it had been danced on o'er and o'er.
To-night I'll try again,
A second night I will not watch in vain."
All day at work love searched him to the core.

At night, his father and his brothers both
Came with him to the holy close to guard;
But long before the midnight many-starred,
His comrades slept, forgetting boast and oath.
The hours went by: he heard
The darkness laughing with the marvellous bird
Who hushed the woodland with her plighting troth.

Then, suddenly, with linnet cryings sweet,
The shapes were near him, putting off their wings;
Then all the close was swift with glimmerings
Of silvery figures upon flying feet
White as the thorn that blows,
Skimming the daisies as the swallow goes
Or as the sunlight ripples upon wheat.

Then, as he stared and prayed, the thought came bold
"There are their wings upon the wall, put by . . .
If I should take them, then they could not fly . . .
But these are gods, immortal from of old,
And they would blast me dead
If I should touch their plumage silver-spread,
Let alone gather it and try to hold."

But as the moth about the candle tries
To know the beauty of the inmost fire,
And feels no burning but his heart's desire,
And even by scorching cannot be made wise,
He took the wings: a lark
Twittered, and colour stood out from the dark;
Those figures sought their wings with passionate cries.

"They are not goddesses," he thought; and then
Seeing who held their wings, those lovely birds
Were pleading with him with caressing words:
"Friend, we shall die if we are seen by men.
Give us our wings, oh, give;
We may not look upon the sun and live:
Sweet mortal, let us have our plumes agen."

Then, to the first, he gave the plumes, from fear;
Then, to the second, gave them out of grace;
Then she, the Queen, was with him, face to face,
Within the touch of hand, she was so near
The two spread wings and sailed
Up to the summer heaven primrose-paled.
"O lovely Queen," he cried, "for pity, hear.

These two nights now I have beheld your dance,
And nothing matters now, but only you;
You are so beautiful, it shakes me through,
The thought of you is my inheritance.
I am unfit to speak
To such as you, but, lovely Queen, I seek
Only to love you, leaving life to chance.

I am unfit to touch your wings; but quake
At thought of losing you; for pity, tell
How I may reach the Kingdom where you dwell,
There to be slave or servant for your sake;
O bird of beauty bright,
Teach me the way, or come again to-night
And have some pity or my heart will break."

Then looking on the lovely lad's distress,
She loved his love for her and pitied him;
But now the morning made the stars all dim;
She took the wings from his unhappiness.
She said, "We have been seen,

We cannot dance again upon this green,
And where I dwell is past the wilderness."

"O tell me where," he cried, "for I shall find
The way there." "Ah," she answered, "way is none.
We dwell South of the Earth, East of the Sun,
Beyond the savage rocks and seas unkind;
You have no wings for flight,
No earthly mortal knows the course aright,
Unless the three Queens have it still in mind."

"And where are they?" he asked. "Far, far," she said,
"Somewhere beyond the sunset in the West;
In seeking me you choose a weary quest.
Now, friend, farewell." "One minute more," he prayed
"Beloved, I shall try . . .
For I shall love you only till I die . . .
And seeking you, I shall not be afraid."

Her glowing face was noble with sweet thought.
"O friend," she said, "the love of me will bring
Loneliness, toil and many a bitter thing;
Nor can the friend you strive to help in aught.
But I will wait you there . . .
Come, even with palsied limbs and snowy hair,
All things are truly found if truly sought."

Then, leaning suddenly, she kissed his lips,
And pressed one glittering feather in his hand,
And swept away above the wakening land
As the white owl at dusk from cover slips . . .
Up the dark wood her gleam
Shone, as adown a basalt shines a stream;
Then she was gone and joy was in eclipse.

At first, he hoped that she would come again:
He watched the next night through: no dancers shone.
Then the next night, until the stars were gone;
Then the third night, but vigil was in vain.
"She cannot come," he cried,
"I will go seek her Kingdom far and wide;
Better to die in search than live in pain."

So at the dowland market he enquired
Of all the tinkers, if they knew the way

South of the Earth? "There's no such land," said they.
"We have gone roving Earth till we are tired
And never heard the name."
The wandering merchants told the lad the same:
They knew all lands, but not the one desired.

And in the inn, a travelling minstrel told
Of lands beyond the sea, both East and West,
Lands where the phoenix has her burning nest,
And trees have emerald leaves and fruits of gold,
But no land East the Sun . . .
"Boy, I have been," he said, "there is not one."
"None?" Kradoc thought, "there must be, to the bold."

He bade farewell to father, brothers, home,
Friends, and the grasses that her feet had pressed;
He sailed to find the Three Queens in the West,
O'er many a billow with a toppling comb,
Till, 'neath the western star,
He trod the forest where the were-wolves are
And spied a hut, as of some witch or gnome.

There sat an old crone wrinkled nose to chin.
"Lady," he said, "since I have gone astray,
Seeking the queens to tell me of my way,
Have you some shed that I can rest me in?
In recompense, I'll cut
Your winter's firing and repair your hut."
"O wonderful," she said, "new times begin.

I have reigned here for twenty oak-tree lives,
Yet never once has stranger spoken thus,
Bowing, uncovered, thoughtful, courteous:
What marvellous young noble here arrives?
One who goes South the Earth!
I govern all four-footed beasts from birth,
To-morrow I will ask them and their wives,

If any know the way to that far land.
Rest here to-night." And when the morrow came
All the four-footed creatures, wild and tame,
Ran thither at the lifting of her hand:
Slink tigers yellow-eyed,
The horse, the stag, the rabbit and his bride,
Fur, antlers, horns, as many as the sand.

246

They listened while she questioned of the way:
"South of the Earth?" they answered. "Madam, no
It is a country where we never go . . .
There is not such a land, the bisons say.
Ask of the birds who fly;
The eagle may have seen it from the sky,
If not the eagle, then the seagull may."

"So," the Queen said, "my people cannot tell
You must away to ask my Sister Queen
To ask her subject birds if they have seen
A country South the Earth where people dwell.
A year hence, travelling hard,
You may be with her, if no ills retard.
Good luck attend. Commend me to her well."

After a twelvemonths' tramp he reached a lake
Wide-shimmering, beyond a waste of reeds;
There by a hovel mouldered green with weeds,
An old hag mumbled, gap-toothed as a rake.
"Lady," he pled. "I pray
You grant me shelter, I have lost my way;
All such requital as I can I'll make.

I will re-thatch your house and cut your corn,
And gather in your apples from the tree."
"O wonderful; new times begin," said she.
"I have lived here since roses had a thorn,
Yet never once till now
Has courteous youth addressed me with a bow.
And you go East the Sun and are forlorn?

I govern all the birds that know the air;
Rest here to-night; to-morrow I will ask
If any of them all can help your task
Or know the ways by which men journey there."
When morning came, she cried
"Come hither, birds," and from the heavens wide
Came erne and geier, heron, finch and stare,

Jay, robin, blackbird, sparrow, croaking crow,
Hawks from the height their talons brown with blood,
Gannets that snatch the herring from the flood,
And fiery birds that glitter as they go.
"East of the Sun?" they said . . .

"We have flown windy space since wings were made . . .
There's no such land. Perhaps the fish may know."

"So," the Queen said, "my subjects cannot guide.
You must go ask my Sister Queen, who rules
The dwellers in the rivers and the pools
And the green seas that waver yet abide.
A year's hard travelling hence
Should bring you there: her Kingdom is immense,
Her folk know every country washed by tide."

After another year he trod the beach
Beside an ocean breaking wave by wave.
There an old hag peered from a dripping cave.
"O ocean Queen," he cried, "grant, I beseech,
That I may rest till day.
To-morrow I will labour to repay
Your kindness to me as your wish shall teach."

"O wonderful; new times begin," she said.
"I have lived here since raindrops became sea;
Yet none till now has spoken thus to me,
Courteous and kind and modest as a maid.
South of the Earth you go?
Rest for to-night; to-morrow you shall know
If those I govern know it and can aid."

When morning came, the Queen gave her command,
And straight the bay was white with many a streak
From the swift fins of those that cannot speak:
Whales, dolphins, salmon, hurrying to the land;
Herrings, the pickerels fierce,
Mackerel with blue flanks writ with magic verse,
And cuttles such as eye has never scanned.

The thought passed to and fro, without a word.
"Ah," the Queen said, "they cannot help you, friend.
Between the world's edge and the ocean's end
No fish, no four-foot beast, no flying bird
Has heard of any place
South of the Earth: you say the human race
Knows no such land. Your seeking is absurd.

Why not abandon what is surely vain?
Why not return to all you left at home,

248

To shear the shining furrow down the loam
Feeling the plough-team lean against the rein?
To marry; and be skilled
In all good crafts, and have your granaries filled
And live till Death comes gently without pain?

Were these not better than the life you choose,
Seeking the thing that is not?" "No," said he;
"This feather, that still shines, she gave to me;
I will go on, though every footstep bruise."
Out in the bay a stir
Broke the land's quiet image into blur . . .
"Wait yet," the Queen said, "something comes with news.

Yes, news of South the Earth . . . the fish that flies,
The thing that beasts and birds and fish disown;
He has a rumour of it, he alone . . .
Go with him therefore, if you think it wise.
These silver wings and fins
Will help you thither; and Desire wins
Though the Desired, won, may prove no prize."

Then with that silvery skimmer of the seas
He sped across the unquiet fatal field,
Now pastured on by haze, now ridged and steeled,
Now low, now loud, but never at its ease;
Till a last leaping flight
Bore him ashore through billows crashing white
Beneath a cliff of granite topped by trees.

And at the scree-top, lo, the crag was sheer.
Hard granite face, nine hundred feet and more,
Gleaming where drifts of cataracts came o'er
And trackless to the foot of mountaineer.
He traced along beneath,
Among the boulders and the stunted heath,
And ever and anon he seemed to hear

From somewhere up above, the cry and bay
Of dogs and hounds together giving tongue,
So that his spirit was with terror wrung
Lest these should be the hunting dogs who slay
Like wolves, what men they meet;
He was defenceless and without retreat,
But thought, "Since hounds are there, there is a way

Up to the summit; and perhaps the hounds
Have huntsmen with them who would succour me."
So thrice he hailed, all unavailingly.
Then o'er the tumbled rocks with leaps and bounds
A dog came swiftly to him,
Barking and wagging tail as though he knew him.
It was his dog, long dead to smells and sounds,

Long buried in that distant Berkshire place,
Now here alive, and crying, "Master, come,
This is our ever-living happy home . . .
Come with me up the track the rabbits trace;
This way, and have no fear.
Climb with me to the forest, Master dear.
We live there always in delightful chase.

All day we hunt whatever game we choose,
Then, in the dusk, we pull it down and eat;
But by the dawn it runs again on feet,
Alive and scattering scent across the dews . . .
Now, up the rock top; lo,
The forest, green as Berkshire long ago.
There run the hounds at game they cannot lose."

And, as he spoke, the precipice was scaled.
There lay a marvellous land of oak trees high,
With grass where hounds were running in full cry
After immortal game that never failed.
All dogs of every kind
Routed or hunted as they had the mind,
And all were glad, for all were waggy-tailed.

"Come with me, Master, through the forest green,"
The little dog said, "as we went of old
Along the Icknield underneath the wold.
Here we forget, in time, what we have been;
But I remember well
The rabbits and the moles and the rich smell
Of those old warrens in that happy scene,

And mind your kindness to me." Then they went
For three long days across the forest land,
Until they reached a desert, white with sand.
"Stay here," the dog said. "Someone will be sent
To guide you further on."

He licked his hand and bounded and was gone.
The desert stretched its desolate extent.

Its saltness nourisht naught but poisonous things,
The moon in silence looked upon its waste,
Then, towards dawn, a something came in haste
Trotting the sand or skimming it on wings:
It was his long-dead mare,
Coming with whinnyings to greet him there,
Dreading no adder's bite nor scorpion stings.

"Master," she said, "I come out of my rest
To bear you hence upon my wings of flame,
For I can fly now, nothing makes me lame . . .
Mount me and lay both hands upon my crest.
O I remember well,
Deep in my spirit, all the Berkshire fell
And you and I at gallop, heading west.

Now for a time I rest me from the past,
But those old days recur; the huntsman's horn,
The opening of the bin-lid for the corn,
The sweet red apples tumbling to the blast.
You with the bit, which I
Dodged, till the oat-sieve shook too temptingly . . .
And all your kindness to me to the last.

Now mount and ride, together we will go
A swifter gallop than we ever knew."
Then, when he mounted, instantly she flew
Over the desert white with salt like snow;
Skimming the sudden whip
Of the blunt adder with the swollen lip;
Making the sage flow back as waters flow.

Till after three long days she made a halt
Upon the beaches of a sea whose waves
Moaned like to cattle in the glittering caves
And fed the tremulous jellies with their salt.
"O Master mine, farewell,"
The mare said. "Now I gallop back to dwell
In far green pastures without any fault.

For there we dwell together in the plain
Unbitted and unshod, in knee-deep grass,

Where never any gad nor botfly was,
But scarlet apples fall and golden grain.
And there we whinny and race
With streaming tails in the delight of pace,
And muse about old harness with disdain."

So with a whinny as of old she sped,
Out of his sight across the desert sand,
Leaving him lonely on the ocean-strand
Where the spent tide its gathered seaweed spread;
Then, gliding over sea,
A woman came to him; no wings had she,
She moved by love, being his Mother dead.

"O lovely son," she said, "who have given all
For love, despite the hardness of the way,
I come to give such guidance as I may,
And be beside your going, lest you fall.
O often I have been
Close, as you travelled hither, though unseen,
And speaking, though you could not hear my call.

I live in the sweet world that love creates.
It is more beautiful than I can tell,
For we can go with water into hell,
With peace to pain, with gentleness to hates.
We have this joy, to strive
To help the grief of everything alive
And show where Heaven shines at open gates.

And some, if truly called by mortal need,
Can come, with light and courage and swift strength,
To vanquish the dull snake whose deadly length
Laps and would coil, round every human deed.
Give me your hand, my son,
The darkness shows that morning has begun,
And we have far to travel: let us speed."

She took his hand, and, lo, they footed sure,
Unsunk upon the unsupporting sea;
They trod the air, unfallen, flying free,
High in the cloudless currents, mountain-pure,
Until a land arose,
Peak upon peak, with pinnacles of snows,
East of the Sun, where happy dreams endure.

His mother kissed his brow and then was gone,
He was alone upon the shore, his sight
Dazzled at first by plenitude of light,
For all things in that happy country shone.
A loitering cataract leapt . . .
A glittering people, crying "Welcome," swept
On wings above him, flying on and on.

"This is the land," he cried. "But where is she?
Where shall I find the wonder whom I love?"
Before him ran a brook out of a grove,
Bringing clear water to the clearer sea.
Within the green grove dim
Someone was singing at a morning hymn:
"O you," she cried, "beloved, answer me."

He thrust aside the myrtle and the rose:
There was his lover stitching, plume by plume,
Bright silver wings that glittered in the gloom,
And singing out her ballad to the close . . .
Seeing him there, she stood;
She shone as though the light were in her blood;
Gone was the waiting time with all its woes.

"I never ceased to trust," she said, "and lo,
The wings which I have wrought for you are made,
Save for one silver feather which I laid
Bright in you hand, beloved, long ago.
You have it still, I see.
We win the lovers' heaven, happy we,
The greatest happiness that heart can know."

Then placing on his shoulders the bright pair
Of wings, she took her lover by the hand
And with him swept above that sunny land,
Thrusting aside, like swans, the rushing air,
To some green place of peace
Where love like theirs forever knows increase,
For nothing sad can ever trouble there.

But sometimes, ere the cuckoos lose their tune,
Ere pink has tinged the snowdrifts of the may
Or seething scythe has gleamed into the hay,
Or nightingales stopped singing to the moon
Whose whiteness climbs and rounds;

Then, in the peace which silences earth's sounds
Save the bird's triumph and the water's croon,

Then, sometimes, in the hush, a glimmering glows
Into a brightness in that Berkshire grass.
Those lovers come where their first meeting was
Beside the spring, within the holy close.
They dance there through the night,
Treading adown in patterns of delight
Moon-daisy, vetch, and fallen hawthorn blows.

ON SKYSAILS

I saw you often as the crown of Queens
As snow upon a mountain, as the rose
Red in the middest summer's many greens
You were the beauty's final grace, as those.

Or as the spire that lifts aloft in heaven,
Or as the wind-vane on the spiry peak,
Or as the glory glimmering in the sweven,
Caught by the dreamer as he wakens weak.

Or as the rapture of the heart at breaking,
Or Power's last touch, or manhood's winning-place
Even so were you that set the shadows shaking.
On ever hurrying sea, to leave no trace.

Far, far, away, the men beholding knew
A queen the more was passing, seeing you.

The west wind blows the smoke among the rain,
The rigging drips, the iridescent dock
Dimples beneath each following pellet's knock.
From each ship's scupper crawls a rusty stain.

The winches rattle cargo; from a shoot
Coal thunders down; a tugboat threshes past
Towing a ship with colours at her mast;
An orange-bearer scents the air with fruit.

Four boys, two ancient riggers and a mate
Heave round upon a capstan, the pawls clink,
The gathered heaves of purchase fall and kink,

The dangling yard goes up into the sky,
Up on its end it goes and swings awry
And settles square, and is a crown of state.

They reared the pine-tree to its height and held
Its slender taper steady with a stay.
What Nature could not compass they compelled,
There the spar stood, since Nature must obey.

Then, turning pride to use, they crossed the yard,
Itself a triumph with its manly gear,
Theirs was a Queen whom nothing should retard,
They set a sail upon the pointing spear:

And there it gleamed aloft, below the flag
Over strange seas, impelled by many airs.
What though the waters raged? What heeds the stag,
Running the hills, of stag-hounds, as he fares?

He pays no heed, but canters, as did she,
Billow by crashing billow, sea by sea.

PAY

The world paid but a penny for its toil,
That which was priceless got the beggar's dole;
Men who fetcht beauty, iron, corn or oil
Scarce could keep beggar's bones about the soul.

I saw those sailing seamen, cotton-clad,
Housed in wet kennels, worm-fed, cheated, driven,
Three pounds a month, and small delight they had,
Save the bright water and the winds of heaven.

Yet from their sweated strength an order rose,
The full-rigged ship in her delightful line,
So beautiful and tranquil in repose
But in supremest action so divine.

For in the trampling seas the beauty stood
Trampling those seas, and made her pathway good.

UNDER LOWER TOPSAILS

Three lower topsails dark with wet are straining
The lower yards to curves, a great sea runs,
Shrouds shriek aloft, the fabric is complaining,
The roaring of the nor'-nor'-easter stuns.

Men stand together waiting for a call,
Their yellow oilskins glisten as they stir.
Each clambering comber toppling wall on wall
Seethes and roars by before its follower.

The ship goes labouring on, until a pause,
A lurch, while a sea mounts and climbs and crowns;
Then like some rapturous instant's loud applause
The thundering billow breaks aboard and drowns:
Flooding the deck rail under, that she lies
Quenched, and the seaman wonders, *Will she rise?*

EIGHT BELLS

Four double strikes repeated on the bells,
And then away, away the shufflers go
Aft to the darkness where the ruler dwells,
Where by the rail he sucks his pipe aglow;
Beside him his relief looks down on those below.

There in the dark they answer to their names,
Those dozen men, and one relieves the wheel,
One the look-out, the others sit to games
In moonlight, backed against the bulkhead's steel,
In the lit patch the hands flick, card by card, the deal.

Meanwhile the men relieved are forward all,
Some in their bunks asleep, while others sing
Low-voiced some ditty of the halliard-fall,
The ship impels them on with stooping wing,
Rolling and roaring on with triumph in her swing.

MINNIE MAYLOW'S STORY

Once (long ago) there was an English King,
Who loved good stories more than anything.

Many a story did the poets tell
To him, who loved their tales and listened well.

But one defect their tales had, that they ended,
Always, at last, the lady was befriended,

The sinner was confounded, lovers blest.
The story's sun went down into the west.

Then the King said, "Would poets could contrive
An endless tale, whose heroes do not wive;

A story ever fresh and never done,
Like the august procession of the sun.

Royally watching mortals from the sky,
That sinks, but rises, and can never die."

Then he proclaimed, "It is our royal will
That poets (duly qualified in skill)

Come to our court, and tell an endless tale."
But those who tried it were of no avail.

Their stories lagged enfeebled and then died,
So that in disappointment the King cried,

"Henceforth it shall be death, to any man,
Who comes to court declaring that he can

Tell me an endless tale and fails therein,
It shall be death, like treason, or great sin,

Upon the headsman's block on Tower Hill.
But any poet who shall have the skill

To tell an endless tale shall have for prize
My daughter's hand and half my baronies;

And, when I die, shall have my crown as heir.
Heralds, go forth: proclaim this everywhere."

It was proclaimed, but, when the threat was known,
The story-tellers left the court alone,

Even though the princess' beauty was so great
As to tempt any poet to his fate.

Though she was known as Emily the Fair,
Heartsease, and Morning Star, and Golden Hair:

Each story-teller feared to lose his head.
Then the King grieved, for his delight was dead.

No story-teller came with thrilling rhyme
To charm his soul with 'Once upon a time'.

Only his Juggler and the Fool remained:
One he disliked, the other he disdained.

Then silence fell upon the palace hall,
Save for the sentry passing on the wall:

Or some old general coming to report
On army remounts at his frontier fort.

Men with most dreary tales of old attacks,
With half their brains gouged by the battle-axe;

Or ministers with courtesies in their spines,
Or Labour members talking about mines;

Or scarlet admirals, whose breezy tone
Made the King thankful to be left alone.

None who could charm him, as in days of old
The poets with the stories that they told.

And Emily the Fair, with downcast eyes,
Guided the bright silk of her 'broideries.

Loving her father, yet, without offence,
Wishing the loved one might have had more sense,

And not be self-condemned to sit like lead,
Dumb by the fire betwixt meat and bed,

Or snarling, as he poked the burning logs,
"This land of mine is going to the Dogs."

One night the porter came before the King,
Saying, "Behold, my lord, a marvellous thing,

Here at your gate a young man brings a tale
That will go on for ever without fail.

He knows the penalty of unsuccess,
His head upon the gate, but none the less

Determines to adventure for the prize."
"Young," said the King. "The young are never wise

And all their stories are but washy stuff:
Still, youth demands until it has enough.

This man shall have enough, like all the rest.
Bid him go see the chaplain; it were best

He make his peace before he make his trial."
"He would not take advice, nor yet denial,"

The porter said: "but hungers to begin."
"Checking a fool in folly is not sin,"

The King replied, "so let him come to me:
Put up your night's embroidery, Emily.

A tale-teller has come to show his skill."
Now the dark palace-hall began to fill,

With knights and men-at-arms and palace dames
And pine logs on the fire cast ruddy flames

That made the shadows dance upon the wall.
Then the King rose and said, "Friends, listen all.

A story-teller comes to-night to try
His fortune in a tale that cannot die.

Where is he, porter? Let the lad appear."
A young man at the entrance answered "Here."

And coming forward stood before the King,
Bright as the golden pheasant in the Spring,

Cool as the antlered royal on the crag,
Tense as the racehorse waiting for the flag.

Then the King said, "You doubtless know the rules
That hedge our Throne from the attempts of fools.

Those who begin and fail in the attempt
Stand self-condemned and none shall be exempt,

Steel lops away the peccant proser's head.
Your person seems unready to be dead."

"Sire," the youth said, "I understand the terms.
I dread no headsman's axe, nor coffin worms,

I venture all things gladly for the stake:—
This fair Princess for whom so many ache.

I do not come for glory nor for land
But as a suitor striving for her hand.

If I succeed, and she will have me . . . well.
If not, come headsman with the burial knell:

And shut me from the presence of her worth.
For the most beautiful princess on earth,

I come to tell a story without end."
Then the King answered, "Very well, my friend.

If you can tell a tale that will endure
Daily as sunrise and as season-sure,

This fair Princess and half my land shall be
Yours, now, and all my kingdom after me.

But if you fail, you die: are you content?"
"Yes," the youth said: "the terms are excellent.

If you permit, I will begin my story:—
Our ancient poets, excellent in glory,

Say that of old this England had a King
Who dreaded Famine above everything . . .

Dreaded, lest anywhere, in toft or street,
Subject of his should lack enough to eat,

And he behold his people wanting food.
So, being eager for his country's good,

He swore, on coming to his father's throne,
That, while he ruled, hunger should be unknown

To woman, child or man throughout his realm.
Then being crowned, and settled at the helm,

He called for England's chiefest architect,
Firstly to draw, and after to erect

A granary with cellars, walls and roof
Water proof, tempest proof, and earthquake proof.

When this was done he bade his Treasury
Purchase all corn, and fill the granary.

The granary was filled, up to the hatch
With peerless wheat and barley without match.

'Now we are saved,' the King cried, 'from our dread
And we can sleep with an untroubled head,

And shall not dream of hunger, nor of towns
With all their people starved to skeletons;

With their lips green from biting on the grass.
Men shall forget that ever Famine was.

This grain will last through ten lean years together;
Let blight, or smut, or rust, or rainy weather,

Or wind, that lays the blade and earths the ear,
Let them all come, I say: We need not fear;

We have destroyed what has destroyed mankind.'
So, with glad heart, contented in his mind,

He bade them seal the granary hatch with lead.
'Let Famine fall,' he thought, 'we shall be fed.'

But mark, O King, upon how small a point
A mortal craft will shipwreck and disjoint.

In that gigantic granary's topmost wall
One tiny scrap of mortar came to fall,

Leaving a chink that no man's eye could see,
Being aloft where men could never be.

Now, King, this vasty mass of gathered wheat
Sent forth a smell, unknown by man, but sweet

To all the locusts of the world, who flew,
Longing to see where so much eating grew.

So that the skies were dark with locusts flying,
Then for three days men saw the locusts trying

To find some entrance to that shuttered store:
And in the end one lively locust tore

Through that small chink from which the mortar fell
And stole away one grain. O King, I tell

Nothing but truth. Another locust came
And struggled through the hole and did the same.
And then another locust did the same.

As secretly as sickness in a bone,
So wrought these locusts utterly unknown.

Who could suspect a cranny? Who suspect
The building Guild, the royal Architect?

Unseen as poison breathed in with the breath;
Each of three locusts dealt a corn a death.

Then came a fourth and took a corn and went
Then a fifth locust who was bulky, bent

And almost blocked the chink, but struggled through
And took a grain, and a sixth locust, too.

And then a seventh crept into the hole;
And then an eighth; and eighth and seventh stole

Each one a grain, and carried it away
And then a ninth one, having seen the way,

Crept in and took a barleycorn and fled.
The tenth was a king-locust, spotted red.

He took three grains, being of royal blood.
The eleventh took a grain and found it good.

Then the twelfth locust, shining in the sun
Crept in and took a grain. The thirteenth one

Followed and took a corn. The fourteenth came
And took a corn. The fifteenth did the same
And then the sixteenth locust did the same.

And another locust carried off another.
And another locust came, the first one's brother.

He took a corn, and then his brother drew
It through the hole, and took another, too.

And then another locust found the place
And another locust followed him in chase,

And another locust followed close behind
And another locust, hungry as the wind,

Leaped in upon his tracks and took a corn
And a battered locust, who was all forlorn

Lame in one leg, and sorry on the wing,
Came in and took another grain, O King.

Sometimes in hot Septembers one may see
On gray cathedral roofs the wasps in glee

Whirling against the blue sky overhead
From papery nests hung underneath the lead,

So men beheld these locusts, but none guesst
That greed of grain had given them such zest.

There came a black Saturnian one, there came
A stalwart Jovian, with crest of flame.

A glittering, dainty Venus-locust flew
Questing for corn, red Martians followed, too.

Each took a grain, and then, a marvellous sight
A locust bowed with age, whose hair was white,

Thrust to the corn . . ."
                But here the King cried, "Hold.
Boy, by our Father's Corpse down in the mould

Stop this unworthy folly of the flies.
Get to your tale." The young man said, "Be wise . . .

Govern your kingdom, Sire, as seems good
But leave a story-teller to his mood.

I tell the tale of what the locusts did.
Another locust crept within and hid,

Under a pile of wheat and took two grains.
And then a locust suffering from pains,

Searched for a peppercorn to warm his marrow:
Then a sow-locust with her twenty farrow

Crept one by one into the chink and stole
And then another locust found the hole,

And crept within and pillaged like the last
And then another locust followed fast.

And then another locust followed soon.
Then one, with wits unsettled by the moon,

Strayed crooning through the hole and did the same.
And then another, and another came.

And then another and another followed
And soon the space between the bricks was hollowed,

So as to hold a locust and a quarter;
And then another locust pressed the mortar.

And then another came and wore it smooth,
And then another came and fleshed his tooth

Right to the bitter kernel of an oat.
Then yet another, with a greedy throat

Came in, and then his cousin, then his aunt."
"Stop!" said the King. The young man said, "I can't

I have to tell my story as it was.
I serve poetic truth, a noble cause.

I will not stop for conqueror or king.
Another locust came upon the wing."

"Silence," the King said. "Silence. Tell me, friend,
How soon this locust incident will end?"

"It will not end," the youth said. "It will go
As it has gone for ever. You will know

All that each locust of those millions did,
Give ear, my King." The King said, "Jove forbid!"

"It is my tale," the youth said, "and you shall.
I staked my life upon it in this hall,

To tell a story for your prize, and now
Many might think you meant to break your vow.

Let me proceed. Another locust came."
"Young man," the King said, "you have missed your aim.

Your story fails, although I grant you clever.
Those locusts could not carry corn for ever.

They might have for a year, but in the end
That granary was bare. What then, my friend?"

"Sire," the youth said, "the King who made the store,
Filled it again, much fuller than before.

And another locust came and took a corn."
"O readiest story-teller ever born,"

The King cried, "you have conquered; we submit
And, as our Daughter seems rejoiced at it,

Son, you shall marry Emily the Fair,
Have half my kingdom now, and be my heir.

My heralds shall design you a device,
On a field wavy, semée wheat and rice,

Three locusts proper, bearing each a grain.
Girl, never let him tell that tale again!"

THE TAKING OF HELEN

Menelaus, the Spartan King,
Was a fighting man in his early spring,
With a war-cry loud as a steer's bellow,
And long yellow hair, so the poets sing.

But he wearied of war, and longed to bide
In quiet at home by his fireside;
He wooed and wedded the beautiful Helen
And carried her home to be his bride.

And little delight was hers, poor thing,
To be tied till death to the Spartan King,
She moved in the cage of the Spartan court
Like a bright sea-bird with a broken wing.

Paris came from a Trojan glen,
The prince of the world's young famous men,
With a panther's eye and a peacock air,
Even the goddesses wooed him then.

He came to Troy to the Spartan port,
He moored his galley: he rode to court
In a scarlet mantle spanged with gold
On a delicate stallion stepping short.

Helen and he knew each from each
That a red ripe apple was there in reach,

The loveliest girl and the loveliest lad
Ready to learn and ready to teach.

He said "O Helen, why linger here
With the King your husband year by year?
What life is this to a star like you,
The brightest star in the atmosphere?

O beautiful girl, I love but you,
And a life of love is your rightful due:
Come with me over the sea to Troy,
Where Queens shall ride in your retinue."

She said to him, "O Paris, my own,
Since I married him I have lived so lone
That life is bleak as a withered bone.
O take me hence into light and life,
My spirit within me turns to stone."

Then Paris said, "But we will not fly
Like thieves that have heard a step draw nigh.
You are the Queen and I am I;
I'll carry you off to my golden ship
At noonday under your husband's eye."

So it was planned, so it was done,
Paris and she were there at one,
The sentry bribed and the door undone,
With a waiting ship and a rising wind
Helen was off with Priam's son.

THE SURPRISE

You have heard the story of the Horse of Troy.

We left him on the sea-beach when we sailed.
We sailed all day, but when the darkness fell
The captains ordered all the fleet ashore.
We beached the black ships out of sight of Troy.

Then quietly the captains of the hundreds
Were told that a surprise would be attempted.
Orders were given: then most stringent watch
Was made, lest any traitor should give warning.

267

We supped and slept, till somewhere after midnight,
Then roused, and tied bleached linen on our arms,
And took short spears and swords: no other weapons:
And forth we went by fifties towards Troy.
Absolute silence upon pain of death
The order was, we crept along like ghosts.

Soon we were in the Plain among the graves
Of men half-buried, whom we used to know,
And how they died, a dozen known to me.
And Trojan bodies, too; familiar landmarks.

It was all cold and windy, with bright stars,
No moon, dry summer going, and the wind
Beating the withered grass and shrivelled leaves.
Then we were at the ford and passing through
I remember water gurgling at a flag-root.

Beyond the ford we were in Trojan land.
There was the black mass of the walls of Troy
With towers (and a light in one of them).
No other sign of life, except a glow,
Before Apollo's temple as we judged,
Some sacrificial fire not yet quenched.
The city was dead still, but for the wind.

They halted us below the waggon track
Between the Spartans and the Ithacans,
And there we huddled in the bitter cold,
Wondering what had happened in the city
And why the city should be still as death:
Whether the Horse were burning in the fire
With all our men inside it sacrificed:
Whether the trap door in the Horse had jammed
So that they could not leave it: or perhaps
(We thought) the Horse is guarded in the temple,
Surrounded by men praying all night long.
Ot had they ventured out, and all been killed?

And if the men were killed, the stratagem
Was surely known, and we half-armed and freezing,
Would be attacked at dawn and ridden down.

A temple bell jangled within the city,
A lesser bell tinkled; then all was silent.

And all this time the little owls from Ida
Came hooting over us: and presently
A mighty, savage owl perched upon Troy
And snapped his iron lips, and flapped, and screamed,
Almost one saw the yellow of his eyes.
Then he launched forth, stealing into the air.

It seemed like many ages in the cold
Before the whisper reached the Ithacans
To creep a little nearer to the wall.
When they had passed, unchallenged, other went.
Word passed that there were sentries on the wall.

And though the orders were against all speech,
Yet whispers let us know that Diomed
Was at the South Gate underneath the tower,
With the picked fighters.
                              Hours seemed to pass
While we froze slowly in our companies.
My eyes were so accustomed to the dark
That I could see the great wall with its ramparts,
A tower, and a gate, close-fastened, brazen,
With men of ours heaped near it like to stones.

Then there was whispering in the ranks behind me:
A captain whispered, "Who knows Diomed?
Do you?" I whispered, "Yes."
                              "Why, then," he whispered,
"Creep forward there, and find him by the gate
Under the tower with the forward party.
Tell him *King Agamemnon is convinced
That this has failed, and that we must withdraw.
Be ready to fall back as we retire.*"

I crept the seventy yards up to the front,
One whispered, "Diomed is on the right,
Nearest the wall." I found him lying there
And whispered him the message of the King.
"What?" he said. "What?" Withdraw from where we are?
Who says so? What authority have you?"
I told him "Verbal orders from a captain."
"Lie still," he said. "And not another word.
I'll learn of your authority when day dawns."
I lay prone on the earth, close at the gate.

Then suddenly there came a little noise.
Someone within the gate was lifting down
The heavy bars that barred it, one by one.
Each of us nudged his fellow and drew breath.
Diomed stood: we other raised ourselves.

One half the narrow brazen door moved back,
Showing a dark gash that grew wider and lighter;
A lamp wavered and flickered in a lane,
The damp glistened on wallwork; a man peered
Round the half-opened door; and "Sst. Sst. Sst,"
He hissed. It was Odysseus, from the Horse.

Diomed signalled to us: he himself
Was first within the gate: I helped him there
To lay the gate wide open to our men.
Then we pressed in, up the steep narrow lane
Past the still flickering lamp, over a Trojan
Sentry or watchman, newly murdered there,
Killed by Odysseus: no one challenged us.
We were in Troy: the city was surprised.

The dogs had all been killed some weeks before,
There were no watch-dogs. When we reached the Ways,
The Wide Ways running round within the walls,
Some horses, tethered there, whinnied and stamped,
And drowsy horse-boys mumbled in their sleep,
But no one challenged; Troy was in a drowse
In the deep morning sleep before the dawn
Now faint upon the distant tops of Ida.

And we were seen by watchmen on the tower
On that side Troy, but none of them suspected
That we were Greeks: they thought that we were Lycians,
Old allies of the Trojans, mustering
Up to the temples for a sacrifice
Before we marched from Troia to our homes.

We were within the second ring of road,
Outside King Priam's palace and the temples,
Before a sentry challenged us, and then
It was too late for the alarm to help.
The man paused at the turning of his beat,
Looked round and saw us, gave a cry, then challenged,
Then died, stabbed through the throat by Diomed.

My party rushed into Apollo's temple
And burst into the palace to the guards
Sleeping in quarters, some of them half drunk,
All without arms: we herded them like sheep.

And by the time the guards were bound, the city
Was lit with blazing thatches, and awake,
Dawn coming, fire burning, women screaming,
And war-cries, and loud trumpets and clashed armour.
There was hard fighting in a dozen spots.

We came out of the guard-room by a gate
Into a blaze all red with fire flying:
A palace court it was, the inner court,
Where Menelaus and his Spartan spearmen
Were killing Priam's sons.
Just as we reached the court a dozen spearmen
Were all attacking young Deiphobus.

I knew the lad by sight, for he had come
On embassy to Agamemnon once,
And Menelaus meant to have him killed
And flung to the camp-dogs, because of Helen.

There he was, fighting for his life with twelve.

A fine young man, like Hektor in the face,
A bright, clean-cut face, tanned with sun and wind,
Smiling and cool and swift with parry on parry.

He had been surprised: he had no body-armour,
Nothing but spear and shield, and there he stood,
Checking each thrust, swift, marvellously.
                                    One minute
He stood, matchless in skill in the red glare,
Then someone crept above and stabbed him down.

The city was all ours in the hour.
Many were killed in fighting: many more
Escaped, during the burning and confusion,
Out of the city by the Eastern gate.
The rest we took: some of the prisoners,
The little children and old men and women,
We drove out of the city to the mountains.

271

The rest we kept; young women skilled in crafts
And men who might make slaves.
                                    We made them quench
The fires that were burning in the city
And then we sacked the city utterly.

When we had sacked her utterly, we forced
Our Trojan slaves to lever down the ramparts
Over the walls, until the city seemed
A mound of fallen stones and roofless houses.
We lit the wreck.

Then as we sailed for home with slaves and plunder,
We saw the ruins burning, and the smoke
Streaming across the sunburnt Trojan plain.
With all that world of murder on our backs
We bore our load of misery from Asia.

AUSTRALIA

When the North Lander saw the rose in blossom,
He thought the bush bore fire, and knelt and prayed.
When first the desert woman saw the sea,
She cried, "O under God, the day and night."

We have but language for the starry Heaven,
And words for continents and emperors.
I have but images within my heart
And words with which to make those images
Form in the minds of others, and, alas,
You are too wonderful and beautiful,
I cannot tell the marvel of your land,
But can be happy with my memories.

I think at first of cities bright with flowers,
Flowers for everybody, everywhere:
Then of a grass unlike the English turf,
"Buffalo grass," you called it, tough and springy:
Then of the birds, the exquisite blue wrens,
The kookaburras laughing in the fig-tree,
The whip birds slashing in the rainy glen,
The blue and scarlet parrots rushing past,
And black swans on the lake at Woolongoon.
Yet of the birds the black-backed magpie seems

The very soul of the Australian scene.
Often in early morning I would hear him
In strange, sweet song, now like to jingling glasses,
Now piping, now like flutes, but always telling
Of morning coming over the world's rim.

Then I remember how upon the hill,
Among the gumtrees, on the holiday,
The car sped past a sunny group of children.
And on the instant as we hurried past,
I heard a little girl cry, "There's John Masefield,"
And knew upon the instant what a power
A language has to give a fellowship
Over the distances of earth and sea.

Next, I remember how the forest stood;
Mile after mile of giant gums, blue-gray,
Glen after glen, blue-gray; peak after peak;
With blackened rampikes from old forest fires,
And bones of dead gums, white as skeletons,
And silence everywhere, not to be broken,
Save by the water in the gully talking.

Then, the great spaces like the Berkshire downs;
Mile after mile, with clumps upon the skyline
Of gumtrees which at distance looked like beech;
The wind-swept, rolling plain, dotted with sheep;
The station buildings here and there: few men,
Perhaps two children upon pony back,
Turning a mob of cattle, or the slow,
Part staggering figures of two sundowners,
Bent underneath the long rolls of their blueys,
Silently moving to a camping-place.

Next, as it were a river of bright flowers
In Earth's most lovely garden, and great rain
Ceasing above a multitude, and sun
Struggling through cloud, and lighting up the scene
Of splendid horses going to the post.

Then in the quagmire of the course, the thunder
Of the great race's passing, with surmise
From all those thousands, of which rider led;
Nothing but distant, flitting, coloured caps,
Shewed in a bunch along the rail; then, lo,

273

They swerved into the Straight, the great horse leading.
He bore topweight; the going was a bog;
He strode at ease, ahead, his ears still cocked.
Had he been called-upon he could have won
By half-a-mile, it seemed: his image stays
Forever in my mind as one of Power
That achieves easily while Weakness strives.

Next, I remember all the sun-swept, wind-swept
Hills of the pasture up above the brook;
No fence in sight; the cattle in small groups
Moving and grazing in the same direction,
And all the landscape stretching on and on,
To unknown mountains, forty miles away,
Where sheep and dogs and cattle, all gone wild,
Ran in the range, men said, and dingoes throve.

There was an ancient tree outside the station,
Which marked (they said) an English convict's grave.
He swallowed stolen jewels and so died.
Often I hope that that free space and light
Have freed him to the lovely universe,
So that he rides upon the wind there, singing
For joy that the old iron of his sins
Is snapped in pieces from his fettered soul.

Always above these memories is the sense
Of charming people, ever kind and thoughtful;
Most generous in thought, in word, in deed,
And faithful in their kindness to the end.
The mind is glad with many memories
Of kind things done and uttered by the race,
Earth's newest race of men, whose bodies' beauty
Surpasses all the peoples of the world;
Whose grace and care and generosity
Though never thanked, can never be forgotten.
A marvellous kind people, beautiful.

I shut my eyes and hear the magpies utter
Their magical, sweet cry like jingling glass,
And see the barren with the whited bones
Of gumtrees stretching to the flood-water,
Where black swans straddle in a line, like men
Pretending to be swans. Beyond the flood
There are the shearing sheds, where men of Anzac,

The shearers about whom the ballads tell,
Wonderful men whose fame this country treasures,
Strip off the fleeces from the sheep as though
Each fleece were but a woolly coat unbuttoned.

And many many other memories come,
Of cities fairer than our country holds;
Of waters gushing among blue-gray gums;
Or mighty pastures, each with lonely horsemen
Loping the morning, singing as they go;
Of beaches where the sun-tanned dare the sharks;
Or bush, the same for miles, all feathery-dim,
Each fathom of it green-gray, feathery-dim,
(Distinct, yet indistinct, almost like seaweed),
Where thirst has killed her hundreds, and will kill.

But among all these memories I hear
From gumtrees dead or blossoming, the magpies,
With that strange song so moving and so sweet,
The very voice of that far distant land,
So sweet that all who hear it must be moved
To hear it once again before they die.

THE WAGGON-MAKER

I have made tales in verse, but this man made
Waggons of elm to last a hundred years;
The blacksmith forged the rims and iron gears,
His was the magic that the wood obeyed.

Each deft device that country wisdom bade,
Or farmers' practice needed, he preserved.
He wrought the subtle contours, straight and curved,
Only by eye, and instinct of the trade.

No weakness, no offence in any part,
It stood the strain in mired fields and roads
In all a century's struggle for its bread;
Bearing, perhaps, eight thousand heavy loads.
Beautiful always as a work of art,
Homing the bride, and harvest, and men dead.

THE SPANISH MAIN SCHOONER

A little wooden schooner, painted white,
Lofty and beamy, likely to be fast,
Lies at the wharf beside the papaw sellers.
She has white wooden after-rails raised high,
A well-steeved bowsprit and a flaring sheer.

She has a deck-house just abaft the mainmast,
It brings the main-boom high above the deck,
The door is open, there are bunks within,
And yellow trousers dangling from a peg.

Outside it, on a box, a shining tin
Of soapy water holds the Captain's shirt.
A cock and hen find pickings on the deck,
Awnings of worn-out sail keep out the sun.

Her gear is white manila, nearly new.
All is in choicest order, the mast-shrouds
Are set-up by a method new to me.
The shrouds turn-in on double purchase-blocks,
The laniards reeve through dead-eyes on the rail.
The masts are raked, each little thing aloft
Is cared for with unusual seamanship.

Her seamen are on deck, four graceful negroes
Wearing white cotton clothing patched with blue,
Their arms are sunburned black up to the shoulder.
They stand below the mainmast, swaying up
Her mainsail white with cotton, the gaff jolts,
The mainsail ripples out, the negroes cry
Ahi, Aho. Upon her transom-stern
In white, on a green oval, is her name,
The SALVADOR DEL MUNDO. Cartagena.

A BALLAD OF SIR FRANCIS DRAKE

Before Sir Francis put to sea,
He told his love, "My dear,
When I am gone, you wait for me,
Though you wait for seven year."

His love, who was redder than the rose,
And sweeter than the may,
Said, "I will wait till summer snows
And winter fields bear hay.

"I'll wait until the ice is hot,
And July sun is cold,
Until the cliffs of Dover rot,
And the cliffs of Devon mould."

Sir Francis went aboard his ship,
Her sails were sheeted home,
The water gurgled at her lip
And whitened into foam.

And months went by, but no more word
Came from that roving soul
Than comes from the Mother Carey bird
That nests at the South Pole.

In the seventh year men gave up hope,
And swore that he was dead.
They had the bell tolled with the rope
And the burial service read.

His love, who was redder than the rose,
Mourned for him long and long,
But even grief for a lover goes
When life is running strong.

And many a man beset her way
Who thought it Paradise
To gaze at her lovely eyes and say
That her eyes were stars, not eyes.

And so she promised a nobleman
When the ninth-year hay was hauled,
And before the harvest-home began
Her marriage banns were called.

The wedding-day came bright and fair,
The bells rang up and down,
The bridesmaids in their white were there
And the parson in his gown.

The rosy bride came up the aisle,
The page-boys bore her train;
She stood by the groom a little while
To be made one out of twain.

Not one of all within the church
Thought of Sir Francis Drake.
A crash made the transept columns lurch
And the central tower quake.

A cannon-ball came thundering by
Between the bride and groom.
The girl said, "Francis wonders why
There's someone in his room.

"Francis is homing from the seas,
He has sent this message here.
I would rather be wife to Francis, please,
Than the lady of a peer."

Ere the priest could start his talk again,
A man rushed in to say,
"Here is Drake come home with the wealth
        of Spain.
His ships are in the Bay."

The noble said with courtly grace,
"It would be a wiser plan
If I let Sir Francis take my place,
And I will be Best Man."

THE *LOCH ACHRAY*

The *Loch Achray* was a clipper tall
With seven-and-twenty hands in all.
Twenty to hand and reef and haul,
A skipper to sail and mates to bawl
"Tally on to the tackle-fall,
Heave now 'n' start her, heave 'n' pawl!"
        Hear the yarn of a sailor,
        An old yarn learned at sea.

Her crew were shipped and they said "Farewell,
So-long, my Tottie, my lovely gell,

We sail to-day if we fetch to hell,
It's time we tackled the wheel a spell."
            Hear the yarn of a sailor,
            An old yarn learned at sea.

The dockside loafers talked on the quay
The day that she towed down to sea:
"Lord, what a handsome ship she be!
Cheer her, sonny boys, three times three!"
And the dockside loafers gave her a shout
As the red-funnelled tug-boat towed her out;
They gave her a cheer as the custom is,
And the crew yelled "Take our loves to Liz—
Three cheers, bullies, for old Pier Head
'N' the bloody stay-at-homes!" they said.
            Hear the yarn of a sailor,
            An old yarn learned at sea.

In the grey of the coming on of night
She dropped the tug at the Tuskar Light,
'N' the topsails went to the topmast head
To a chorus that fairly awoke the dead.
She trimmed her yards and slanted South
With her royals set and a bone in her mouth.
            Hear the yarn of a sailor,
            An old yarn learned at sea.

She crossed the Line and all went well,
They ate, they slept, and they struck the bell
And I give you a gospel truth when I state
The crowd didn't find any fault with the Mate,
But one night off the River Plate.
            Hear the yarn of a sailor,
            An old yarn learned at sea.

It freshened up till it blew like thunder
And burrowed her deep, lee-scuppers under.
The old man said, "I mean to hang on
Till her canvas busts or her sticks are gone"—
Which the blushing looney did, till at last
Overboard went her mizzen-mast.
            Hear the yarn of a sailor,
            An old yarn learned at sea.

Then a fierce squall struck the *Loch Achray*
And bowed her down to her water-way;
Her main-shrouds gave and her forestay,
And a green sea carried her wheel away;
Ere the watch below had time to dress
She was cluttered up in a blushing mess.
  Hear the yarn of a sailor,
  An old yarn learned at sea.

She couldn't lay-to nor yet pay-off,
And she got swept clean in the bloody trough;
Her masts were gone, and afore you knowed
She filled by the head and down she goed.
Her crew made seven-and-twenty dishes
For the big jack-sharks and the little fishes,
And over their bones the water swishes.
  Hear the yarn of a sailor,
  An old yarn learned at sea.

The wives and girls they watch in the rain
For a ship as won't come home again.
"I reckon it's them head-winds," they say,
"She'll be home to-morrow, if not to-day.
I'll just nip home 'n' I'll air the sheets
'N' buy the fixins 'n' cook the meats
As my man likes 'n' as my man eats."

So home they goes by the windy streets,
Thinking their men are homeward bound
With anchors hungry for English ground,
And the bloody fun of it is, they're drowned!
  Hear the yarn of a sailor,
  An old yarn learned at sea.

TRADE WINDS

In the harbour, in the island, in the Spanish Seas,
Are the tiny white houses and the orange-trees,
And day-long, night-long, the cool and pleasant breeze
  Of the steady Trade Winds blowing.

There is the red wine, the nutty Spanish ale,
The shuffle of the dancers, the old salt's tale,

The squeaking fiddle, and the soughing in the sail
   Of the steady Trade Winds blowing.

And o' nights there's fire-flies and the yellow moon,
And in the ghostly palm-trees the sleepy tune
Of the quiet voice calling me, the long low croon
   Of the steady Trade Winds blowing.

SEA-FEVER

I must go down to the seas again, to the lonely sea and the sky,
And all I ask is a tall ship and a star to steer her by,
And the wheel's kick and the wind's song and the white
      sail's shaking,
And a grey mist on the sea's face and a grey dawn breaking.

I must go down to the seas again, for the call of the running
      tide
Is a wild call and a clear call that may not be denied;
And all I ask is a windy day with the white clouds flying,
And the flung spray and the blown spume, and the sea-gulls
      crying.

I must go down to the seas again, to the vagrant gypsy life,
To the gull's way and the whale's way where the wind's
      like a whetted knife;
And all I ask is a merry yarn from a laughing fellow-rover,
And quiet sleep and a sweet dream when the long trick's
      over.

THE WEST WIND

It's a warm wind, the west wind, full of birds' cries;
I never hear the west wind but tears are in my eyes.
For it comes from the west lands, the old brown hills,
And April's in the west wind, and daffodils.

It's a fine land, the west land, for hearts as tired as mine,
Apple orchards blossom there, and the air's like wine.
There is cool green grass there, where men may lie at rest,
And the thrushes are in song there, fluting from the nest.

281

"Will you not come home, brother? you have been long away,
It's April, and blossom time, and white is the may;
And bright is the sun, brother, and warm is the rain,—
Will you not come home, brother, home to us again?

"The young corn is green, brother, where the rabbits run,
It's blue sky, and white clouds, and warm rain and sun.
It's song to a man's soul, brother, fire to a man's brain,
To hear the wild bees and see the merry spring again.

"Larks are singing in the west, brother, above the green
       wheat,
So will you not come home, brother, and rest your tired feet?
I've a balm for bruised hearts, brother, sleep for aching eyes,"
Says the warm wind, the west wind, full of birds' cries.

SPANISH WATERS

Spanish waters, Spanish waters, you are ringing in my
       ears,
Like a slow sweet piece of music from the grey forgotten
       years;
Telling tales, and beating tunes, and bringing weary thoughts
       to me
Of the sandy beach at Muertos, where I would that I could
       be.

There's surf breaks on Los Muertos, and it never stops to
       roar,
And it's there we came to anchor, and it's there we went
       ashore,
Where the blue lagoon is silent amid snags of rotting
       trees,
Dropping like the clothes of corpses cast up by the seas.

We anchored at Los Muertos when the dipping sun was
       red,
We left her half-a-mile to sea, to west of Nigger Head;
And before the mist was on the Cay, before the day was
       done,
We were all ashore on Muertos with the gold that we had
       won.

282

We bore it through the marshes in a half-score battered
  chests,
Sinking, in the sucking quagmires to the sunburn on our
  breasts,
Heaving over tree-trunks, gasping, damning at the flies and
  heat,
Longing for a long drink, out of silver, in the ship's cool
  lazareet.

The moon came white and ghostly as we laid the treasure
  down,
There was gear there'd make a beggarman as rich as Lima
  Town,
Copper charms and silver trinkets from the chests of Spanish
  crews,
Gold doubloons and double moidores, louis d'ors and portagues,

Clumsy yellow-metal earrings from the Indians of Brazil,
Uncut emeralds out of Rio, bezoar stones from Guayaquil;
Silver, in the crude and fashioned, pots of old Arica bronze,
Jewels from the bones of Incas desecrated by the Dons.

We smoothed the place with mattocks, and we took and
  blazed the tree,
Which marks yon where the gear is hid that none will ever
  see,
And we laid aboard the ship again, and south away we
  steers,
Through the loud surf of Los Muertos which is beating in
  my ears.

I'm the last alive that knows it. All the rest have gone their
  ways
Killed, or died, or come to anchor in the old Mulatas Cays,
And I go singing, fiddling, old and starved and in despair,
And I know where all that gold is hid, if I were only there.

It's not the way to end it all. I'm old, and nearly blind,
And an old man's past's a strange thing, for it never leaves
  his mind.
And I see in dreams, awhiles, the beach, the sun's disc
  dipping red,
And the tall ship, under topsails, swaying in past Nigger
  Head.

I'd be glad to step ashore there. Glad to take a pick and go
To the lone blazed coco-palm tree in the place no others
    know,
And lift the gold and silver that has mouldered there for years
By the loud surf of Los Muertos which is beating in my ears.

CARGOES

Quinquireme of Nineveh from distant Ophir
Rowing home to haven in sunny Palestine,
With a cargo of ivory,
And apes and peacocks,
Sandalwood, cedarwood, and sweet white wine.

Stately Spanish galleon coming from the Isthmus,
Dipping through the Tropics by the palm-green shores,
With a cargo of diamonds,
Emeralds, amethysts,
Topazes, and cinnamon, and gold moidores.

Dirty British coaster with a salt-caked smoke stack
Butting through the channel in the mad March days,
With a cargo of Tyne coal,
Road-rail, pig-lead,
Firewood, iron-ware, and cheap tin trays.

THE EMIGRANT

Going by Daly's shanty I heard the boys within
Dancing the Spanish hornpipe to Driscoll's violin,
I heard the sea-boots shaking the rough planks of the floor,
But I was going westward, I hadn't heart for more.

All down the windy village the noise rang in my ears,
Old sea-boots stamping, shuffling, it brought the bitter
    tears,
The old tune piped and quavered, the lilts came clear and
    strong,
But I was going westward, I couldn't join the song.

There were the grey stone houses, the night wind blowing
    keen,

The hill-sides pale with moonlight, the young corn springing
    green,
The hearth nooks lit and kindly, with dear friends good
    to see.
But I was going westward, and the ship waited me.

SEEKERS

Friends and loves we have none, nor wealth nor blessed
    abode,
But the hope of the City of God at the other end of the road.

Not for us are content, and quiet, and peace of mind,
For we go seeking a city that we shall never find.

There is no solace on earth for us—for such as we—
Who search for a hidden city that we shall never see.

Only the road and the dawn, the sun, the wind, and the
    rain,
And the watch fire under stars, and sleep, and the road again.

We seek the City of God, and the haunt where beauty dwells,
And we find the noisy mart and the sound of burial bells.

Never the golden city, where radiant people meet,
But the dolorous town where mourners are going about the
    street.

We travel the dusty road till the light of the day is dim,
And sunset shows us spires away on the world's rim.

We travel from dawn to dusk, till the day is past and by,
Seeking the Holy City beyond the rim of the sky.

Friends and loves we have none, nor wealth nor blest abode,
But the hope of the City of God at the other end of the road.

A CREED

I held that when a person dies
    His soul returns again to earth;

Arrayed in some new flesh-disguise
    Another mother gives him birth.
With sturdier limbs and brighter brain
The old soul takes the roads again.

Such was my own belief and trust;
    This hand, this hand that holds the pen,
Has many a hundred times been dust
    And turned, as dust, to dust again;
These eyes of mine have blinked and shone
    In Thebes, in Troy, in Babylon.

All that I rightly think or do,
    Or make, or spoil, or bless, or blast,
Is curse or blessing justly due
    for sloth or effort in the past.
My life's a statement of the sum
Of vice indulged, or overcome.

I know that in my lives to be
    My sorry heart will ache and burn,
And worship, unavailingly,
    The woman whom I used to spurn,
And shake to see another have
The love I spurned, the love she gave.

And I shall know, in angry words,
    In gibes, and mocks, and many a tear.
A carrion flock of homing-birds,
    The gibes and scorns I uttered here
The brave word that I failed to speak
Will brand me dastard on the cheek.

And as I wander on the roads
    I shall be helped and healed and blessed;
Dear words shall cheer and be as goads
    To urge to heights before unguessed.
My road shall be the road I made;
All that I gave shall be repaid.

So shall I fight, so shall I tread,
    In this long war beneath the stars;
So shall a glory wreathe my head,
    So shall I faint and show the scars,

Until this case, this clogging mould,
Be smithied all to kingly gold.

FRAGMENTS

Troy Town is covered up with weeds,
   The rabbits and the pismires brood
On broken gold, and shards, and beads
   Where Priam's ancient palace stood.

The floors of many a gallant house
   Are matted with the roots of grass;
The glow-worm and the nimble mouse
   Among her ruins flit and pass.

And there, in orts of blackened bone,
   The widowed Trojan beauties lie,
And Simois babbles over stone
   And waps and gurgles to the sky.

Once there were merry days in Troy,
   Her chimneys smoked with cooking meals,
The passing chariots did annoy
   The sunning housewives at their wheels.

And many a lovely Trojan maid
   Set Trojan lads to lovely things;
The game of life was nobly played,
   They played the game like Queens and Kings.

So that, when Troy had greatly passed
   In one red roaring fiery coal,
The courts the Grecians overcast
   Became a city in the soul.

In some green island of the sea,
   Where now the shadowy coral grows
In pride and pomp and empery
   The courts of old Atlantis rose.

In many a glittering house of glass
   The Atlanteans wandered there;
The paleness of their faces was
   Like ivory, so pale they were.

And hushed they were, no noise of words
  In those bright cities ever rang;
Only their thoughts, like golden birds,
  About their chambers thrilled and sang.

They all knew all wisdom, for they knew
  The souls of those Egyptian Kings
Who learned, in ancient Babilu,
  The beauty of immortal things.

They knew all beauty—when they thought
  The air chimed like a stricken lyre,
The elemental birds were wrought,
  The golden birds became a fire.

And straight to busy camps and marts
  The singing flames were swiftly gone;
The trembling leaves of human hearts
  Hid boughs for them to perch upon.

And men in desert places, men
  Abandoned, broken, sick with fears,
Rose singing, swung their swords agen,
  And laughed and died among the spears.

The green and greedy seas have drowned
  That city's glittering walls and towers,
Her sunken minarets are crowned
  With red and russet water-flowers.

In towers and rooms and golden courts
  The shadowy coral lifts her sprays;
The scrawl hath gorged her broken orts,
  The shark doth haunt her hidden ways.

But, at the falling of the tide,
  The golden birds still sing and gleam.
The Atlanteans have not died,
  Immortal things still give us dream.

The dream that fires man's heart to make,
  To build, to do, to sing or say
A beauty Death can never take,
  An Adam from the crumbled clay.

IGNORANCE

Since I have learned Love's shining alphabet,
    And spelled in ink what's writ in me in flame,
And borne her sacred image richly set
    Here in my heart to keep me quit of shame;

Since I have learned how wise and passing wise
    Is the dear friend whose beauty I extol,
And know how sweet a soul looks through the eyes
    That are so pure a window to her soul;

Since I have learned how rare a woman shows
    As much in all she does as in her looks,
And seen the beauty of her shame the rose,
    And dim the beauty writ about in books;

All I have learned, and can learn, shows me this—
How scant, how slight, my knowledge of her is.

C. L. M.

In the dark womb where I began
My mother's life made me a man.
Through all the months of human birth
Her beauty fed my common earth.
I cannot see, nor breathe, nor stir,
But through the death of some of her.

Down in the darkness of the grave
She cannot see the life she gave.
For all her love, she cannot tell
Whether I use it ill or well,
Nor knock at dusty doors to find
Her beauty dusty in the mind.

If the grave's gates could be undone,
She would not know her little son,
I am so grown. If we should meet
She would pass by me in the street,
Unless my soul's face let her see
My sense of what she did for me.

What have I done to keep in mind
My debt to her and womankind?
What woman's happier life repays
Her for those months of wretched days?
For all my mouthless body leeched
Ere Birth's releasing hell was reached?

What have I done, or tried, or said
In thanks to that dear woman dead?
Men triumph over women still,
Men trample women's rights at will,
And man's lust roves the world untamed.

O grave, keep shut lest I be shamed.

THE WILD DUCK

Twilight. Red in the west.
Dimness. A glow on the wood.
The teams plod home to rest.
The wild duck come to glean.
O souls not understood,
What a wild cry in the pool;
What things have the farm ducks seen
That they cry so—huddle and cry?

Only the soul that goes.
Eager. Eager. Flying.
Over the globe of the moon,
Over the wood that glows.
Wings linked. Necks a-strain,
A rush and a wild crying.

A cry of the long pain
In the reeds of a steel lagoon,
In a land that no man knows.

SIXTY ODD YEARS AGO

Much worth was in the country: yet, today,
That long dead England seems a land astray.
Backward and blind, and proud of being both,
Toiling to death the fundamental sloth,

Governed by cackle-shops, whose fatal fun
Pretended that scheme cackled was thing done.
Muddled, yet meddling in affairs not ours
With vestry morals and a eunuch's powers;
Vain of a chaos of mean cities filled
With any squalor any cared to build;
Vain of a drunken untaught multitude
Who breathed not, ate not, drank not, one thing good.

Such seems the England of that distant past:—
Prepared for war, (the war before the last);
Prepared for peace, that should create a race
Of cringing starvelings haggard in the face;
Unlettered, unimpassioned and unled
Want in the heart and clap-trap in the head;
Working at games, despising art and thought,
Its over-toiling millions making naught,
Naught, for their lives' exhaustions put in pay,
That thinking man would wish to see today.

Times were to come to shock the land awake.
Danger of death displayed us our mistake.
When death came striding, England let men see
Patience and courage changing destiny.
When death is winning and disaster shews,
Then England lightens and her sign's the rose.

We, who have seen this England left alone
And felt the nations count us overthrown,
And seen the greedy vultures stretching neck
And gaping beak, for pieces of the wreck,
And heard the exultation of the cur
Yap the hyacnas on to finish her,
We know the nature of the sign we bear
A deathless rose that winter makes more fair.

When our survivors stand among their dead,
At some path's end where lunacy has led,
When courage learns, it cannot alter fate
Unweaponed, unsupported and too late;
When allies fall, and friends account it wise
To do the biddings of our enemies,
Then, our hope kindles; then we truly are;
Darkness must fall before we seem a star.

GALLIPOLI, 1915

Even so was wisdom proven blind;
So courage failed, so strength was chained;
Even so the gods, whose seeing mind
Is not as ours, ordained.

ON THE DEAD IN GALLIPOLI

They came from safety of their own free will
To lay their young men's beauty, strong men's powers
Under the hard roots of the foreign flowers
Having beheld the Narrows from the Hill.

from
ON THE HILL

No I know not;
Yet the framework has a beauty and an order
Over which illusion passes in the never-counted leaves,
That are whirled away in Autumn, if they go not
From Nature any further than the border
That re-gives as it receives.

Bare the hill stood.
Rabbit-scuffled chalk was on its trenching;
And the leafless beeches listened to the silence of the sky.
Purple as a cloud of thunder brooded Kills Wood;
In the Vale, a running white of smoke was blenching
As the West Express went by.

No; I knew not;
But the setting had a vastness and a power,
And the long illusion passing never passed, though
    seemed to pass.
It was green a little season, and then grew not:
Fruited sometimes; often never came to flower,
Then was wind above dead grass.

No; I see not
More than this, a living greatness of procession,
Part of infinite procession hurled in fire through the sky,
Bearing things that seem to be, then seem to be not,

Human things, in living faulty with obsession,
Leaving anguish when they die.

THE HILL

This remains here.
This was here, I well remember, over fifty years ago.
Subject to untiring Nature as to many dying creatures,
Altered always, crop and colour, but preserving living
    features
That we love and seem to know.

Here the Norther
Brings its death upon the bastion till the laurustinus dies.
Here the Easter comes with coughings and the tower
    death-bell tolling,
Here the Souther drives the rain-streaks out of darkness
    over-rolling,
And the Wester clears the skies.

Thought is nothing
To this scene on which the plant of man puts out its
    million leaves
It has neither brain nor feeling; neither planning nor
    progression;
Only infinite diversion of an on and on procession
Heedless of what man believes.

I am of it.
Know that I am wholly kin, if partly set astray.
Know that in it is the healing of the sorrow of a nation,
And the glory of deliverance from crime and usurpation
With Eternity today.

Man is nothing
To this quiet, full of power, to this effort, full of peace,
Nothing, even as a rebel, blind with anger and forgettal;
Nothing, even as a turmoil that his madness cannot settle
That his death makes swiftly cease.

But the power
And its quiet and its effort reassert a silent sway.
Man by man a spirit listens, soul by soul, a mortal answers,

Then a cry for better order moves the frenzy of the
      dancers
And the madnesses obey.

I am gazing
Into what is man's foundation, the enduring scene that
      stands,
Comforted by sun and water, glad of either in their
      season,
Something that outlasts our minute, and has majesty for
      reason,
While its granites wear to sands.

Much I wonder.
Much I long for this to speak, for an Incarnate Scene
      to come
With a word for me to utter: so I ponder; so I hearken,
Watching closely that I see it ere my fading eye-balls darken,
And repeat, ere I be dumb.

All my knowledge,
All my being is summed up in this, the scene, that is a
      friend
That is comfort through the evil and the agony of living,
That, if heeding, and if judging, seems forgetting and
      forgiving
And will seem so to the end.

Here I leave it.
Here it leaves me in the twilight, the imperfect wax it
      prest;
Knowing this, that it has shaped me, or mis-shaped me,
      for the telling
Of the purpose of the spirit that possesses this, in-
      dwelling,
Knowing change, but never rest.

Is it heedless?
Is it heartless, or unjudging, or forgetful, or immune?
Do we apprehend its nature, can we comprehend its
      power,
We, as mortal as the sparrow, and as fading as the
      flower,
And as changing as the Moon?

Let them answer
Who reply to every question, as befits an iron time.
I can only see a valley with a million grass-blades blowing
And a hill with clouds above it whither many larks are
   going
Singing paeans as they climb.

JOUNCER'S TUMP

My grand-dad said, to Sis and me,
"In yonder tump, or mound,
An ancient hero buried be,
With gold all wrapped around:—
A thousand pound."

My grand-dad died, as reason bade,
Since man but mortal is.
The only thing of him that stayed,
Was just that word of his,
To me and Sis.

And I went east and then went west,
A soldier of the Queen;
Sis married twice, and then had rest
As though she hadn't been
Upon the scene.

And I, returning from the war,
One-legged, (that went with two),
Found none to love or sorrow for,
And nought for me to do,
But barley-brew.

So, sitting in the HOB & JILL
At my eleventh cup,
"In Jouncer's Tump" (I said to Bill)
There lies a golden tup.
Let's dig him up."

"Come on", said Bill: the rest said "No . . .
It's all to rouse the dead.
What's put below should lay below
Until the world is sped . . ."
Much more they said.

But out went Bill and out when I
Into the moonlit way
The full moon revelled in the sky
The tawny owl said "Hey . . .
Hoo Hoo. Hurray."

So, pick and shovel being had,
We went by the Red Lane
To where the Jouncer's Tump stood sad
Between a field of grain
And Charles's Wain.

And when we saw it close at hand
That great mound with its trees,
So grim, it put us to a stand,
For human marrows freeze
At things like these.

For many hundred men had wrought
To heap that barrow grim;
And he, inside, though out of thought,
Had once been passing trim,
With life in him.

For otherwise, not thus would men
Have piled such sods and stones
High up, to half the county's ken,
Above his breathless bones.
This, the world owns.

This man had been a King indeed,
And now, to break his tomb,
Was something to make mortals heed . . .
A cloud came by like doom
And brought a gloom.

Then Bill: "It seems to me" (he said)
"That yonder lies the door.
There, where the rabbit burrows be.
And what men venture for
Leads to their score."

With that, he leapt into the ditch
And picked, like a man mad,
The Jouncer Barrow's sloping pitch . . .

For Bill was a live lad.
Great might he had.

And after scrabbling tons of earth
Lo, there a doorway shewed,
Ample for any mortal girth,
In, to the King's abode,
An open road.

Bill lit the candle in his hat
And in he crawled and scraped
We shovelled like the mole or rat
And there the passage shaped
The doorway gaped.

And when the fallen earth was cleared
That long dead men had strown,
A kind of corridor appeared,
Empty and dry as bone
In well laid stone.

Roofed with it, paved and walled; and we
Pushed-in, but half in dread
Of what our eyes might shortly see,
And what might soon be said
There, by the dead.

Then, lighting all the light we had,
We reached the room four-square,
In the grave's heart, and stood adrad
At what we had laid bare,
The dead King there.

For there . . . the first, this myriad year,
Did our four eyes behold
Big bones, a sword-hilt and a spear,
Beneath a mail of gold
As grand-dad told.

Then Bill, who feared not dead nor quick,
After his first surprise,
Said, "Take his hat for candle-stick,
And now, to strip the prize,
From where it lies."

So while the candles waved and dripped
We did our robbers' deed,
That golden coat of his we stripped,
Urged to a double speed
By fear and greed.

Then out we dragged it to the night,
Before the east was gray,
An owl glid to us into sight,
And called and glid away,
Hoo Hoo Hurray.

We shovelled out our marks and went
Away, all mucked and hot.
And Bill said, "Now, my first intent
Is, put the spoil to pot,
And melt the lot."

And this, ere daylight came, we did.
We melted and we shared,
And each his portion took and hid,
Nor told what we had dared,
Nor what had bared.

Yet, later, as I shook my sack,
What seemed a coin of gold
Fell on the flooring with a clack
And on its edging rolled,
Till I caught hold.

It was a coin, or link, or flake,
Stamped with an ear of corn,
A marvel of an ancient make
By men of heretoforn . . .
None recent-born.

None, for a thousand years or two,
Had had the skill to leave
That golden corn-ear done so due,
From some long-mouldering sheave.
It made me grieve,

That neither of us once had seen
That mail with any care;

That neither knew what it had been
Nor what its beauties were
That we laid bare.

All of the coat, for all I knew
Had once been subtly wrought
Of links each beautiful and new
Like this one, (as I thought)
And now was nought.

I put the little link aside . . .
And lo, an earnest drove
Of angry men of law who tried
To trace the treasure-trove,
And did, by Jove.

For people of the HOB & JILL
Had talked, and news had spread . . .
The constables had taken Bill,
"O wicked," (people said)
To rob the dead."

And both our shares of gold they took.
They called us "Thief" and "Knave"
For having dared to break and look
Within a dead man's grave.
Much jaw they gave.

They made us shut the barrow door
And smooth the barrow side
Much neater than it was before:—
And talk went far and wide.
At last it died.

But two strange things there be; the one
That the lone golden link
That I had saved, was somehow gone
Through chance or theft or chink,
Where, I can't think.

The other, that my grand-dad told
Full forty years ago,
About the hero wrapped in gold
That we discovered so.
How did he know?

For he had never searched the mound;
None had, the scholars showed,
Since first the King went underground,
And Jouncer's Tump was strowed,
For his abode.

And scholars said the golden King
By what might still appear,
Had slumbered there a little thing
Of twice a thousand year,
Or very near.

And how my grand-dad knew that fact,
As fact we proved it be,
Two thousand years after the act,
Not any man can see.
It staggers me.

THE BLUEBELLS

We stood upon the grass beside the road,
At a wood's fence, to look among the trees.
In windless noon the burning May-time glowed.
Gray, in young green, the beeches stood at ease.
Light speckled in the wood or left it dim:
There lay a blue in which no ship could swim,
Within whose peace no water ever flowed.

Within that pool no shadow ever showed:
Tideless was all that mystery of blue.
Out of eternities man never knew
A living growth man never reaped nor sowed
Snatched in the dim its fitness from the hour
A miracle unspeakable of flower
That tears in the heart's anguish answered-to.

How paint it; how describe? None has the power.
It only had the power upon the soul
To consecrate the spirit and the hour,
To light to sudden rapture and console,
Its beauty called a truce: forgave: forgot
All the long horror of man's earthly lot,

A miracle unspeakable of flower
In a green May unutterably blue.

For what, for whom, was all the beauty spread,
This colour, that had power to dissolve
Man's fugitive dismays into resolve
And be a balsam upon hearts that bled?
In all the mile of marvel, what immense
Current of life had power so intense
To wrest such bounty out of sun and soil?
What starved imagination ached to feed?
What harassed heart implored for an assoil?

Who can behold it on this lonely hill,
Here in the one week when the wonder shows,
Here, where old silence waits on the wind's will,
Where, on the track, none but the postman goes,
Where upon mouse or bird the kestrel drops,
Or spotted 'pecker burrowing his bill
Furrows the bark, or the red squirrel hops
Or hunting vixen lifts a questing nose,
What other seer can the beauty thrill?

None, in the day; and, when the beauty dims,
When moonlight makes the still un-leafy tree,
A spell-bound ghost that cannot move his limbs,
What other passer can be here to see?
The new-come night-jar chirring on the branch?
The nightingale exulting in his hymns?
The wood-mice flitting where the moon-beams blanch?
The wind, in the few fir-trees, like a sea
On which the pale owl like a feather swims?

For none of these can such a marvel be.

Has it a source in a forgotten scene?
Is it a mark of vital methods taken,
Of choices made, at turning-points of Fate
Whether to know the Earth or seek the Queen?
Is it but yearly gladness of bonds shaken?
After a prison, an apparent gate?
Or is this miracle of blue and green
A symbolling of what it all may mean,
When the Queen comes and all we dead awaken?

IN PRAISE OF NURSES

Dedicated to
MARY CLIFFORD
LAURA FRANKLIN
HELEN McKENNA
PHYLLIS SIMMONDS
JOANNA WILLS

Man, in his gallant power, goes in pride,
Confident, self-sufficient, gleaming-eyed,
Till, with its poison on an unseen point
A sickness strikes and all his strengths disjoint.
Then, helpless, useless, hideous, stinking, mad,
He lies bereft of what he was and had,
Incapable of effort, limb and brain,
A living fog of fantasies of pain.

And yet, today, as ever, since man was,
Even mad Man a healing impulse has.
Doctors there are, whose wisdoms know and check
The deadly things that bring the body's wreck,
Who minish agony, relieve and heal
Evils once mortal in Man's commonweal.
All honour Doctors; let me honour those
Who tend the patient when the doctor goes.

Daily and nightly, little praised or paid,
Those ordered, lovely spirits bring their aid,
Cheering the tired when the pain is grim,
Restoring power to the helpless limb.

Watching through darkness, driving away fear
When madness brings her many spectres near;
Cleansing the foul, and smiling through the pique
Of nerves unstrung or overstrained or weak,
Bringing to all a knowledge, hardly won,
Of body's peace and spirit's unison;
And blessing pillows with a touch that brings
Some little ease to all man's broken strings.

All that they do is utter sacrifice
Of all themselves and precious beyond price;
And what a joy, through them, to re-survey

That narrow, sweet, now half-forgotten way
Of selfless service as a way to live
Based not on what you win but what you give.

Daily these gentle souls give pain relief:
Deferring dying they diminish grief;
The one they succour need not be a friend,
Only a wreck with anguish to amend.
Anguishes such as lately made me see
Such day-and-night-devotion given to me.

To you, most beautiful, devoted friends,
My gratitude will go until life ends.

Never, while living, may I fail to bless
The thought of you about my wretchedness.

I thank and bless you: that I write at all
Is, by itself, your work's memorial.

ON PILOTS

Pilots, those unknown beings, who remove
All ships and seamen from the homes of love,
Yet, still unknown, at long last, cheer the sight,
Like the first sounding or the Bishop Light,
And bring them home, to the desired place.

O memory, praise them, before Death efface.

Many have watched the Channel Pilot leave
His plunging charge at setting-in of eve,
Have heard his cry of 'Letters for ashore',
While the unsheeted topsails slat and roar,
He, gathering letters, hurrying good-byes,
Leaps to his boat on some well-taken rise,
And so away, while she, (his charge) again
Bows to blue water to the south of Spain.

O, to how many, nearing coast or port,
On some keel-trodden way of ship-resort,
The Pilot-Schooner has appeared, displaying
Skill in the sea-arts beyond mortal telling;

Some daughter of the pine-woods near the sea,
Each timber shaped by him who felled the tree,
On Massachusetts coast, or colder Maine.

There the sweet sea-horse leant against the rein;
She with a feather whitening at her lip,
Sure as a sea-gull sidling to her ship,
And then away, upon another quest,
A swimming sea-bird seemingly at rest,
One with the water, yet the water's Queen.

Can the old Hoogli pilots still be seen?
The Brig-Men, studying the hourly change
Of depth, of current-speed, of current-range,
Of shoals becoming deeps; of deeps that filled
(Nor warning given), as the River willed;
Of sands engulfing any ship that struck,
In depthless unplumbed squotulence of muck,
Leaving but eddies wrinkling under sky,
Wrinkling away, with bodies floating by?

They held half England's shipping in their hands,
Both up and down, and saved it from the sands.
Where pilots now have engines that prevail,
Those pilots handled charges under sail.
Often, in channels without room to turn,
They sailed them in and backed them in astern,
And plucked them outward on the sailing day.

Power has given man an easier way
These many years, but we should keep in mind
When weakness was and every way was blind,
When England's shipping had no mark to bless
Between Old London Bridge and Dungeness,
When all that seamen's threat had no defence
Save common sense and too uncommon sense;
When the young Nelson, still a growing boy,
Learned to be pilot groping in a hoy.

No easy task for lads in such a school,
To take a ship in charge in London Pool,
To seize the ebb, and pull her from the herd:
Perhaps at quiet dawn when no wind stirred,
To tide her down, her only strength an oar,
Tugged, to change course, twixt Wapping and the Nore.

So, loitering down, with fifty loitering down,
The gallows-beaconed road from London town,
Nearing collision, but by luck and skill
Just scraping clear as clever pilots will,
Catching a moment's gust, an instant's chance,
By doing hand and understanding glance.

Then, perhaps, drifting into fog not knowing
What lay ahead, or near, but keeping going
The instinct, ear, and scent alike at strain
For some least hint that made the matter plain;
Perhaps a cock-crow from a Kentish Farm,
(Even a mooing cow has given alarm)
Or whiff from hayfield, lime-kiln, bonfire-smoke.
Each, coming when it did, a voice that spoke.

He who has drifted thus in fogs, unseeing,
Has touched his spirit's unseen Greater Being.

Was there not once (some generations since)
An invitation from a foreign Prince
Sent to an English Fleet to make a stay
In some close harbour for Regatta Day?
Himself, the foreign Prince, would pilot all,
Proud, in his yacht, lest dangers should befall,
He, the land's Prince, would greatly, kindly, lead
To that snug cove, the anchorage decreed.

Then, as the teller told, a fog ensued,
Fog in her unity of solitude,
Dumb as old Death, save where the bell-buoys tossed
Their desolate lamentings of things lost.
Fog covered land and water, beast and man,
Blurring both anchorage and royal plan.
'So,' the Prince said, 'we cannot steam today,
To pilot-in the English to the bay.
Well . . . they must wait . . . the fog will lift anon.'

A night went by; a struggling sunbeam shone,
Or seemed to shine: upon a little wind,
Hardly a breath, the nulling dimness thinned,
A summer brightness shone on all the bay.
There in the cove appointed, our fleet lay,
Anchored, aligned, in order, distance kept,
Self-piloted through fog while landsmen slept.

There comes a memory from the long-since seen;
The *Waterwitch*, the Pilot's barquentine,
In summer sunset gliding like a ghost
Under all sail along the English coast.

Who did not envy those aboard her, then,
The lads there training to be pilot-men
Whose books were Nature's doings, seamen's guides,
Shallow and depths, sea-currents, set and tides;
Rocks breaking and rocks hidden, where the tint
Upon the water's surface gave the hint;
And all that wisdom gathered from the lead
When sudden fog engulfed what lay ahead;
Their life's communion with the Greater Mind
That told the courses when the way was blind;
The acute senses that receive and fuse
At once, the fifty signs to one of use?
What happier life for youth, than to engage
To spend a twelvemonth learning pilotage?

'By God and guess,' the seaman's proverb said,
So are paths found, where paths were never made.
By thought's intensity transcending thought,
The way is found, the ship to safety brought,
Or sent away, with every hope to thrive
Breasting blue water like a thing alive.

OLD RAIGER

Prologue:

Good Old Man Raiger, raging in his rage,
He raged to rights, considering his age.
He was a cough-drop, raging, as all said,
A rage like his would strike a tombstone dead.
When he was raging under Wood Top Hill,
Old Parson trembled and the chimes stood still,
He sent his rage afore, Old Raiger done.
He scared 'em stiff, one son and t'other son.

This raging Raiger, who and what was he?
A widower, with Tom and Charles his sons,
Owning some land and having ships at sea.

The two sons, not yet wed,
The younger having heart, the elder head,
In quarrel, not at daggers drawn, but guns.

Tom, heir and elder, still in some disgrace,
For some low love-affair, out eastward way,
Now sought to oust his brother from the place
Courting the girl Charles wooed.
Charles was a bailiff altogether good.
The loved-one was the country beauty, May.

One of old Raiger's ships was due to sail,
On a time-charter, from the port near by.
Successions of small crosses turned the scale,
She missed her tide and stayed.
The message (telling Raiger) was delayed.
He heard of stoppage, not the reasons why.

Thinking at once, 'The charter may be lost',
(Two days already had been stricken null),
His fury sought for someone to be tosst.
The houschold heard his cries
Cursing his Captain's being, lungs and eyes,
The ship, her charter, mates and crew and hull.

Trembling, they heard Old Raiger leave his room,
Calling his sons to have the carriage brought;
He bellowed like the trumpeting of doom,
But neither son replied.
So, raging to their door, he flung it wide;
There, rolling on the floor, the brothers fought.

Tom, the beneath one, gasped, 'I am the heir,
'You're just an unpaid bailiff to the Farm.'
Charles said, 'I'll teach you, here or anywhere.
'You shall not trouble May.
'Marry your baggage there, out Pightle way.'
Then tooth and nail replied to knee and arm.

Old Raiger tore the two apart, and sent
Each, as he bid; and when they brought the chaise,
Mounting, he asked them what their fury meant,
Fighting like two mad curs.
'I'll disinherit both if this recurs,
Mark that, you dogs' . . . and galloped off ablaze.

But, soon as he had gone, the angry two
Were at each other's throats upon the floor
Seeking the answer which of them should woo
The lovely dark-haired May;
Tom cried, 'We'll settle this at break of day.
'Tomorrow, up at Wood Top, half past four.'

'Right,' Charles agreed. 'Roof-rifles, twenty paces,
'We'll walk apart, then turn; let lead decide.
'May shall not have to suffer your disgraces.
'Our rifles are a pair.'
Tom answered, 'Dawn tomorrow: I'll be there
'And lead shall settle . . . Wood-Top-covert-side.'

Some little grief for brotherhood of old
Was with them both at moments in the night . . .
Charles wakened early in the April cold
A little before day.
He took his gun and went the woodland way
In dripping dew and the beginning light.

There, upon Wood Top, Brother Tom was waiting,
Nursing his gun, with his back turned to him,
The blackbirds cackled for the night abating,
And now, as Charles drew near,
The figure turned, and struck him dumb with fear:
It was not Tom, but Raiger, mad and grim . . .

Mad beyond speech, but no one could mistake
The wordless rage, the fury of command,
The hell-fire tempest, just about to break,
His childhood's utmost dread.
Charles quailed and shrank although no word was said;
He backed, obedient to the pointed hand.

He backed before the fury to the gate,
Terrified, as in childhood, like a hound
Suddenly sick with terror at a rate,
Crouched to the lifted whip . . . .
But what had brought the Raiger from the ship?
How had he learned of duel, time and ground?

He shrank along the border of the wood,
Back, through the swing-gate, in among the scrubs,
Terrified still, but in the ride he stood,

To plead his desperate case.
In childhood, truth had often won him grace,
The old dog barked but didn't bite his cubs.

But this time, 'No,' he thought, 'No pardon, now.
'This is detection in a plotted crime . . .
'He has discovered it, I marvel how . . .
'This ruins both of us . . . .
'I've seen him rage of old, but never thus . . .
'And now we're ruined to the end of time.'

A minute passed, but Raiger did not come . . .
No sound of footsteps came from Wood Top field,
The rage of outraged fatherhood was dumb . .
'He's had a stroke,' Charles thought . . .
'Father,' he cried; but Father answered naught.
A rabbit's hopping paused, a blue jay squealed.

'Father,' he cried again. No Father followed.
This was unlike the Raiger when ablaze.
His furies ravened when his devil holloaed.
'Father, I'm here,' Charles cried.
'He's had a stroke,' he said, as none replied.
He ran to see, but lo, to his amaze . . .

No human being showed, alive or dead;
The mighty paleness of the Wood Top bare
Was desolate, save where a rabbit sped.
Of Raiger, no trace, none . . . .
Where he had raged was nothing but Tom's gun,
Tom's very gun and Tom's own footprints there.

There in the dew, where Raiger's shape had glared,
None but Tom's footprints darkened in the dew.
Now with another terror Charles was scared:
'But I saw Father here . . . .
'It was himself, and he is dead, I fear . . .
'Dead at our duel that he somehow knew . . .'

Taking Tom's gun, he said, 'We are accurst' . . .
— When, lo, there in the dew, was Jill, the maid,
Crying, 'O Master Charles, before the worst,
'Come quick, before he dies . . . .
'For Master Tom, at home, a-dying lies . . .
'He came in dying, like his wits were strayed.'

They raced for home and there was Tom in bed,
Saying, 'I took my gun, and Father came,
'Speechless with anger, Charles, a thing of dread,
'A bombshell blazing bright . . .
'I am the wicked one, and you're the right . . .
'Soon he'll be here, Charles, and he'll strike us dead.'

'No, no,' Charles said. 'Shake hands, and let's be friends.'
The hands were shaken and the feud was done.
'Where did you see him, Tom?' 'At Wood Top Ends,
'Where I was waiting you.
'Lord knows how he discovered, but he knew,
'I ran for home and flung away my gun.'

'I have your gun,' Charles said, 'And Father's rage
'Is nothing now — our quarrel's set aside . . . .
'When he has blown his blast, he will assuage,
'Lie quiet and let be . . .
'I'll find him, Tom, — he never bothers me.'
But in his heart he thought, 'Father has died.

'Somehow, in death, he knew what we had planned
'And fury at our folly dealt the stroke . . . .
'And he the justest spirit in the land,
'Raging beyond all bounds,
'Panted to cudgel his two crazy hounds,
'And in the agony his great heart broke.

'That was his spirit sent for us to see
'To terrify and keep us from a crime.'
'Now, Tom,' he said, 'let bitter bygones be,
'All will be well . . . I'll out . . .
'I shall have news of Father without doubt.
'And food's a stand-by in a troublous time.'

So, rousing Tom from bed, and ordering food,
He went to ask had any seen or heard
Of Raiger back at home, in field or wood,
Or inns where mail-teams change . . . .
No one had news, all thought the question strange;
He hurried back to Tom without a word.

But news was coming, to make all alive;
While Tom and Charles took breakfast as of old,
A pair of grays came smoking up the drive,

It was The Game-Cocks' team.
Someone was coming thither in a steam,
Crunching the gravel, scattering the mould.

'Here's Father, then,' the Brothers spoke as one;
They heard an oath: the door was opened wide.
'Ha,' roared the Raiger, 'so the quarrel's done.
'I thought you two mad goats
'Had taken knives and cut each other's throats.
'Go, May's without; don't let her stay outside.'

They brought a blushing May: they offered chairs.
All trembled as the Raiger drew his breath;
He froze the Brothers with ferocious glares.
'You two blind jangling jays . . .
'You've nearly killed me with your crazy ways.
'But, Sirs, I'll stop your folly before death.

'Give me some coffee, May . . . the foes are friends,
'For all my gallop in the dark, they're cool.
'But hark 'ee, Masters, this your quarrel ends.
'You cocks, red in the comb,
'Will keep this not a cockpit but a home.
'I stand no nonsense more from either fool.

'No more such madness. Firstly, Tom the heir.
'Your girl, out at the Earls, is married now,
'The Pightle Inn man's wedded to her there.
'It must be understood
'That all that rotten gossip stops for good:
'The matter ends, I care not why nor how.

'You'll leave her there, whatever may have been,
'Of young man's folly or of woman's lies.
'Take it from me, you'll marry as I mean . . .
'Jemina . . . understand.
'You'll go today to ask her for her hand.
'You'll link the two estates, Sir: so be wise.

'I met Jemima's father, coming here.
'Your marriage with Jemima is arranged
'(All but the wedding-day and ringers' beer).
'I know you like the lass.
'(A cut above you, too, but let that pass . . .
'The glass has risen and the wind has changed.)

'Now, lovely May, daughter of my old friend,
'Forgive these fore-words; now I come to you . . .
'Men make the ruins that the women mend.
'This ruin here of ours,
'With you, may soon be beautiful with flowers;
'Charles isn't much, but can be made to do.

'Now, Charles, you don't deserve, but will, in time;
'I know you love this sweet beloved Spring,
'You'd marry her, but haven't got a dime.
'Now the Home Farm is yours.
'Whatever follies happen, land endures;
'Ask her, arrange the banns, and buy the ring.'

He rose and thrust Charles down upon his knees.
There at May's feet, and May was not unkind.
Tom blushed and paled and shuffled, ill at ease.
'Sir,' he said, 'Sir, forgive . . . .
'We three are pledged to friendship while we live.
'By tea-time I will know Jemima's mind.'

'Good,' said Old Raiger. 'Now, my bantam cocks,
'Eat . . . then I'll sleep . . . I've had a wearing night.
'The charter's safe, apart from Ocean's knocks. . .
'No need to call me hence.
'But suddenly I had a shocking sense
'That you two crazy bull-calves meant to fight.

'Duel, in fact at dawn, beyond the wood . . .
'(I was at Docks, with thirty miles to go)
'I swore I'd stop your folly if I could . . .
'So off, with a fresh team.
'Clear roads and moonlight we could put on steam.
' "Those fools,' I said, 'I'll stop their folly, though.' "

'Mind, it was not impossible to do,
'I thought we'd do it, but we met delays . . .
'Slowing for sloughs, and casting of a shoe,
'And ostlers all asleep,
'Myself, all mad at you two silly sheep,
"All dynamite, exploding into blaze.

'But morning caught me, as I might have known
'At Scrobbles (Squire's Gate) you know the place,

'And there stood Squire waiting all alone
'The Morning Mail to town.
'It seemed insanity, but I got down
'And settled with him in Jemima's case.

'"Crazy," you'll say, "to settle Tom's affair.
'"Just when already (haply) Charles and he
'"Had blown their silly ghosts into the air."
'Yes . . . but I next fetched May,
'She might be having a most tragic day,
'And where was comfort for her, save in me?

'By George, you two have given me a dance,
'And all for nothing, for you've made a peace,
'And tragedy collapses in romance.
'Now, I'll to bed to rest.
'Tom, off to see Jemima, it were best.
'Charles, tip the driver till the horses prance.'

Epilogue:

That's what the tale says Raging Raiger did
To stop his sons from doing what's forbid.
Finding he couldn't get to 'em, he sent
His spirit from him, and his spirit went
And scared 'em proper out of their two skins.
A terror will work wonder against sins.

He stopped them doing murder, that's a fact;
And stopping murder is a righteous act.
Many (as disliked Raiger) would admit
The old dog came with credit out of it.

But the two wild-cat boys got wives of sense.
Jemima brought th' estates into one fence,
And some (as disliked Raiger) sorrowed sore
To know he'd got the grass he lusted for,
Old Butter Pastures, that he'd longed-for long.

Raiger, if you'll permit me, he was strong.
Not in weight-lifting, nor in pitching hay,
But bowing all things down to have his way.
You wouldn't think it, not to see him, quite;
He never fought, he never had to fight.

313

But what he had in mind he had in mill,
Grinding all cross-conclusions to his will.
Maybe for thirty years his will was burning,
And all the thirty years the lane was turning.
'Nothing turns lanes, but will,' Old Raiger said . . . .

'Willing a thing, and knowing how to wait,
'And passing time, make many crookeds straight.
'But Willing is the Boy,' Old Raiger said.

A many sorrowed for Old Raiger dead.

THE ALONG-SHIPS STOW

Treacle, treacle, little ship,
Hither, mariners, and sip,
Buckets, mariners, and dip.

I was the Second in the *Captain Bold*,
Bound north, with general freight, from
                    Port of Peace,
Myself the very youth, the ship was old;
And leaving port, the wind on the increase,
I, fresh to berth and ship,
Knew from the dances she began to skip
That if she had a fault, it was, she rolled.

And as the gale increased, I thought the more
About the casked molasses we had stowed,
Up to the hatches there at Sugar-Shore . . .
A danger-freight for any ship to load.
I had stowed thwart-ship tiers . . .
Then the old mate had come about my ears
Swearing along-ships was the proper mode.

Well, seniors order, second mates endure,
Molasses tests the methods and decides;
The weather would be wicked, that was sure,
In wicked weather nothing wrong abides.
Things worsened, the glass fell;
The squallings stiffened into steady yell,
The forward well-deck often took it pure.

314

At first the rainfall kept the sea in check,
As rainfall will, but as the day went by,
Men needed life-lines on the open deck.
Then, what seemed smoke came skimming over sky . . .
Galloping smoke at first,
Then blackness, wilderness and thunder-burst,
And sea-hounds crying for a ship to wreck.

Well . . . as it worsened, nothing could be done
But lay her by and listen while it raved.
The Old Man shouted, 'Mister . . . listen, son . . .
'Find if those 'tweendeck casks are getting staved.
'It's certain to blow worse.
'Molasses in a cargo is a curse.
'Before it lulls, she'll stave a hundred ton.'

So down I went in semi-dark, and clung,
Under a man-hole peering to observe,
My feet jammed on the uprights of the rung,
My body bracing to her heave and swerve.
I saw a great grim cave
Where every inch a moaning whimper gave
For every inch was hurt and giving tongue.

Within the stifling tumult of the cave,
Along the 'long-ship-tiers the Mate had stowed,
Barrel on barrel had begun to stave,
And others strained to travel the same road.
The treacle struggled through
The started staves in seepages of glue
Which pressed, and, bursting bonds, became a wave.

Everywhere, treacle-tear and treacle-drip,
Staves, bungs and dunnage whelmed in a thick heave,
Dense treacle feelers getting a good grip;
I cannot tell it, nor can you believe . . .
Slow-loitering, surging swift
According to the plunging or the lift
Of the tormented, (haply dying) ship.

Below, the 'long-ship-tiers my thwart-ships stow
Still stood the strain (so far as I could see).
The truth about them nobody could know
But they were standing as it seemed to me.

As for 'a hundred ton',
The Old Man's guess, I reckoned every one
Was doomed to perish; all the lot would go.

Aghast, I watched the treacle as it oozed,
As roll or squatter made the barrels grind
Beyond the competence of things ill-used . . .
I cannot lose the picture from my mind . . .
The 'tweendecks of an ark
Hot, screaming dimness suddenly made dark
For suddenly the 'tweendecks lighting fused.

Straight, I reported that the 'tweendeck stow
Was staving, piece-meal, as it seemed to me.
A hundred casks had gone and more would go,
Destroyed between the devil and the sea.
'It must just take its way,'
The Old Man said, 'and if it spills, it may.
We cannot trim it till it stops to blow.'

So there we rolled, and took it green, and lay,
In a great roaring in a sea gone mad,
Unknowing whether it were rain or spray
That drenched us in the sousings that we had.
The Chief sent up to tell,
'A lot of treacle's got into the well.'
'Then pump and clear the muck', we sent to say.

The pumps began, but as the proverb tells,
'The blow comes on the bruise', and so with us.
Things worse than treacle get in pumps and wells,
Rupture and wreck and cloggings ruinous.
We felt the pump-throb beat,
Thumping the planking underneath our feet,
Suddenly stop, and stay stopped, 'twixt two bells.

'What stops the pump?' the Old Man said to me,
'Go down and find . . . and how's the treacle there?
'The Devil's always where he shouldn't be,
'And treacle is a devil everywhere.'
Below, I was appalled
To find a stokehold floor where treacle crawled,
A teatime tide out of a soupy sea.

I trod in treacle over my boot's sole,
Treacle was oozing out of chinks and seams.
Some pump-repairers, crouched against the roll,
Sweated in heat beyond the devil's dreams.
They fingered filth and curst.
One of them said, 'Then it's the sprangle burst . . .
'It's only treacle, this, with bits of coal.'

I asked the Second, when the leak began.
He answered: 'Find out, if you want to know.
'This hooker is an obsolete tin can,
'Fit for the knackers twenty years ago.
'She's rolled her fixings loose,
'And what we treat in is her vital juice.
'Report it, with our love, to the Old Man.'

The Old Man said, 'You know that treacle burns,
'And what may come at sea one never knows.
'Man never knows the ocean, but he learns,
'You'll learn where treacle gets to when it flows.
'If it should reach the fires,
'This ship will be a sight as she expires,
'This morning in the Bay of No Returns,

'To burn in treacle isn't to my mind,
'Somehow a lot of it has found its way . . .
'Whatever way it comes, the rest will find
'And we must bale it till the pump can play.
'By all I can observe,
'This storm is making her Atlantic swerve,
'We'll see a star (or Heaven) before day.

'Go, muster every bucket, scoop and broom
'And bale the stuff and dump it as she dips.'

I took the watch into the engine-room,
And we and treacle fairly came to grips.
We scraped what wouldn't yield,
We poured what wouldn't empty as she heeled,
And this in tropic heat and treacle-drips.

At first, when we were fresh, new to the toil,
Glad of the chance of something to be done,
More than just holding on and dripping oil,
We formed the bucket-chain and thought it fun.

317

Then when fatigue began,
I tried a song, as when a shanty-man
Bids halliard-haulers stretch along the coil.

'O treacle is the life of man,
'Treacle. Jemima.
'O treacle is the life of man,
'Treacle for Jemima.

'I scoop it up in an old tin pan,
'Treacle. Jemima.
'I scoop it up in an old tin pan,
'Treacle for Jemima.'

And as we shantied, stuck with treacle and sweat,
I heard a stoker grubbing in the pipes
Growl, 'Why, they haven't tried the sprangle yet . . .
'The sprangle's bust and tore the dick to stripes.'
The Chief replied, all-glowing:
'While you're aboard here, keep your clock from going.
'Springle your sprangles elsewhere . . . don't forget.'

Indeed, the strain had made all bearings hot.
The chorus failed, the shanty-singing died.
It made a fellow's very heart-blood clot
To get one bucketful tipped overside.
Then, suddenly, a flood
Of treacle hideous as an ogre's blood
Surged from a dozen barrels gone to pot.

Just on despair-point the disaster fell.
'Together, boys', we cried, and all together
We grappled with that new attack from hell,
All gasping at the ending of our tether.
Against Death's self we baled;
The stuff would reach the fires if we failed.
And failure neared, as any fool could tell.

And then the Old Man with his steward came,
Hot coffee mixed with rum, a mugful each:
A respite in the crisis of the game,
Life in the rum and comfort in the speech.
'By all I can observe,
'This storm has taken her Atlantic swerve.
'It blows like Barney's Bull, though, all the same.'

318

But with the strength thus given we returned
To bucket up the surgings of the gum
And still the rolling hooker plunged and churned
And pitched us, man and bucket, in the scum.
And still, in the black pit,
The engineers still struggled to re-fit
The thing without which we might all be burned.

Sea-knowledge knows that when the glasses rise
The strongest winds come, and the seas are worst;
Then comes the moment when the hooker dies,
Propellers drop away and hatches burst.
That very worst we felt;
Down went the swearing searchers as they knelt,
The treacle took us, as a gum takes flies.

We slithered all to leeward where we lay,
Heaped in a jam from one appalling blast.
I thought 'Here endeth; this is Judgment Day,
'She'll never weather this . . . this is the last.'
She lay beam-ended, thrust
By one long roar of never-ending gust,
Such as puts shipping into Dead Man's Bay.

How long she cowered I shall never know
But after a long age, slowly, she crawled
Into a weather-roll, but O so slow . . .
I wondered still . . . and then, I was appalled:
As she rolled back I saw
Molasses in a tidal wave of awe,
All the last barrels of the 'long-ships stow.

A stoker cried, 'It *was* the sprangle, then.'
The sprangle didn't move me: treacle did.
I called, 'Together, now . . . Up buckets, men.'
Slowly they formed the chain on being bid,
In treacle a foot deep,
Their eyes all treacle, strain and want of sleep,
I hope never to see the like agen.

But now the game was up, the treacle gained,
The hands worn out, and no relief remaining,
Dogged and dripping, done and over-strained,
The weather worse, the treacle ever gaining.
'No, not another turn,'

The leader said at last. 'We'll have to burn.'
Out of a new seam spurts of treacle rained

'Come, boys, it's bale or broil,' I said, but no,
They were good men, but finished; they were done.
It was so odd to see the buckets go,
Flop in the treacle there from everyone.
And then to see them float
As the ship rolled, each like a listed boat.
Mind, it was light now, morning had begun.

'We're done, sir,' a man said, 'we're beaten out.
'Not one of us can do another turn.
'Our number's up and fortune's up the spout.
'And if it's burn or baling, we must burn.'
I said, 'Wait till I come . . .
'Spell-O a while . . . I'll muster for some rum.
'Another lively spell may end the bout.'

Just as I seized the iron rail to climb
Men fitted a new sprangle in the dim.
The treacly engineers all black with grime
Made the pump chug and started on a hymn.
She chugged with steady thrill . . .
All hands again upped buckets with a will,
It was just Christmas-time and Easter-time.

And then, with clearing squalls, it ceased to blow,
The tropic sunlight burned, the sea went down,
Soon we had revelled in a watch below,
Soon we were clean and smartened up for town,
How Peace dissolves ill spells.
Saint Nicholas' and Woodside Ferry bells
Made all that treacled night seem long ago.

LINES FOR THE RACE OF SAILING SHIPS,
LISBON TO THE HUDSON BRIDGE, NEAR
MANHATTAN, 1964.

Once, they were Queens, triumphant everywhere,
In every port their countless house-flags flew;
Wherever wind blew billows they were there
Smashing their shadows as they thrusted through.
All the world's commerce was their occupation,

Men cheered them going forth and entering in,
Each venture showed another crown to win.

I, who beheld them in their pride of old,
Cannot forget their splendour as they came
Superb, out of the perils never told,
Hoisting their colours and the four-flag name,
And the cable-rattle of their exultation
As anchor fell ere anchor-watch was set;
Who that beheld such vision can forget?

Today, the few survivors show again
Their glory of man's triumph over force;
Over the tumult of the seas they strain
Against the westers battling out the course,
The world's great sailing ships in emulation,
Their seamen praying to be first to hail
A New York pilot-schooner under sail . . .

Soon they will reach into the wondrous Bay,
The harbour, Mannahatta, the world's pride;
There, be the racer's fortune what it may,
Glory and grace attend on every side;
The flags of the great ships of every nation;
The towering City shining in the sun;
And the dear quiet after effort done.

There, each in place, the contestants will moor
Beneath the Statue lightening the world . . .
Masters and mates and men will make all sure,
All square the mighty yards, all canvas furled.
Then, with three cheers, the seamen each in station
Will haul the colours down and hoist the lights
And beating bells begin the festal rites.

REMEMBERING DAME MYRA HESS

Most beautiful, most gifted, and most wise,
How shall man word the wonder that you were,
Now that your grace no longer blesses eyes,
Your presence nulls no care?
You are set free, as music that you played,
Made life a glory as your fingers bade,
You are alive with all that never dies.

For surely now you are among the rays
That guide and bless our darkness, as we grope
From wreck to ruin in life's tangled maze,
Lighting the paths of Hope . . .
Wisdom that sent you still directs your giving
The Courage that determines all things living
To seek for beauty and to light the ways.

I see you, as upon your stage alone,
In the great breathless silence that awaits
You, with the touches that make beauty known
Unbarring the shut gates . . .
You, the clear-eyed, who saw, in the attempt,
Eternal sparks illumine the dream dreamt,
The starry hand that scattered the seed sown.

FOR LUKE O'CONNOR

One early Summer, when the times were bad,
In 'Little Old New York', long years ago,
I looked for work, an ignorant raw lad,
Knowing no craft, nor knowing how to know.

There, up and down, in the exciting Sun,
I offered help that no one seemed to need,
Then suddenly success came; Life had won;
Luke offered work, and I was saved indeed.

Saved and restarted, with the golden chance
(At last) of learning what mankind has wrought
In all his centuries of ignorance;
To light his darkness with the stars of thought.

These are belated thanks, but let me say,
'For seventy years I've thanked you every day.'

THE SHROPSHIRE FRIENDS

Long since, when coming from the West,
With England near, I could not rest,
Though night time fell,
So near the two that I loved best.

322

There, somewhere, nor-nor-east from me,
Was Shropshire, where I longed to be,
Ercall and Mynd,
Severn and Wrekin, you and me.

So up I went, to walk the deck,
To gaze, with eager aching neck,
For England's Lights,
The Lighthouses preventing wrecks.

Far forward I would crane, to spy
Those fixed stars of the sailor's eye,
His most loved stars,
And feel their beauty drawing nigh.

There, while the beating engines shed
The mumble of their trampled tread,
The ship's great heart,
I stared into the night ahead.

Into a darkness now I stare
Towards where Wrekin lifts in air
And Severn glides,
I know that you are somewhere there.

A FELLOW MORTAL

I found a fox, caught by the leg
In a toothed gin, torn from its peg,
And dragged, God knows how far, in pain.

Such torment could not plead in vain,
He looked at me, I looked at him.
With iron jaw-teeth in his limb.

'Come, little son,' I said, 'Let be . . .
Don't bite me, while I set you free.'

But much I feared that in the pang
Of helping, I should feel a fang
In hand or face . . .
                   but must is must . . .
And he had given me his trust.

So down I knelt there in the mud
And loosed those jaws all mud and blood.
And he, exhausted, crept, set free,
Into the shade, away from me;

The leg not broken . . .
                              Then, beyond,
That gin went plonk into the pond.

THE STARS THAT SHONE

Now that I cannot get about
And know what I must do without,
I think of men of long ago
Whom I was privileged to know,
The men, like stars, showing the way.
They were Life's masterpieces; they . . .

Most, now, for many years have lain
Out in the churchyards in the rain,
In villages where clocks are slow.
And some where men no longer go
Now that a peace has been declared,
And times have changed since many cared.

Musicians, painters, poets, men
Who made the world more lovely then,
The story-tellers beyond price,
Bringing the news from Paradise,
Men from whose handiwork we see
Horizons in eternity.

Now that my roving days are over,
And all my frontiers stop at Dover,
I think of what Life used to mean
When all these fellows trod the scene
And Life was in myself with them
In Troy, in Greece, and Bethlehem.

Rich was the Life they let me share
Those spirits of the days that were.
Those dippers in the wells of art,

That found such cures for broken heart.
And such variety of friend
From Broken Heart to the World's End.

Their portraits still display the men . . .
Who, now, can match with those of then?
Those men who tamed the unbacked beasts,
And spoke the witty word at feasts,
And made the wicked world go round
Twixt Chance's Pitch and Lobs's Pound?

Some knew the seas whose Westers toss
The mollyhawk and albatross,
Whose mates the yellow fever killed
For graves that yellow fever filled.
Destroying strength, annulling youth,
From Benin Bight to Vera Cruz.

But all are gone, for the world turns,
And Change is what all living earns,
Change, and the Hope, that we may meet
Such lovely friends in a new street,
And share their never-ending joy
In Bethlehem, and Greece, and Troy.

AN EPILOGUE

I have seen flowers come in stony places
And kind things done by men with ugly faces,
And the gold cup won by the worst horse at the races,
So I trust, too.

INDEX OF FIRST LINES

John Masefield O.M. 1878-1967

John Masefield was born on 1st June, 1878, at Ledbury in Herefordshire. Educated at King's School, Warwick, and on H.M.S. *Conway*, he first went to sea at the age of fifteen on a windjammer. He succeeded Robert Bridges in 1930 as Poet Laureate and was awarded the Order of Merit in 1935. Widely travelled in his youth, he lived the last twenty-eight years of his life in Abingdon, Berkshire, where he died on 12th May, 1967.